SOME GREAT POLITICAL IDEALISTS
OF THE CHRISTIAN ERA

Some
Great Political Idealists
of the Christian Era

By

F. J. C. HEARNSHAW

M.A. LL.D. Litt.D.

EMERITUS PROFESSOR OF HISTORY IN THE UNIVERSITY OF LONDON
AND FELLOW OF KING'S COLLEGE

GEORGE G. HARRAP & COMPANY LTD.
LONDON   BOMBAY   SYDNEY

First published 1937
by GEORGE G. HARRAP & Co. LTD.
182 *High Holborn, London, W.C.*1

*Made in Great Britain. Printed by Western Printing Services, Ltd.,
Bristol*

PREFACE

NEARLY every year during the decade 1923-33 the Department of Mediæval and Modern History at King's College, London, arranged a series of free public lectures on the social and political ideas of a group of great thinkers of the Christian era. There were eight courses in all, and between them they covered the whole of the long period from St Augustine to Herbert Spencer. It fell to my lot, as head of the department, to deliver one or more of the lectures in each of these courses. In so far as I had a free choice of subject I made it my business to select for special study a thinker whose social and political ideas were novel, and one whose influence upon the actual course of events was considerable. Thus it came to pass that I dealt successively with Wycliffe, Machiavelli, Grotius, Bolingbroke, Rousseau, Burke, Austin, and Spencer. In this series of studies St Augustine at first had no place. The exposition of his system of thought, as displayed in the *De Civitate Dei*, was kindly undertaken by a distinguished Oxford scholar, one of the highest of living authorities on mediæval political theory. Most unfortunately, however, this eminent scholar was suddenly taken ill, and—at little more than an hour's notice—I was compelled to act as his deputy. In the circumstances my treatment of the difficult saint was inevitably thin, and, although I have striven by subsequent reading to make it more substantial, I nevertheless feel that I am less sure of him than I am of any of the other members of my company.

It was suggested that, although my company of nine is obviously a scratch team, it does by a happy chance display so great a variety of interest, and so wide a compass of political and social speculation, that it might be worth while to collect the nine studies from their several volumes and

5

issue them as a connected series. Hence the present volume, which I hope may be regarded as not wholly superfluous.

I think that it will be found that there are not many of the major problems of society that are not discussed by one or other of the nine thinkers under review. The relation of Church to State; the relation of State to individual; the relation of ethics to politics; the relation of politics to law; the bases of political authority; the rights of the subject; the conflict between principle and expediency—all these and many others are discussed in detail by one or more of my thinkers.

I have taken the opportunity to revise all the studies, and in particular to enlarge the Book Lists by the addition of important works published in recent years. The study of St Augustine has been largely rewritten.

F. J. C. HEARNSHAW

OXTED, SURREY
April 1937

6

CONTENTS

I

ST AUGUSTINE AND THE CITY OF GOD [1]

ST AUGUSTINE (A.D. 354–430), the greatest of the Fathers of the Latin Church, lived at one of the most critical periods of the world's history. It was the period during which Western Europe was passing from the tutelage of the Roman Empire into the disorderly liberty of mediæval Christendom. At the time of Augustine's birth the imperial power of the Cæsars seemed to be re-establishing itself in virtue of the masterly reorganisation of Diocletian and Constantine. When, seventy-five years later, his long and laborious life drew to a close, the vision of a revival of the Roman dominion in the West had proved to be a mirage. The very city in which he died, his African bishopric of Hippo, was at the moment of his death beleaguered by a horde of savage Vandals. The Roman frontiers had been broken, and hosts of barbarians—Visigoths, Sueves, Alans, Burgundians, Franks, and others—were pouring into Dacia, Mœsia, Illyricum, Italy, Gaul, and Spain. Civilisation and Catholicism alike appeared to be doomed. To St Augustine, who was both a great Roman and a great Christian, fell the tremendous task of interpreting to his contemporaries the meaning of the awful catastrophe. He had to explain the fall of the Empire whose dominion had been regarded as eternal. He had to portray the polity of the future; to depict the ideal towards which the Church—which alone had spiritual power—should urge its way; to expose the

[1] From *The Social and Political Ideas of Some Great Mediæval Thinkers* (Harrap, 1923). The other studies in this volume are: "Mediæval Political Thought," by Ernest Barker; "John of Salisbury and the 'Policraticus,'" by E. F. Jacob; "St Thomas Aquinas and the Papal Monarchy," by F. Aveling; "Dante and World-empire," by E. Sharwood Smith; "Pierre Du Bois and the Domination of France," by Eileen E. Power; "Marsilio of Padua and Mediæval Secularism," by J. W. Allen; "John Wycliffe and Divine Dominion," by the editor.

foundations and make clear the structure of the City of God.

The fall of the Roman Empire in the West was the outstanding fact of the time. It is difficult for us—the heirs of so many subsequent ages—to realise the magnitude of the portent, as it appeared to men of that age, and particularly to members of the Christian Church. From the first the Church had been dominated by the Empire. Christ Himself had been born a Roman subject, had lived under the protection and restriction of Latin law, had suffered death at the mandate of an imperial official. The early apostles, and in particular St Paul, had found their evangelistic activities wholly conditioned by the institutions and ideas of the Roman administrative system; in the main, they concluded that the discipline of Rome prepared men for Christ, and that the justice of Rome was a defence against the fury of the unbelievers. Later, however, the government of the Cæsars developed hostility to the Christian community. The causes have often been canvassed and are not far to seek. The Cæsars instinctively perceived, and correctly judged, that the Empire as established by the craft of Augustus, and the Church as moulded by the imperial genius of St Paul, could not exist side by side. Each claimed a sovereignty which was fatal to the other. Hence the great persecutions of the Church by the State, and the great conspiracies against the State by the Church. The dualism became complete, and the furious conflict of the two rival authorities reached its climax in the half-century which began with the Emperor Decius and ended with the Emperor Diocletian (A.D. 250–304). The pagan State exerted all the power which it still possessed to crush the Christian Church out of existence.

It failed; and its failure was marked by the resignation of Diocletian and the conversion of his successor, Constantine. The Church and the Empire were reconciled. Three centuries of dualism were brought to an end. A *Respublica Christiana* was, in theory at least, set up—a Christian State in which the Emperor as *pontifex maximus* became *episcopus episcoporum*, and presided at œcumenical councils. The Church, filled with a sense of triumph and inspired by confident hope, supported by Cæsar and in grateful return exalting his prerogative, advanced to complete its capture of the State and its evangelisation of the world. It counted without misgiving upon the permanence of Rome and upon its own unbreakable unity.

Both the grounds of its assurance proved to be unsubstantial. On the one hand, the Empire no sooner had become Christian than it began to totter to its fall. On the other hand, the Church no sooner had attained security than it began to be split in irremediable schism. To the Emperors, in all probability, the feature of the Church which had most impressed them had been that infrangible solidarity which had given it success in the face of the most ferocious assaults. The storms of controversy, the fires of persecution, the upheavals of mob-violence, all had assailed it in vain. It had stood, massive in its patient fortitude; a corporation stronger in the unity of its will, the singleness of its faith, the concentration of its loyalty, than the Empire itself. But with the removal of the external pressure of adversity that solidarity ceased. Differences of doctrine, particularly that which divided Arius from Athanasius, caused irreconcilable breaches; doubtful problems of discipline, particularly that associated with the Donatists, led to schismatical dissent; conflicts for office, emolument, property, power, distracted the episcopate, scandalised the faithful, and amazed the world. The Emperors, who, in the presence of external foes, above all things needed internal peace and unity, were profoundly disappointed and disgusted. As to doctrine, they did not mind what the bishops said, so long as they all said the same thing; as to discipline, they were indifferent what rules the Church laid down, provided it acknowledged the supreme authority of the State; as to property and power, they were willing richly to endow the episcopate, if only it would agree within itself as to the partition of the spoil. The Emperors, however, appealed in vain to the wrangling hierarchs. The Church victorious, instead of becoming, as had been hoped, a new source of strength and bond of union to the Empire, became a fresh cause of dissension, disintegration, and disaster. Constantine's son and successor signalised his disillusionment by proclaiming himself a heretic; the next of the great Emperors of the fourth century, Julian, apostatised altogether.

Meantime, while controversy and confusion prevailed within the Empire, the threat of the barbarians beyond its river-frontiers became more and more insistent. An immense movement of the nations was in process, originating apparently in some gigantic upheaval among the nomadic hordes which occupied the pastoral tablelands of Central Asia. At length the Huns, expelled from their native steppes, made their way through that ancient gateway of wandering peoples which lies between the Ural Mountains and the Caspian Sea, and fell like a hurricane upon the already troubled West. The weakened barriers of the Roman dominion could no longer stand the strain. The Danube and the Rhine were crossed by barbarian invaders, and the Latin civilisation was threatened with submergence by floods of Teutonic savagery. First and most notable of these alien hosts were the Visigoths. Having crossed the Lower Danube in A.D. 376, and having defeated a great Roman army at Adrianople two years later, they were allowed to settle in the two provinces of Dacia and Mœsia (the northern regions of modern Serbia and Bulgaria). In A.D. 395, weary of peace and inactivity, they broke loose, and for nearly twenty years wandered and wasted, until they came to final rest in the valley of the Garonne. Macedonia, Thrace, Thessaly, Greece, Italy, Gaul, Spain, all experienced the horror of their depredations. But of all their deeds the one which caused the greatest stir in the world was the sack of the city of Rome in A.D. 410.

No city in the world had ever risen to such eminence as Rome. For eight centuries (since her capture by the Gauls in 390 B.C.) she had been inviolate. She had become the centre of the vastest and most powerful empire which had ever been established among mankind. The wealth of the world had been poured into her lap, and it had been used to adorn her with temples and palaces which were among the marvels of the earth. All roads led to her; all men looked to her for guidance and control; she was regarded as the symbol of all that was most potent and most enduring. True, she had suffered some loss of prestige and influence when Constantine (A.D. 330) built a 'New Rome' on the Bosphorus, and made this Christian capital the seat of his government. But no imperial favour could transfer to the city of Constantine the loyalty and reverence which for many successive generations had gathered round the ancient city of the Seven Hills.

The departure of the Emperor; his conversion to Christianity; his founding of a new capital where churches and not temples had the places of prominence and honour— all these things tended to make Rome with its Senate the representative of the old order, and the place where the worship of the old gods was maintained in the greatest vigour. For eighty years (A.D. 313–392) Christianity and the Cults were allowed to live side by side in the Roman Empire. Then came, as the culmination of a long series of religious enactments increasingly favourable to the new faith, the edict of Theodosius I, totally prohibiting and proscribing the practice of paganism. Two years later, as we have seen, the ravages of the Visigoths began, reaching their climax in the sack of Rome itself (A.D. 410).

The sack of Rome caused almost equal consternation to pagans and to Christians. The devotees of the old gods— exasperated, humiliated, dispossessed, persecuted—raised aloud the cry, "Rome has perished in the Christian days." They pointed to the victories which their fathers had won in the days when Jupiter, Neptune, Mars, and their fellows were venerated and served; they enumerated the regions which had passed under Roman control through the divine favour of Cybele, Isis, Mithras, and the Syrian Baal; they lauded the unity and strength which the Empire had derived from the worship of the spirit of the city and the genius of its prince; they attributed all the calamities of their own dark days to the abandonment of the old faiths and to the

13

consequent anger of the deserted and insulted deities. The Christians, for their part, though they repudiated the arguments of the pagans, were troubled to think that the conversion of the Empire had not sufficed to save it from this overwhelming and spectacular disaster, and were still more perturbed to realise that the imperial power in which they had trusted for temporal security and world-wide dominion was unable to save even itself from destruction.

St Augustine heard both the cry of the pagans and the plaint of the Christians. He was in a position to understand each of them. The son of a pagan father and a Christian mother, he himself had passed from paganism—by the graded way of Manichæism, Scepticism, and Neo-Platonism —to the full confidence of Christian faith. Feeling the urgency of the problem to which the fall of Rome had given rise, he set himself to deal with it in all its aspects. The main appeal of the pagans had been to history. To history, then, he too would go. He set himself to survey—so far as his knowledge went, and his purpose required—the records of the human race. He made explicit what had been implicit in Christianity from the beginning, viz., a philosophy of history. He sought to interpret the course of mundane affairs, including the catastrophes of his own day, in terms of the eternal will of God. In his hands the story of mankind became a narrative of the unfolding in time and space of the eternal purpose of the Creator. He laid down the lines of that theodicy which, from the ampler stores of information afforded by later research, was developed by Bossuet in his *Discours sur l'histoire universelle*, by Vico in his *Nuova Scienza*, and by Schlegel in his *Philosophie der Geschichte*.

St Augustine began the writing of his *De Civitate Dei* in the year 413; it occupied him, with many intervals and much interruption, until 426. To this long and broken period of construction, with its distractions and discontinuities, is no doubt due the fact that it is one of the most difficult of books to read, that its definitions are vague and variable, that its argument is obscure, that its conclusions are still a subject of interminable controversy. Nevertheless,

14

in spite of grave defects both in design and in execution, it stands among "the few greatest books of all time." Its grand idea is clear. It traces from the day of creation to the day of final judgment the history of the two societies whose conflict had been the outstanding feature of the four centuries of the Christian era. The one, the *Civitas Dei*, had its origin with the creation of the angels; the other, its rival, the *Civitas Terrena*, commenced with the fall of Satan. On earth, the one was founded by the pious Abel, the other by the impious Cain.

The story of these two societies is pursued in twenty-two books. These books fall into two main groups. Books 1–10 are defensive: they are concerned with rebutting the pagan charge, "Rome has perished in the Christian days." They show that the fate of Rome was not peculiar; that earlier empires (in particular, the Assyrian) had suffered extinction from causes other than Christian; that Rome herself (*e.g.*, in 390 B.C.) had experienced calamities as great as that of A.D. 410, in days when the old gods were in the height of their ascendancy; that, in general, the fall of earthly states could be adequately explained by, and indeed was directly attributable to, the vices which paganism bred—cruelty, extortion, pride, luxury, debauchery. They end by carrying the controversy into the pagan camp, and by contending that the catastrophe of 410 was mitigated, rather than caused, by the religion to whose authority the Gothic conquerors were constrained to render some obedience. Books 11–22 are constructive. They ask and answer the question, "If it is the fate of earthly dominion to pass away, is there a city which endures?" Yes, replies Augustine, the city which shall have no end is the *Civitas Dei*. It is here, when Augustine touches the height of his great argument, and justifies the ways of God to men, that he becomes at once most magnificent and most obscure. What does he mean by the *Civitas Dei*, and what by the *Civitas Terrena*, which is its damned antithesis? What are the two *civitates* to whose origin, whose history, and whose destiny he so constantly recurs?

II

It must be confessed that St Augustine is far from consistent in his conception of the *Civitas Dei*. Sometimes he treats it as synonymous with the 'Christian religion' in opposition to paganism.[1] At other times he identifies it with the visible and militant Church as opposed to the world. On one occasion, indeed, he says explicitly, *ergo et nunc Ecclesia regnum Christi est, regnumque caelorum.*[2] But commonly and normally the *Civitas Dei* is regarded as equivalent to the *communio sanctorum*—the society of saints—as opposed to the *communio perditorum*, or company of the lost. This *communio sanctorum* consists of those predestined from all eternity to everlasting felicity. It thus far transcends the limits of the visible militant Church, for it includes not only the innumerable multitudes of the elected dead and the unborn who are foreordained to bliss, but also the holy angels and all the company of heaven.[3] On the other hand, it does *not* include many of the living who are members of the visible militant Church, for this Church, as Augustine expressly states, "has in her communion and bound to her by the sacraments, some who shall not eternally dwell in the lot of the saints."[4] Hence in this world the two *civitates*—the *communio sanctorum* and the *communio perditorum*—are inextricably mixed up, like wheat and tares, waiting the explication of the final Day of Judgment. Nevertheless, although the fallible tests of human science are unable to distinguish the saved from the lost, to the eye of God the lines of demarcation are clear. He knows His own elect, for He Himself, by His inscrutable decree, has determined who from among the fallen and depraved human race shall be saved by grace, cleansed from sin, and conveyed to Paradise, so as to occupy the mansions vacated by the rebellious angels. All such as are not thus

---

[1] *Retractations*, ii, 43.

[2] *De Civitate Dei*, xx, 9.

[3] Augustine no doubt regarded himself as among those foreordained to bliss; nevertheless, not until he was thirty-three years old was he baptised into the visible militant Church.

[4] *De Civitate Dei*, i, 35. *Cf.* also xviii, 49.

16

singled out and—without any merit or motion on their own part—saved are involved in Adam's guilt and Adam's doom; they form the lamentable *communio perditorum*. Such, in substance, is the Augustinian conception of the two societies, or *civitates*.

It is a horrible idea, a veritable nightmare of a theology. It cast an awful shadow over the Dark Ages, blackening the gloom caused by their ignorance and lawlessness. Relieved to some extent by the mediæval penitential system which provided inexpensive means for circumventing the decrees of inexorable fate, it returned with aggravated horror in the system of Calvin, and for some centuries held a large part of Protestant Europe under its malignant spell. Just as its sharp-cut dualism—reminiscent of Augustine's nine years' enslavement to Manichæism—helped to precipitate the long mediæval conflict between the Empire and the Papacy, so does it lie near the root of the ubiquitous modern struggle between Church and State.

Nevertheless, it must be carefully borne in mind that in Augustine's scheme the antithesis between the *Civitas Dei* and the *Civitas Terrena* is *not* precisely the antithesis between either Empire and Papacy, or State and Church. The Papacy had not yet developed, and Augustine recognised no sort of supremacy in the Bishop of Rome. As to the Roman Empire, with which he had much to do and concerning which he had much to write, his attitude varied according to circumstances. *Pagan* Rome, he reluctantly admits, was representative of the *Civitas Terrena*. He admits it reluctantly because, like St Paul, he was proud of his Roman citizenship, and he recognised the fact that the Romans of the republican period were distinguished by the possession of many virtues. Nevertheless, since the inspiring principle of their lives was glory (the praise of man) and not justice (the service of God), they could not be regarded as belonging to the *Civitas Dei*. All the same, the virtues— courage, honesty, patriotism, sense of duty—with which Divine Providence endowed them raised them high above such unmitigated reprobates as the Assyrians, and made them worthy to be the people among whom the *Civitas Dei* should be developed.

Pagan Rome, however, was in Augustine's day passing away and was being converted into a Christian Empire. Constantine had recognised and legalised Christianity in A.D. 313. Gratian and Theodosius, his successor, in a series of edicts issued during the decade 382–392, had pro-scribed paganism—closing the temples, prohibiting their sacrifices, and confiscating their endowments—and had made Christianity the sole lawful religion throughout their vast dominions. Paganism, it is true, died hard. In some respects, indeed, it secured for itself an enduring lease of life by transmuting itself subtly into apparently Christian institutions. Nevertheless, in its open and avowed forms it rapidly became extinct. It is estimated that it had dis-appeared from the towns of the Empire before A.D. 415. It lingered longer among the *pagani*, or country-folk.

The new Christianised Roman Empire occupied a very different position from its pagan predecessor. It supported the Church; it patronised the Church; it accommodated its laws to Christian standards; it endowed bishoprics and monasteries; it conferred large governing powers upon high-placed ecclesiastics. Hence, if the Empire had not yet become wholly a member of the *Civitas Dei*, it had obviously ceased to be merely a limb of the *Civitas Terrena*. It occupied an intermediate or transitional position. It took its place among those persons and institutions who were in process of being saved. Hence Augustine—especially in those writings of his that relate to the Donatist schism—did not hesitate to appeal to the secular power to aid him in his conflict with the enemies of Catholicism. He reverted to the attitude of St Paul: regarded the half-converted Empire as working for the same ends as the Church, although on a lower plane; commended it in so far as it sought to main-tain peace and enforce equitable law; admitted that its authority was in accordance with the Divine Will; sup-ported its claim to the loyal obedience of the faithful.

What has just been said concerning Augustine's attitude

towards the Roman Empire applies more generally to his view of the State as an institution universal among civilised men. He quotes Cicero's famous definition of a State, which describes it as "an assemblage bound together by a common acknowledgment of right and by a community of interests."[1] He argues, however, that since Cicero's day, under the influence of divine revelation, the idea of 'right' has been immensely extended. The words *jus* and *justitia* no longer mean merely the rendering by each man of his due to his neighbour; they include, and indeed connote primarily, the rendering by man of his service to God. If, however, the word *justitia* be used in this enlarged Christian sense it is plain that it can no longer be employed as a criterion of the State as such. For, if only those assemblages of people who render due service to God are recognised as true States, then no true States will be found in the world. But States are recognised in the Holy Scriptures: Christ Himself admitted the authority of Pilate and said, "Render unto Cæsar the things that are Cæsar's"; St Paul bowed down before the majesty of the execrable Nero, and maintained that "the powers that be are ordained of God." It is clear, then, that *justitia* must be omitted from the essential characteristics of a State. Of course, its presence is eminently desirable, for without it States are indistinguishable from organised banditries.[2] But, whether banditries or not, they exist universally; they arise from man's natural need of community; their existence and their authority are in accordance with the Divine Will. Their essential characteristic, in Augustine's view, is *agreement* on the part of their constituent members. His amended definition runs, "A State is an assemblage of reasonable beings bound together by a common agreement concerning the objects of their love."[3] Augustine, in short, is feeling his way towards a

---

[1] " Coetum juris consensu et utilitatis communione sociatum " (*De Republica*, ii, 21).

[2] " Remotâ justitiâ quid sunt regna nisi magna latrocinia? Quia et latrocinia quid sunt nisi parva regna? " (*De Civitate Dei*, iv, 4.)

[3] " Populus est coetus multitudinis rationalis, rerum quas diligit concordi communione sociatus " (*op. cit.*, xix, 24).

contract theory of the origin of the State. He had already foreshadowed this movement in his *Confessions*, where he speaks of "a general agreement among human beings to obey kings."[1]

Thus we see that if the *Civitas Dei* is normally *not* the Church the *Civitas Terrena* is *never* the State. The State—even when under rulers such as Nero it is but a *magnum latrocinium*—is an institution in accordance with the Divine Will. Bad as it may be, it is better than the anarchy which is its only alternative. It keeps some sort of order; it maintains some kind of peace; it provides some measure of defence against lawless men and foreign foes; it secures conditions amid which the good life is more possible than it would be in the unmitigated licence of Nature; it is, however oppressive and unjust, a schoolmaster to bring men to Christ.

In Augustine's view, then, Church and State are not sharply divided the one from the other. He follows St Paul in regarding them as natural allies. And in his day, even more than in St Paul's, they were closely associated. If St Paul had found indifferent Roman governors useful as protectors of himself and his infant churches from the fury of the Jews, much more did Augustine find Christian emperors valuable agents for the suppression of Donatist schismatics, the excommunication of Pelagian heretics, and the extinction of Manichæan unbelievers. It is lamentable indeed that after 398 Augustine came more and more to rely on the secular arm to effect purifications of the Church which he was unable to effect by means of his own logic and eloquence. Relying on that terrible text "Compel them to come in," he became a persecutor, the spiritual father of the Inquisition. Further, just as the Church used the State to crush heresy, unbelief, and schism, so did the State—from 313 onward—increasingly employ officials of the Church in administrative work. Bishops became Ministers of State, defenders of cities, judges of civil courts. Priests were made guardians of orphans, relievers of the poor, educators of the ignorant. More and more as the Roman Empire waned

---

[1] " Generale pactum humanæ societatis obedire regibus" (*Confessions*, iii, 8).

and as the darkness of the Middle Ages settled down upon the Western World did the distinction between Church and State become blurred, until finally it was completely obliterated in the mediæval *Respublica Christiana*.

BOOK LIST

A. PRIMARY SOURCES

Augustinus, Sanctus Aurelius: Opera Omnia. 11 vols. Paris, 1679–1700.

Augustinus, Sanctus Aurelius: De Civitate Dei. Ed. E. Hoffmann. 2 vols. Vienna, 1898.

DODS, MARCUS: *The City of God:* A Translation into English. 2 vols. Edinburgh, 1897.

HEALEY, JOHN: *The City of God:* A Translation into English. 2 vols. London, 1610.

WELLDON, J. E. C. (ed.): *S. Aurelii Augustini Episcopi Hipponensis de Civitate Dei contra Paganos.* Libri xxii. 2 vols. London, 1924.

B. SECONDARY SOURCES

ANGUS, S.: *The Sources of the First Ten Books of Augustine's City of God.* Princeton, 1906.

BAYNES, N. H.: *The Political Ideas of St Augustine's "De Civitate Dei."* London, 1936.

CUNNINGHAM, W.: *Saint Austin and his Place in the History of Christian Thought.* Cambridge, 1885.

DAWSON, C.: "St Augustine and his Age" (in *A Monument to St Augustine*). London, 1930.

DORNER, I. A.: *Augustinus.* Berlin, 1873.

FIGGIS, J. N.: *The Political Aspects of Saint Augustine's City of God.* London, 1921.

GÖLLER, E.: *Die Staats- und Kirchenlehre Augustins.* Berlin, 1930.

HERTLING, G. VON: *Augustin.* Mainz, 1902.

HUMPHREYS, E.: *Politics and Religion in the Days of Augustine.* Columbia University, 1912.

LEISEGANG, H.: "Der Ursprung der Lehre Augustins von der 'Civitas Dei'" (in *Archiv für Kulturgeschichte*). Berlin, 1925.

McCABE, J.: *Saint Augustine and his Age.* London, 1902.

MAUSBACH, J.: *Die Ethik des heiligen Augustinus.* Freiburg, 1909.

REUTER, A.: *Augustinische Studien.* Gotha, 1887.

SCHOLZ, H.: *Glaube und Unglaube in der Weltgeschichte.* Leipzig, 1911.

SEIDEL, B.: *Die Lehre des heiligen Augustinus vom Staate.* Berlin, 1909.

THOMAS, F.: *S. Augustin, La Cité de Dieu.* Geneva, 1886.

TRÖLTSCH, E.: *Augustin, die christliche Antike und die Mittelalter.* Berlin, 1915.

II

WYCLIFFE AND DIVINE DOMINION [1]

THE interval between St Augustine and John Wycliffe is a long one. It comprises, indeed, almost the whole of the thousand years that divided the decline of the ancient Roman Empire from the rise of the modern national States. That mediæval millennium, however, rich though it was in epoch-making events, was not fruitful in political ideas. It saw the establishment of the barbarian kingdoms in Western Europe; the rise and spread of Islam; the incursions of the Vikings; the settlement of the Magyars in Hungary; the organisation of Christendom for discipline under Pope and priesthood, and for defence under Emperor and knighthood; the feudalisation of society; the wild adventure of the Crusades. It was, indeed, an epoch of intense and varied activity, of fierce energy, and of vast achievement. But it was an epoch of deeds rather than of words; of institutions rather than of ideas. Lord Bryce has described it as "essentially unpolitical," and it was so in the sense that it was engaged in constructing states and not in formulating political theories.

It is regrettable that the Middle Ages were not more articulate. They were dominated by notions so alien from our modern modes of thought that, in the absence of express statement, it is difficult for us to realise or formulate their creeds. No doubt, for example, there were political principles of some sort inherent and implicit in feudalism—ideas of suzerainty as based on contract, of the mutual responsibility of rulers and ruled, of hereditary right, of territorial dominion, of power as property. But so long as feudalism prevailed they were never made explicit. Not until feudalism

---

[1] From *The Social and Political Ideas of Some Great Mediæval Thinkers* (Harrap, 1923). For the other studies in this volume see p. 9.

had decayed and was passing away were its fundamental theories extracted, examined, classified, and systematised. The 'feudal system,' as Professor Maitland has told us, was introduced into England by Sir Henry Spelman in the seventeenth century. Similarly, I think, it might be contended that the Holy Roman Empire was established by Lord Bryce in 1864, and that the *Respublica Christiana* was invented by Father Figgis in 1910. The men of the Middle Ages did not clarify their thoughts: the majority of them had no thoughts to clarify. They lived by instinct and tradition, like the higher animals. One has to infer their motives from observation, as M. Maeterlinck infers the polity of the bees.

Soon after the passing of the millennial year (A.D. 1000), however, the inarticulate era came to an end; silence gave place to sound. The first utterances of political significance were, it is true, more like the roars of infuriated bulls, or the screams of exasperated eagles, than the speeches of rational men: they were the alternate anathemas and blasphemies which marked the Investiture Controversy. These elemental utterances, however, unedifying as they were in themselves, stirred the mediæval mind to political speculation. They compelled attention to the problem of the relation of Papacy to Empire, of spiritual to temporal authority, of Church to State. At first the ecclesiastical theorists had it all their own way. They alone possessed such knowledge of letters as survived from classical times; they still commanded the consciences of men. Hence the cause which they supported emerged substantially triumphant from the Investiture struggle; the victorious Papacy increased in splendour and power until it reached its culmination of might, majesty, and dominion under the great Innocent III. The theory of papal sovereignty is well expressed and enforced by John of Salisbury and St Thomas Aquinas, as also by others, such as St Bernard and Ægidius Romanus.

The age of St Thomas and his faithful henchman Ægidius was the high-water mark of mediæval Christendom. The rebellious empire of the Hohenstaufen had been destroyed: the Papacy reigned apparently supreme in all causes both spiritual and temporal. Secular philosophy had been sub-ordinated to divine theology; Aristotle had been made to acknowledge the overlordship of Augustine: the *Summa* of St Thomas contained the complete, unified, and harmonised *corpus* of human knowledge, which it was supposed would never have to be supplemented or superseded. The great thirteenth century, however, had no sooner come to an end than new revolt, disorder, heresy, schism, set in. The age of assured faith, implicit obedience, disciplined activity, gave place to one of doubt, discord, and destruction. The ideal unity of Christendom was dissolved in the confusion of national states; the vision of the peace of God faded before the reality of the strife of men. In the Jubilee of 1300 the Papacy, in the person of Boniface VIII, appeared to touch heights of imperial power never attained before. In 1303 the tragedy of Anagni, with its sequel of confusion, com-promise, and captivity, revealed the deceptiveness of the appearance, and displayed the true impotence of the Papacy in temporal concerns. The Papal Monarchy was at an end; the effort of the Church to unify and govern the world had failed; the nations and their kings had refused to follow the way of peace which St Thomas Aquinas had marked out for them.

The problem of the fourteenth century was how to restore tranquillity to the distracted and demoralised fragments of what had lately been Christendom. Dante saw the one and only way of hope in the reunion of Christendom under the Holy Roman Emperor; Pierre Du Bois, perceiving that the mediæval Empire had passed away even more irrevocably than the mediæval Papacy, urged a reconstruction of Christendom under the most potent of its rulers, the king of France; Marsilio of Padua, wholly rejecting the idea of any reunion or reconstruction of the Church-state of the Middle Ages, looked forward to the establishment of a Peace of the People. We have now to inquire how John Wycliffe envisaged the problem of his time, and what were the political ideas which seemed to him to point the way to peace and progress.

II

Wycliffe was born in the North of England about the year 1324. As he grew up to manhood the evils which had marked the opening of the fourteenth century became manifestly worse. In particular, the Papacy, exiled from Rome and established at Avignon (1309–76), having been robbed of its temporal suzerainty, lost also its spirituality, and sank into a deplorable condition of religious apathy, moral corruption, and intellectual contempt. It also passed under the control of its destroyer, the king of France, and seemed to be degraded to the ignominious position of a mere tool of his policy. At the same time its departure from Italy involved the loss of the revenues of the Papal States, and this necessitated a formidable increase in the demands for money made upon the faithful in northern lands. England, in particular, which had been recognised as a fief of the Papacy by King John, was drawn upon heavily to support the growing expenses of the papal court: French cardinals became the absentee holders of the richest English benefices; curial agents collected in this country for the advantage of Avignon a larger sum than flowed into the coffers of the king himself.[1] The exasperation which in any circumstances would have been caused by the loss of English patronage and the drain of English wealth was incalculably aggravated when the Hundred Years War broke out (1337). From that time onward it was felt that the papal overlord of England was the pliable dependent of England's most deadly foe; and that the ecclesiastical treasure of the nation was being prostituted to the comfort and encouragement of the enemy.

[1] " At Salisbury in 1326 the dean, the precentor, the treasurer, two archdeacons, and twenty-three prebendaries were papal nominees" (Capes, *English Church*, p. 86). Fifty years later " The income of the French clergy alone accruing from English livings was estimated at £60,000 a year " (Lechler, *John Wycliffe*, p. 168). Absentee French cardinals held the deaneries of York, Carlisle, and Lincoln; the archdeaconries of Canterbury, Durham, Suffolk, and York; besides many prebends and other benefices (Lewis, *John Wicliffe*, p. 34).

In the midst of these disaffections and discontents fell the Black Death (1349). This colossal catastrophe, which so well-informed an historian as Professor Thorold Rogers regarded as the most momentous event recorded in English history, had a profound and far-reaching effect in the religious sphere, as well as in the spheres of politics, economics, and society. It shook the ecclesiastical system to its foundation. It destroyed the faith of the common man in the efficacy of prayer, in the virtue of priestly ministrations, in the benefits of pilgrimages and penances, in the value of piety and the worth of good deeds. A blind, cruel, and irresistible Fate seemed to sweep away good and bad indifferently to a single swift and abominable doom. To the religious man it raised problems which had slumbered since the days when Augustine had sought to solve the mystery of the agony in which the old Roman world was perishing. Was man in any sense the arbiter of his own destiny? Was there such a thing as free will? Was not the whole course of every creature, both in this world and the next, foreknown and foreordained from the beginning? Were not the pretences of the priests to affect the welfare of any body, or the fate of any soul, by means of masses, absolutions, penances, fastings, and the like, palpable absurdities and execrable frauds? These were questions, and this was a temper, that went far deeper into the abysses of doubt than those which merely concerned papal patronage, or ecclesiastical jurisdiction, or the revenues of an alien hierarchy. While the new spirit of national patriotism menaced the temporalities of the Papacy, the revival of the Augustinian conception of the Church as the community of the predestined elect laid an axe to the root of the spiritual claims of the mediæval priesthood, and prepared the ground for the growth of Lollardy and Calvinism. Such were the circumstances in the midst of which Wycliffe grew up. It was an age wherein an old order was visibly breaking up. What part did Wycliffe play in either discerning or determining the lines along which the new order would frame itself?

III

Into the details of Wycliffe's life it is not necessary to enter here. Many of them still remain obscure,[1] owing partly to the fact that the reformer had not sufficient personal fascination to make men wish to remember much about him,[2] and partly to the fact that the destructive inquisition of the later mediæval clergy went far to obliterate all traces of his abhorred activity. The sixty-odd years of his earthly span can be divided into four periods as follows: (1) his juvenile career, c. 1324–35; (2) his academic career, 1335–74; (3) his political career, 1374–78; and (4) his anti-papal career, 1378–84.

Neither the exact date nor the precise place of his birth can be determined with certainty; but evidence seems to point to the year 1324 and to Spresswell, near Old Richmond, in the North Riding of Yorkshire.[3] Of his parentage, his home life, and his early education nothing is known; but it is probable that he lived and learned somewhere in the valley of the Tees, until, about 1335, he was enrolled as a member of Balliol College, Oxford. Balliol was the college of the Northerners: it stood for Teutonism as against Latinism; for national independence as against the ultramontane cosmopolitanism of the *Respublica Christiana*; for the realism of Duns Scotus as against the prevailing nominalism of William of Ockham. Its great rival and antagonist was Merton, the college of the Southerners, the champion of *sacerdotium*, universalism, and tradition. All Wycliffe's associations were with Balliol; his spirit was the Balliol spirit; his attitude throughout life the Balliol attitude. He rose to be Master of the college in 1361—the first sure date we have in his recorded biography. Much complication has been caused

---

[1] It is reported that at a recent examination the only thing about which one of the candidates was quite certain was that Wycliffe was " the editor of the *Morning Star* "!

[2] We have no record of any friendships of his. Among his numerous writings not a single letter is to be found.

[3] See discussion in G. Lechler's *John Wycliffe*, pp. 79–84, and in H. B. Workman's *John Wyclif*, i, 21–28.

by the fact that the name 'John Wycliffe' (spelled variously)
has been found in the contemporary registers of both Merton
College and Queen's College. The older biographers of
Wycliffe tried to fit all the entries into the story of the
reformer's life: the result was chaos and hopeless perplexity.
The recent researches, however, of Mr Courthope, Dr
Reginald Lane Poole, Dr Hastings Rashdall, and others,
have made abundantly clear the curious fact that in the
middle of the fourteenth century there were no fewer than
three persons of the same name resident simultaneously in
the university. One was the reformer; the second was a
Fellow of Merton College who for a brief period was Warden
of Canterbury Hall and who finally died Prebendary of
Chichester and Rector of Horsted Keynes in Sussex in 1383;
the third was an obscure almonry boy of Queen's College,
known only as a renter of rooms in the college, and as a
person who omitted to pay his debts. It is eminently satisfactory and disembarrassing to have got the reformer clear
of both the obscurantism of the Merton Wycliffe and the
insolvency of his namesake at Queen's. For Wycliffe, as we
have already remarked, was essentially a Balliol man. Now
to be essentially a Balliol man is to be portentous. The
typical Scholar of Balliol is a youth distinguished by ominous
brilliance; the typical Fellow of Balliol is a meteor of high
magnitude; the typical Master of Balliol—well, Wycliffe
was the typical Master of Balliol, luridly luminous, heretic-
ally vaporous, the Great Nebula itself in the constellation of
Lucifer.

In Oxford, during the forty years of his association with
the university, Wycliffe rose to a position of the highest
eminence. Even his enemy, Henry de Knyghton, acknowledged that "in philosophy he was reckoned as inferior to
none, and as unequalled in the exercises of the schools,"
and spoke of him as "a man of profound wit, exceptionally
strong and effective in disputations—one who was regarded
by the common sort of divines as little less than a god."
One of the severest of his modern critics similarly admits
that he was "the leading figure in the academic circles of

his day; one of the last of the great schoolmen."[1] He was "the Evangelical Doctor," the teacher who increasingly tended to bring all things to the test of the Gospel, until finally, at the end of a long and painful evolution, he proclaimed the Scriptures as interpreted by human reason to be the supreme standard of verity. He was not an original thinker: he followed Plato in his exaltation of Ideas; Augustine in his conception of the Church; Grossteste (whom he considered a greater man than Aristotle[2]) in his antagonism to the Papacy; Bradwardine in his leaning towards predestination; Ockham in his insistence on priestly poverty; Fitzralph in his theory of dominion. What *was* original in him was the intellectual fearlessness which pushed premises to their logical conclusion, the rationalism which refused to bow to authority, and the moral courage which defied the terrors of the Inquisition. It is noteworthy that all through the academic period of his career, and indeed to within three years of his death, he carried the university with him. He was regarded by doctors and scholars alike as the champion of the freedom of the *studium* against the mortifying restraints of the *sacerdotium*; as the exponent of the claims of philosophy against the ascendancy of theology; as a defender of the rights of the secular clergy against the encroachments of monks and friars; above all, as the invincible maintainer of a lofty realism against the decadent nominalism of the rival University of Paris. This reputation became wide as Christendom itself, and he, more than anyone else, gave to Oxford the intellectual glory of this its Golden Age. It was unfortunate for Oxford that the liberty which she enjoyed in the middle of the fourteenth century should have become associated with deadly heresy on Wycliffe's part, with Lollard schism, with the Peasants' Revolt, and with world-disorder generally. For these things made it possible for Archbishop Courtenay to establish in 1382 an Inquisition which effectively stifled freedom

---

[1] W. W. Capes, *The English Church in the Fourteenth and Fifteenth Centuries*, p. 110.

[2] " Plato, Augustinus, Lincolniensis, sunt longe clariores philosophi."

of thought. From that date Oxford ceased to be the national centre of progressive ideas; she became, what she long remained, "the home of lost causes and impossible beliefs."

IV

To return to Wycliffe. During the years when he was teaching philosophy at Oxford stirring events were transpiring in the larger world. In particular, the Hundred Years War was running its evil and lamentable course, involving the English nation in ever-widening circles of animosities. Among these animosities the most serious was that which sundered England from the Papacy. The Papacy had been growing in unpopularity throughout England ever since that fatal year, 1213, when Innocent III had extorted from the renegade King John a recognition of the papal suzerainty over his realm. The increasing claims to jurisdiction and the insatiable demands for money which resulted from John's surrender had roused a swelling indignation among the people. The annual tribute of 1000 marks (700 for the kingdom of England, 300 for the lordship of Ireland) which John had agreed to pay to the papal court as a symbol of his submission was frequently withheld after 1272, and in 1333 was wholly suspended. In 1343 Parliament petitioned the King against papal provisions, and in 1351 passed the Statute of Provisors. The year 1353 saw the first Statute of Præmunire, designed to restrict foreign jurisdictions in England; in 1365 this general statute was pointed by another which expressly prohibited the carrying of suits to papal courts. This direct challenge roused Pope Urban V to action: he demanded payment of the tribute, together with arrears due since 1333. A special Parliament was called by Edward III to deal with this demand. It met in May 1366, and after due deliberation rejected the papal claim on the ground that John's surrender, with its attendant promise, was *ultra vires* and in violation of his coronation oath. Urban V felt it inadvisable to press the matter farther in face of the strenuous national resistance. Not so, however, his successor, Gregory XI, eight years later.[1]

In 1374, when the papal demand for the tribute (with its implication of feudal dependence) was renewed, the position of England was appreciably weaker. On the one hand, the nation was no longer united: a formidable conflict was raging between a clerical party, headed by William of Wykeham, and an anti-clerical party, headed by John of Gaunt, Duke of Lancaster and son of King Edward III. On the other hand, the French were recovering victory in the great war, and were rapidly driving the English out of their land. In these circumstances, the Papacy, with French support, resumed the practice of provisions, ignored the prohibitions of *præmunire*, and redemanded the Johannine tribute. The once glorious King of England, hero of Crécy and Poictiers, now rapidly sinking into senile incompetence, was eager for tranquillity on almost any terms. Hence in 1374 he sent two missions to Bruges, one, under John of Gaunt, to treat of a truce with the French; the other, under the Bishop of Bangor, to reach an accommodation with the Papacy. With the Bishop of Bangor went John Wycliffe. This event probably marks his first emergence from academic into political life.

Neither of the two missions of 1374 achieved any conspicuous success. We are not now concerned with the humiliating terms which the Duke of Lancaster had to accept from the French king. As to the Bishop of Bangor's business, so little did he press the matter of provisors, and so agreeable did he make himself to the papal representatives, that on his return to England he was at once 'provided' by the Pope with a more lucrative bishopric than the one he held! The question of the tribute and its feudal implication was, however, better managed. This, apparently, was Wycliffe's special concern. He had made himself master of both the law and the philosophy inherent in the idea of dominion, and he put up an unanswerable case against the papal overlordship. Behind his logic, moreover, making it doubly

[1] See the continuation of *Eulogium Historiarum*, iii, 337.

effective, was the passionate resolve of the English nation not to admit its political subjection to the court of Avignon —which was regarded as itself subject to the King of France. Wycliffe's arguments against the feudal dominion of the Papacy over England are summarised in a document entitled *Determinatio quædam Magistri Johannis Wyclif de Dominio contra unum Monachum*—a document to which Dr Loserth conclusively assigns a date subsequent to 1374.[1] It appears that a certain monk—probably William Wadford, the opponent with whom Wycliffe crossed swords in his *De Ecclesia* and his *De Civili Dominio*—had had the temerity to support the papal claim to feudal suzerainty over England, and to contend that, as the Pope had conferred the government of England upon the King on condition of the payment of the annual tribute, and as the tribute had ceased to be paid, the King had forfeited his title to the crown. Wycliffe, as the expert on this problem of dominion, was commissioned to answer the audacious ecclesiastic. He did so in this remarkable *Determinatio*, wherein he describes himself as *peculiaris regis clericus talis qualis*—a curious expression which probably means no more than that he had been the King's representative at Bruges in 1374. The *Determinatio* is constructed in the form of a series of speeches delivered in Parliament by seven lords.[2] At one time it was thought to be a veracious report—the earliest extant—of a genuine parliamentary debate. It is, however, too good to be true. It is too logical for lords; too consecutive and coherent; too free from tautology and irrelevance. It resembles those admirable eighteenth-century parliamentary reports which Dr Johnson wrote after he had been sound asleep during the whole

[1] Loserth, in *English Historical Review*, April 1896. The document itself is printed, not very correctly, however, by Lewis in his *John Wicliffe* (1720), pp. 363–371. Emendations in the text are made by F. D. Matthew, *English Works of Wyclif* (1880), p. v. Summaries of the arguments will be found in R. Vaughan's *Tracts and Treatises of John de Wycliffe* (1845), pp. xix–xxiv, in G. Lechler's *John Wycliffe* (1884), pp. 124–130, and in Workman's *John Wyclif*, i, 231–239.

[2] "Primo ergo transmitto doctorem meum reverendum ad solutionem hujus argumenti quam audivi in quodam consilio a dominis secularibus esse datam."

evening, when (having escaped the distraction of the speeches) he woke up refreshed and full of lusty resolve that the Whig dogs should not have the best of the argument. The *Determinatio* is Wycliffe pure and undiluted. The seven secular lords are but a ghostly bodyguard arrayed before him in the hope of averting from himself the dreadful thunderbolt of papal excommunication. He was not yet a rebel against the Papacy; he had not yet challenged any article of the Catholic faith; he still (in this very document) described himself as *humilis et obedientialis filius Romanæ Ecclesiæ.*

The arguments advanced against the papal suzerainty were briefly these: first, the kingdom of England had been obtained by conquest and not by papal grant; secondly, feudal relations were mutual, the lord was bound to protect his vassal, and the Pope gave the king of England no such protection; thirdly, so far was he from protecting him that he actually fostered and encouraged his mortal enemies; but fourthly, so vast were the estates of the Church in England that the Pope was rather the sub-tenant of the king than his suzerain; fifthly, if the Pope pardoned John in 1213 in consideration of his promise to pay 700 marks a year he was guilty of simony; sixthly, 700 marks was an absurdly inadequate sum for a fief so magnificent as the kingdom of England; finally, John had no right or power to pledge his monarchy, or to surrender its independence. This utterance is obviously that of the *peculiaris regis clericus* rather than of the *filius Romanæ Ecclesiæ*, and when he followed it up by formal and formidable dissertations, *De Dominio Divino* and *De Civili Dominio*, he could not possibly hope to escape papal censure and episcopal condemnation. No camouflage of secular lords could conceal or protect his irreverent and revolutionary head. From covertly denying the particular papal claim to lordship over England he had gone on to assail the whole system under which religious men exercised temporal power and possessed mundane property. This general attack on ecclesiastical politicians and clerical wealth excited immense interest. It was an assault led, not by an obscure fanatic like John Ball, but by the foremost

schoolman of the age. It was couched, not in wild vernacular tirades, but in the ponderous logic of the latest and
most approved academic Latin. It commanded attention,
and it demanded energetic repulse. Its menace to the
hierarchy was all the more formidable because, although
Wycliffe's theory of dominion was unintelligible to the multitude, his denunciations of the worldliness and wealth of the
clergy were greeted with the warmest approval by the party
of John of Gaunt, by the majority of the Parliament, and by
the commonalty generally. Hence in 1377 it was necessary
for the Church to act, and to act with decisive vigour.

V

The year 1377—the year of Edward III's death and
Richard II's accession—was the culminating point of
Wycliffe's career. He was at the height of his powers. He
had not as yet broken with the Church or committed himself
to either heresy or schism. He was the idol of Oxford
University, the hero of London City, the *protégé* of the Duke
of Lancaster, the adviser of the House of Commons, and even
the ally of the friars in their advocacy of apostolic poverty.
So strong was his position that the first attempt to silence
him entirely failed. It was made in February 1377 by the
masterful and inquisitorial Courtenay, Bishop of London,
who summoned him to appear in the cathedral church of
St Paul, in order to answer for his anti-clerical teachings.
He duly came, but he brought with him not only friars of
the four orders to assist him in his arguments, but also the
Duke of Lancaster and the Earl Marshal with a company of
armed men to guard him from perils more imminent than
failure in debate. The sacred court speedily became a scene
of furious wrangling, in which the fiery bishop and the
impious duke were the protagonists. It broke up in wild
disorder before ever its cause of convocation had been so
much as stated. Wycliffe, who seems to have been a passive
spectator of the unseemly brawl, was conveyed into safety
by his anomalous friends.

The second attack came from the Papacy itself. No doubt it had been inspired by the clerical party in England; but apparently not by either Courtenay of London or Sudbury of Canterbury, for both were roundly rebuked for slackness in dealing with this dangerous rebel. On May 22, 1377, Pope Gregory XI (lately returned to Rome from Avignon) issued no fewer than five bulls directed against Wycliffe, who was accused of reviving and disseminating the perverse opinions and unlearned doctrine of Marsilio of Padua, *damnatæ memoriæ*, and his collaborator, John of Jandun. Three of the five bulls were addressed to the prelates of Canterbury and London. They provided them with three different courses of action. According as circumstances suggested, they were authorised and commanded to arrest and imprison Wycliffe; or to get the King to do so; or to cite him to appear at Rome. The situation was evidently a delicate one: the anti-clerical party was strong and vigilant, and the penalties of *præmunire* were not to be lightly incurred. The fourth of the bulls was addressed to the King: it exhorted him to aid the bishops in their pious task. The fifth was directed to the delinquent University of Oxford: it sternly rebuked the Chancellor and his Fellows for permitting tares to grow amid the pure wheat of their doctrine, and ordered them, on pain of the loss of their privilege, to extirpate the pernicious vegetation, and to hand over the sowers of it to the papal commissioners, viz., the Archbishop of Canterbury and the Bishop of London.[1]

Accompanying the bulls was a list of nineteen articles (reduced in subsequent recensions to eighteen) culled from Wycliffe's works and declared to be damnable. It is notable that all but one of these obnoxious propositions were derived from the treatise *De Civili Dominio*. It is further remarkable that no questions of Catholic faith were involved in them; they referred exclusively to problems of politics, principles

---

[1] The text of the bulls is to be found in Walsingham, *Hist. Ang.*, i, 345 *et seq.*; also in the St Albans *Chronicon Angliæ*, p. 174 *et seq.*; and again in the appendix to Lewis's *Wicliffe*, pp. 254–264. Summaries of their contents are given in Lechler's *Wycliffe*, pp. 162–165, and in Sergeant's *Wyclif*, pp. 175–177.

of property and power, relations of Church and State.[1] They were not arranged in any logical order; they were not criticised or explained; the grounds of their condemnation were not stated. It must be confessed that, like much of Wycliffe's writing, the meaning of some of them is extremely obscure. This much is clear, however. They exalt the State above the Church; they subject the clergy to the judgment of the laity; they recognise the right and proclaim the duty of secular lords to confiscate ecclesiastical property when it is abused.[2] It will be seen that two tremendous issues were raised by this controversy of 1377—the one by Wycliffe himself, the other by his opponents. On the one hand, Wycliffe called upon the State to reform a Church corrupted by worldly power and temporal possessions. On the other hand, in self-defence, the menaced Church sought to introduce the papal Inquisition into England, with power to arrest, imprison, try, and punish those who thus assailed its prerogatives.

The five bulls and the nineteen articles probably reached Canterbury some time in June 1377; but for six months nothing was done with them. The occasion was not auspicious for their publication. Edward III died on June 21, and a regency was established much less disposed than the old King had been to act as jackal to the Papacy. In October a Parliament was called which declared itself emphatically on Wycliffe's side. It received from Wycliffe a paper in which he stated and defended his position.[3] It further consulted Wycliffe respecting the lawfulness of with-

[1] For the text of the articles see Walsingham, *Hist. Ang.*, i, 345–353, or Lewis, *Wicliffe*, pp. 266–267. Compare also Shirley, *Fasciculi Zizaniorum*, p. 484. Lewis translates the articles with comments, pp. 42–46; and he further gives, from Walsingham, a paper purporting to set forth Wycliffe's own explanation of their meaning, pp. 54–63. Summaries are provided by Lechler, pp. 165–167, by Sergeant, pp. 177–179, and by Workman, i, 293–300.

[2] Perhaps the three most offensive articles were No. 6, " Domini temporales possunt legitime ac meritorie auferre bona fortunæ ab ecclesia delinquente "; No. 17, " Licet regibus auferre temporalia a viris ecclesiasticis ipsis abutient-ibus habitualiter "; and No. 19, " Ecclesiasticus imo et Romanus Pontifex potest legitime a subditis et laicis corripi, et etiam accusari."

[3] *Libellus Magistri Johannis Wycclyff quem porrexit Parliamento regis Ricardi contra statum Ecclesiæ.* See Shirley's edition of *Fasciculi Zizaniorum*, pp. 245–257.

holding treasure from the Pope, and when he replied that—according to natural reason, the command of the Gospel, and the law of conscience—it *was* lawful it welcomed and accepted his opinions.[1] Not until this anti-papal Parliament was prorogued did the papal commissioners venture to act. Then, on December 18, 1377, they sent a mandate to the University of Oxford, together with the bull and the articles, ordering the university (1) to inquire into Wycliffe's opinions, and (2) to cite him to appear to answer for his views before the papal commissioners in St Paul's.[2] The university intensely resented this papal and episcopal interference with its liberties, and this attack upon its most illustrious teacher. It held the inquiry, however, and declared its finding to be that what Wycliffe said was true, though not very happily expressed: his nineteen propositions are pronounced *veras esse sed male sonare in auribus auditorum*! With this qualified benediction Wycliffe was sent by the university to appear before the papal commission at St Paul's.

For some reason or other, however, the commission did not sit at St Paul's. It sat at Lambeth; probably because the attitude of London was disquieting. Both populace and Government were in fact alive to the menace of the papal Inquisition. An anonymous tract in the English language, usually attributed to Wycliffe himself, had been widely circulated in the city, calling upon all good Christians to rally in defence of the conclusions of Wycliffe and the independence of the English Church. The appeal was effective. No sooner was the court set (early in 1378) than it was surrounded, filled, and overawed by a howling multitude which had poured over London Bridge and made its way tumultuously through the Borough into the Liberties of the Archbishop. Not only was the timid Sudbury terrified into ineptitude, but even the haughty and domineering

---

[1] *Responsio Magistri Johannis Wyccliff ad dubium infrascriptum quæsitum ab eo per Dominum Regem Angliæ Ricardum secundum et Magnum suum Consilium, anno regni ui primo.* See Shirley, *op. cit.*, pp. 258–271.

[2] For the mandate see Spelman, *Concilia*, i, 625, or Wilkins, *Concilia*, iii, 123, or Lewis's *Wicliffe*, p. 264. It will be noted that the course pursued was not any one of the three indicated in the bulls. *Cf.* Workman's *John Wyclif*, i, 305.

Courtenay was too much scared to act. Their discomfiture was completed when a messenger arrived from the mother of the young King, prohibiting the court from pronouncing any sentence upon Wycliffe. Hence, as Walsingham indignantly tells us, the words of the two would-be inquisitors were "softer than oil, to the public loss of their own dignity, and to the damage of the Universal Church." Wycliffe was merely ordered to refrain from preaching and lecturing on the subjects embodied in the nineteen propositions before the court. Then he was allowed to go forth a free man.

The rebuff to the Papacy and its agents was a severe one. Wycliffe had been merely irritated and alienated, not in the least injured, by the feeble performances of the five bulls and of the two commissioners in charge of them. The measure of Wycliffe's immunity was no doubt also the measure of the exasperation of the baffled Sudbury and Courtenay. What next they intended to do remains in doubt; for on March 27, 1378, Pope Gregory XI died, and their commission lapsed. Wycliffe thus secured a further term of impunity. The death of Pope Gregory XI, moreover, had another important effect upon his career. It gave rise to the awful schism of the Papacy which for the next thirty-nine years (1378–1417) rent in suicidal civil war an already distracted Christendom. Before the end of 1378 there were two rival Popes, Urban VI at Rome, and Clement VII gravitating towards Avignon, engaged not in tending the sheep of the Church, but in tearing one another, anathematising one another, and calling one another 'Anti-Christ.' Hitherto Wycliffe had been, at any rate in profession, *humilis et obedientialis filius Romanæ Ecclesiæ*. In 1378 he ceased to be such. He repudiated the Papacy, and applied to both the Popes the epithets which they were applying to one another. They became, in his increasingly lurid language, "monsters," "limbs of Lucifer," "vicars of the fiend," "men glowing with Satanic pride," "sinful idiots," "horrible idols." Their trains of conflicting cardinals were described by him as "incarnate devils" and "hinges of Satan's house."

The remaining six years of Wycliffe's life were a headlong rush, with a gathering velocity, down the steep place of heresy into a sea of a protestantism much more profound than ever Luther's became. No sixteenth-century reformer, indeed, ever divested himself more completely of the whole mediæval system than did Wycliffe during this brief delirious span. Into the details of Wycliffe's career as a religious revolutionary we are not here called upon, or indeed permitted, to enter. Suffice it to say that this closing period of his life (1378–84) was one of almost incredible activity and productivity. He poured forth pamphlets in the vernacular; he composed massive theological treatises in Latin; he organised a translation of the Bible; he trained a band of itinerant agitators. He ultimately laid his axe to the root of the whole sacerdotal overgrowth when he denied and denounced the doctrine of transubstantiation—a doctrine (comparatively recent in its formulation) which he attributed to the direct inspiration of the devil after he had been let loose to deceive men at the close of the first Christian millennium.

VI

This closing period of Wycliffe's career added very little that is new to his social and political teaching. He was absorbed in theological controversies and ecclesiastical conflicts. His *Trialogus* (1382), which contains incomparably the best exposition of his ultimate religious negations, is almost silent on the doctrine of dominion and its implications, which had played so large a part in the utterances of the years when he was *peculiaris regis clericus*. Another cause besides theological preoccupation, moreover, may have tended to keep him quiet respecting dominion. The Peasants' Revolt had broken out in 1381, and the sanguinary communism of the revolutionary boors was by many attributed to the pernicious working of the Lollard leaven, which seemed to increase in virulence as it passed from Latin into English, and from the lecture-rooms of Oxford into the hovels of the villanage.[1] Now Wycliffe, like Luther after him, was a strong believer in order and in firm authoritarian government. He did not admit that his doctrine of dominion had properly any such application as John Ball and the raging peasants gave to it. But he recognised that it was difficult to safeguard it from misapprehension and abuse; hence he ceased to press it or proclaim it. Nevertheless he could not escape the odium which the subversive tenets and violent deeds of the rebels brought upon him, and this, when added to the odium generated by his deadly heresy, soon alienated from him all his early supporters and friends. John of Gaunt, the young King and his mother, the Council of Regency, the Parliament, all felt it impossible to continue to countenance a man whose teachings tended towards revolution in this world and perdition in the next. The friars turned against him with transubstantial fury. The University of Oxford, which protected him as long as it dared, and followed him as far as it could, was at length forced to stop, as it contemplated with horror the abysses of rationalism into which he was descending. Even of his own Poor Priests—the Lollard preachers of the new revolt—the more cultured leaders fell away and made their peace with the Church. He was left at the end of his life a very lonely man, in the midst of alienated friends and ravening foes.

How did he escape destruction? It is not easy to say. Some of his biographers—for example, Foxe, the martyrologist, and Burrows, his quincentenary eulogist—evidently regret that he was not called upon to make an edifying termination at the stake. His story thus concluded would have pointed a more effective moral of the sort which they desired. The fact, however, remains that, stricken down by paralysis in his church at Lutterworth, he died a natural death on the last day of the year 1384. But, though he was

---

[1] There is, as a matter of fact, no communism in Wycliffe's works. Those who have supposed that there is have merely—by giving a material meaning where Wycliffe intended a spiritual one—misinterpreted such passages as "Fidelis hominis totus mundus divitiarum est, infidelis autem nec obolus." In Wycliffe's view every Christian man ideally possesses everything. This is not communism. It is merely individualism gone mad.

spared the fiery trial of martyrdom, his followers were not. In 1382, amid the alarm caused by the Peasants' Revolt and the horror generated by the Lollard attack upon the sanctities of the Mass, Courtenay—now Archbishop in the place of Sudbury, murdered by the peasants—was able to retrieve his discomfiture of 1378. Describing himself as *per totam nostram provinciam Cantaburiensis Inquisitor hæreticæ pravitatis*, he summoned a synod to the Blackfriars in London. As the result of eight sessions (May 17 to July 12, 1382) he secured the condemnation of twenty-four of Wycliffe's conclusions— ten as heretical, fourteen as erroneous. Further, on May 26, 1382, he obtained from the King and the Lords an ordinance ordering the sheriffs throughout England to arrest, imprison, and hand over to the bishops any persons whom they might accuse of heresy. Here, indeed, was the Inquisition in full force. Fortunately for the liberties of the country, the Commons, who had not been consulted, took alarm, and when Parliament met in October they compelled the withdrawal of the obnoxious ordinance, saying in notable words: "It is not the intention of the Commons to be tried for heresy, nor to bind over themselves or their descendants to the prelates, more than their ancestors had been in time past." It is an interesting example of the instinctive English appeal to precedent (invented, if necessary, for the occasion). By a succession of such appeals, as has been remarked by Tennyson and others, English freedom has broadened down. In this instance, Courtenay, checked in his hope of commanding secular aid in his hunt for heresy, had to content himself with a royal writ authorising the bishops themselves to arrest heretics if they could catch them. But this was a far inferior concession; for the bishops lacked the secular paraphernalia of the chase. All the same, he was able to exercise a pressure which before his death in 1396 laid Lollardy very low.

The accusations brought against the Lollards, however, were exclusively theological in character. Hence they lie outside our present sphere. All that now remains for us to do is first to attempt a summary of Wycliffe's social and political ideas, and secondly to form an estimate of his character and achievement.

VII

It has been remarked that all Wycliffe's significant activities lay within the last ten years of his life. If he had died in 1374 his name would have passed into complete oblivion; even if he had lived but till 1378, with his works on dominion composed, he would have been recollected dimly and uncertainly, merely as a second and inferior Marsilio, *damnatæ memoriæ*. It was the enormous and feverish output of the years 1378–84 which made him an everlasting portent and a purging power. Not often does it happen that a man radically changes his profession, materially alters his mode of life, or effectively shakes the world out of its old form when he is sixty years of age!

The political and social ideas of Wycliffe, therefore, formulated as they were for the most part during the penultimate period of his career, are not among those thoughts of his which have had the greatest influence upon mankind. They are in the main academic in character; they are expressed in highly technical scholastic Latin; they are obscure both in substance and in accidents. Nevertheless, one of them, viz., the doctrine of dominion, which was at the basis of them all, is recognised as an important and curious contribution to sociological theory. The only trouble is that no one can quite understand what the doctrine is, or on what principle Wycliffe applied it.[1] It was not, however, a doctrine original to Wycliffe. He had learned it from Fitzralph, Archbishop of Armagh, who had developed it in his conflicts with the friars; while Fitzralph himself claimed for his views

[1] The best discussions of Wycliffe's doctrine of dominion are to be found in the following works: R. L. Poole, *Illustrations of the History of Mediæval Thought and Learning*; W. W. Shirley, introduction to *Fasciculi Zizaniorum*; R. L. Poole, preface to Wycliffe's *De Dominio Divino*; R. L. Poole, *Wycliffe and Movements for Reform*; W. A. Dunning, *A History of Political Theories, Ancient and Mediæval*; G. V. Lechler, *John Wycliffe and his English Precursors*; H. B. Workman, *John Wyclif*, i, 257–274, and ii, 20–30.

the venerable authority of St Bernard, St Augustine, and the Gospels. Only gradually, moreover, did Wycliffe unfold the doctrine of dominion. He was an ecclesiastical politician before he was a political philosopher. He arrived at theory by way of practice. His early utterances, therefore, are clearer than his later. Hence to understand him it is best to watch his ideas as they grew in the hothouse of circumstances and in the forcing-ground of political controversy.

First and foremost, then, he was a *nationalist*. Brought up during the Hundred Years War, and at a time when the Papacy appeared to be merely a French institution, he seems to have had no conception of Christendom as a whole, or of a Universal Church; still less of a united Humanity. His ideal was a national State with a national Church subordinate to it. He spoke of endowments as given *non cuicunque ecclesiæ sed singulariter ecclesiæ Anglicanæ*. He ended by urging that the English Church should reassert its independence of Rome and should live *more Græcorum sub propriis legibus*. It was his nationalism and his exclusively insular patriotism which commended him to the court of Edward III, and caused him to be sent as the English champion to the Conference of Bruges.

Closely allied to his nationalism was his '*étatism*.' In the exaltation of the State and the ascription to it of sovereignty his writings anticipated *The Prince* of Machiavelli, the *Republic* of Bodin, the *Von Weltlicher Oberkeit* of Luther, and *The Leviathan* of Hobbes.[1] He based the duty of obedience to the civil authorities, not on his abstract theory of dominion —this he reserved exclusively for ecclesiastical purposes—but on the clear commands of Scripture and on the unequivocal examples of Christ and the Apostles. He agreed with Augustine and the Fathers generally that the Fall of Man necessitated and caused the institution of the State.[2] He regarded it as part of the divine scheme to bring man back to righteousness. So emphatic appeared to him to be the

[1] Note particularly *De Civili Dominio*, Book I, ch. xxviii, and the tract *De Dominis et Servis*.

[2] " Dominium civile est dominium occasione peccati humanitus institutum " (*De Civ. Dom.*, Book I, ch. xviii).

inspired injunction to obey "the powers that be" on the ground that they were "ordained of God," that he held it to be obligatory on Christian men to reverence the authority of even wicked tyrants, even as St Paul reverenced the authority of Nero. Nay, he went so far as to say, in words which scandalised the elect, that in certain circumstances *Deus debet obedire diabolo*. As to the form of government: in a better state of affairs a theocracy such as that depicted in the Book of Judges would be the ideal; but in the actual sinfulness of the world a strong monarchy was essential.[1]

Appendant to his '*étatism*' was his *Erastianism*. He was Erastian both in the exact and in the popular sense of the term. In the exact sense he was Erastian in that he held that persuasion and not force was the proper method of the Church. In the popular sense, also, he was Erastian in that he held that the State was omnicompetent, having authority in all causes whether temporal or spiritual. This latter view—which Professor Maitland rightly calls Byzantine rather than Erastian—was expressly set forth in his *De Officio Regis* (1379). It portrays and advocates a relation of Church and State essentially identical with that later established by Henry VIII: it displays the king as supreme over ecclesiastical persons, ecclesiastical property, ecclesiastical courts. It exalts the State as against the Church, even going so far as to say that the State represents the divinity of Christ, while the Church represents but His humanity. The king is God's vicar in the government of his people, and bishops derive whatever authority they may have through him and him alone. This is more than even Hooker urged.[2]

From this extreme utterance it will be further evident that Wycliffe was not merely an Erastian but also an *anti-sacerdotalist*. His mind, for all its mediæval trappings, was essentially the lay mind. It instinctively revolted against all the pretensions of priestly authority. It was the Renaissance

---

[1] See *De Civili Dominio*, Book I, ch. xxvi and xxvii.

[2] The following is a significant passage from the *De Officio Regis* (ch. vi): "Episcopi, sui officiales et curati sui, tenentur in qualicunque tali causa spiritualiter cognoscere auctoritate regis; ergo rex per illos. Sunt enim tales legii homines regis."

mind not yet disentangled from the meshes of scholasticism. It came to the conclusion that the root of all sacerdotal superstition lay in the illusion that a person upon whom episcopal hands had been placed was anything which a layman was not; or could do anything which a layman could not do. This conclusion led inevitably to the repudiation of the whole sacramental system, and particularly to the denial of transubstantiation—that daily miracle of the Mass, the performance of which raised the lowest priest above the highest king.

Wycliffe's anti-sacerdotalism was only another aspect of his intense *individualism*. Wholly abandoning the common mediæval conception of the Church as an ark manned by a clerical crew busily engaged in rescuing a perishing humanity from a devil-infested flood, he reverted to the Augustinian idea of the Church as the communion of the elect, known only to God, and bound each one of them immediately to his Maker by the personal tie of grace. This indeed was the vital principle which underlay the obscure verbiage of the doctrine of dominion. Every man who rightfully exercised any authority or possessed any property held it directly, without any intervening lords, from the supreme *Dominus Capitalis*, the Creator of the Universe, to whom alone properly belonged all might, majesty, dominion, and power.

Wycliffe's individualism—perhaps his most remarkable characteristic in that age of old-established collectivism— was intimately associated with a *passion for righteousness*. The theory of dominion was not only a theory of personal relation; it was also a theory of moral responsibility. The condition under which every creature held property and power from God was obedience to His holy will. Hence mortal sin entailed entire forfeiture. *Peccans mortaliter non habet dominium* was one of his striking sayings; and, again, he contended *quod nullus existens in peccato mortali est dominus, sacerdos, vel episcopus*, and even *quod si papa sit præscitus et malus homo ac per consequens membrum diaboli, non habet potestatem supra fideles Christi ab aliquo sibi datam, nisi* [shades of Innocent IV and Boniface VIII!] *forte a Cæsare*. Here again was another blow at the sacerdotal system. For who could tell where and how

45

often by mortal sin the chain of sacramental efficacy had been broken? The truth seems to be that nothing scandalised Wycliffe's righteous soul more in that sinful age than the dissociation of religion from ethics, and the spectacle of corrupt priests (whose every act proclaimed their devotion to the world, the flesh, and the devil) maintaining that the validity of their official performances was not affected by their unofficial depravities. "By life been preestes known," he contended.

This brings us to another prominent article of Wycliffe's creed, viz., his strong and reiterated insistence on the *duty of the clergy to withdraw themselves from secular concerns and to surrender their mundane possessions*. They were to give themselves to good works and sound teaching, and to live by the charity of their flocks. He dated the decadence of the Church from the day of the Donation of Constantine, when the devil "bi Silvestre preest of Rome brought in a new gile and moved the Emperour of Rome to endowe the Churche in this preest." He contended again and again that the spheres of clergy and laity are distinct and separate. The functions of the clergy are purely spiritual; to them not *dominium* but *ministerium* is assigned as a duty; they should abjure earthly lordship and devote themselves to the service of their flocks. So urgent did Wycliffe regard the divestment of the spirituality of their terrestrial endowments that he called loudly upon the secular lords, to whom mundane property and power had been committed as an inalienable trust, to strip the clergy of their entangling wealth, if they would not strip themselves thereof. The secular lords, headed by John of Gaunt, indicated their readiness to render this little service to their religious brethren.[1]

VIII

This sketch of Wycliffe is already too long. But it must not be brought to a close without some brief attempt to estimate the character and influence of the reformer. Much

[1] Two notable tracts on this topic are printed by F. D. Matthew in his *English Works of Wycliffe*, pp. 359–402 and pp. 405–457.

traversing of the dull and dreary wastes of Wycliffe's writing has brought me to the suspicion—I might even say the conviction—that Wycliffe was not a religious man at all. This, I submit, is also the opinion of the Christian world— the Catholic section of it explicitly; the Protestant section tacitly. For, though 'Wycliffe Halls' may be founded for the training of Protestant clergy, no one dreams of studying Wycliffe's works therein; though 'Wycliffe Preachers' may be instituted to combat the teachings of Rome, no one of these preachers ever thinks of quoting a word that Wycliffe said; though 'Wycliffe Societies' may be founded to put the multitude of his manuscripts into print, no single tract is ever considered edifying enough for general circulation. In fact, two separate 'Wycliffe Societies' (1844 and 1884) have already languished in the effort to get people to read, or even to buy, the soulless stuff he wrote. Much of it, after five centuries, is still unprinted, and (probably to no one's loss) likely to remain so.

Wycliffe, it is true, dealt largely with religious topics, and quoted Scripture freely to his purpose. But that does not compel us to call him religious. He was an academic theologian, a scholastic philosopher, a thinker whose interest in his theme was purely moral and intellectual. He seems to have had no religious experience; no sense of sin; no consciousness of conversion; no assurance of salvation; no heart of love; no evident communion with God. He made no emotional appeal; he roused no spiritual response in the souls of those to whom his dry syllogisms were addressed. He was, indeed, a rationalist, born before his due season. His affinities were with the eighteenth century, and in the eighteenth century not with John Wesley but with David Hume. If he had lived in the nineteenth century he would have been the head, not of the Evangelical Alliance, but of the Rationalist Press. His definition of revelation would have satisfied the French Encyclopædists: revelation to him was merely a higher power of reason—*lumen supernaturale est forma perfectiva luminis naturalis*.[1]

[1] *De Dominio Divino*, Book I, ch. xi.

47

The motive force behind the enormous activities of his closing decade was antagonism to Rome. He was anti-papal, anti-clerical, anti-monastic, anti-sacramental, all but anti-Christian. He was merely negative and destructive. His Bible was but a weapon of offence; his pamphlets were violent polemics; his Poor Priests were not evangelists but revolutionary agitators. The hungry sheep whom temporarily he drew from their old pastures looked up to him and were not fed; and most of such as did not perish in their disillusionment made their way back to the fold where at any rate some scanty nutriment could be gained. Wycliffe belonged to the Renaissance rather than to the Reformation. Not, of course, to the Renaissance of Southern Europe with its art, its poetry, its music, its soft and tender humanities; but to the Renaissance of Northern Europe with its passion for truth, its instinct for science, its anarchic freedom, its stern zeal for righteousness.

He was a dour fighter, and he had to contend against foes of limitless malignity and power. To stand, as he did at the end of his life, almost solitary yet entirely undismayed, in the midst of enemies so many, so merciless, and so mighty, argues a courage little less than sublime. That he failed to appreciate the good qualities of his opponents was in the circumstances natural. It no doubt is difficult rightly to estimate the virtues of people who are plotting your destruction in this world and predicting your perdition in the next. Nevertheless it is regrettable that he should have called the clergy "fiends of hell," without recognising the greatness of the work which they had accomplished in civilising mediæval Europe; and that he should have denounced the monks as "gluttonous idolaters" without taking into account all that the monasteries had stood for through long centuries of rapine and war. Above all, it is regrettable that in his far-sighted anticipations of the remote future, with its national states, its Erastian churches, its autocratic monarchs, and its civil clergy, his very modern mind should have had so small a conception of the grandeur of those mediæval ideals of the Christian Commonwealth and the Church Universal which

48

had filled the vision and inspired the pens of thinkers such as St Thomas Aquinas and dreamers such as Dante.

BOOK LIST

A. PRIMARY SOURCES

WYCLIFFE: *De Dominio Divino.* Ed. Poole, 1890.
    De Civili Dominio. Ed. Poole and Loserth, 1885–1905.
    De Ecclesia. Ed. Loserth, 1886.
    De Officio Regis. Ed. Pollard and Sayle, 1887.
    English Works. Ed. Matthew, 1880.
Fasciculi Zizaniorum. Ed. Shirley, 1858.
Concilia Magnæ Britanniæ. Ed. Wilkins, 1736.

B. SECONDARY SOURCES

BIGG, C.: *Wayside Sketches.* 1906.
BROWN, E. (editor): *Fasciculus Rerum Expetendarum et Fugiendarum.* 1690.
BUDDENSIEG, R.: *Johann Wiclif und seine Zeit.* 1885.
CAPES, W. W.: *The English Church in the Fourteenth and Fifteenth Centuries.* 1900.
CREIGHTON, M.: *History of the Papacy,* vol. i. 2nd edition, 1897.
—— *Historical Essays and Reviews.* Ed. L. Creighton. 1902.
DUNNING, W. A.: *A History of Political Theories, Ancient and Mediæval.* 1910.
FIGGIS, J. N.: "John Wyclif" in *Typical English Churchmen,* Second Series, 1909.
LECHLER, G. V. (translated by P. Lorimer): *John Wycliffe and his English Precursors.* 1878.
LEWIS, J.: *Life of Wicliffe.* 1720.
LOSERTH, J.: Article "Wiclif" in Herzog-Hauck, *Realencyklopädie.*
LYTE, H. C. M.: *History of the University of Oxford.* 1886.
POOLE, R. L.: *Illustrations of the History of Mediæval Thought and Learning.* 2nd edition, 1920.
—— *Wycliffe and Movements for Reform.* 1888.
—— Article "Wyclif" in *Encyclopædia Britannica.* 1911.
RASHDALL, H.: *The Universities of the Middle Ages.* 1895.
—— Article "John Wycliffe" in *Dictionary of National Biography.* 1900.
SERGEANT, L.: *John Wyclif.* 1893.
TREVELYAN, G. M.: *England in the Age of Wycliffe.* 1899.
VAUGHAN, R.: *Life and Opinions of Wycliffe.* 1828.
WORKMAN, H. B.: *The Dawn of the Reformation,* vol. i. 1901.
—— *John Wyclif: a Study of the English Mediæval Church.* 1926.

III

MACHIAVELLI AND THE NON-MORAL STATE [1]

No one who visits Hereford Cathedral can fail to be struck by the marvellous *Mappa Mundi* of Richard de Haldingham, which adorns the south choir aisle. It represents the theological conception of the world at the close of the thirteenth century. The habitable earth which it portrays is flat and circular, like a rimless plate, surrounded by a narrow fringe of ocean. At the centre of the circle stands Jerusalem; at the extreme east the Garden of Eden: midway between the two the Tower of Babel. Round the margin at different points are situated such places as the peninsula in which Gog and Magog were interned by Alexander the Great, the Earthly Paradise discovered by St Brandan, and the British Isles. On various otherwise unoccupied spots in Asia and Africa are to be found such interesting curiosities as the kingdom of Prester John, the realm of the Amazons, the granaries of Joseph, and the land of the Sciapodes, those fascinating one-legged folk whose solitary foot was so large and adaptable that it not only carried them about with incredible celerity, but also served them when they rested as a shelter from the tropical sun. It would be difficult to conceive any map which, in all its details, is more widely and wildly remote from correspondence with geographical reality. For, even when it does present such features as the British Isles or the Mediterranean Sea which undoubtedly

[1] From *The Social and Political Ideas of Some Great Thinkers of the Renaissance and the Reformation* (Harrap, 1925). The other studies in this volume are: " Introductory: The Renaissance and the Reformation," by the editor; " Nicolas of Cusa," by E. F. Jacob; " Sir John Fortescue," by Miss A. E. Levett; " Sir Thomas More," by A. W. Reed; " Desiderius Erasmus," by J. A. K. Thomson; " Martin Luther," by J. W. Allen; " John Calvin," by W. R. Matthews.

exist, it presents them in such forms and positions as make them almost unrecognisable. We may safely say that not even in the thirteenth century did it ever occur to any master mariner to borrow this map, or make a copy of it, for purposes of navigation. We may also confidently assert that if he had done so his voyage would have resulted in speedy and irretrievable disaster.

At the very time, however, when the pious prebendary of Haldingham was concocting from the Scriptures and the mythologies this fantastic travesty of the world as it actually exists, Italian seamen—particularly those of Venice and Genoa—on the basis of careful observation and repeated experiment, were constructing for practical purposes *portolani*, or mariners' charts, which give an amazingly accurate and minute representation of that Mediterranean basin wherein the main maritime commerce of the Middle Ages was concentrated. Free from prejudice and prepossession, unhampered by the postulates of theology, they depicted lands and seas as they really were, and so laid the foundations of the modern science of navigation.

All which is a parable and an analogy. Richard de Haldingham was a contemporary of St Thomas Aquinas and Dante. While he was drawing his fantastic map they were expounding the principles of politics. And the principles of politics as expounded by them bore, in respect of remoteness from reality, a striking resemblance to Richard's cosmology. They both lived ideally in a unified and symmetrical society—the *Respublica Christiana*—whose supreme ruler was God, and whose final law was His Holy Will. This society was administered mediately by two human agents, the Pope and the Emperor, the one exercising divine authority over all causes spiritual, the other over all causes temporal. Under the Pope served a hierarchy of cardinals, bishops, and clergy; under the Emperor a corresponding hierarchy of kings, nobles, and knights. The only serious problem that disturbed the beatific serenity of either St Thomas or Dante was the problem of the relation between the two powers, the spiritual and the temporal. Were they co-ordinate and equal, or was one superior to the other? How were the spheres of their jurisdiction delimited? As to these problems the views of St Thomas and Dante differed. To the one the Papacy from its very nature was the higher power; to the other the Empire had an immemorial claim to universal authority. The arguments by which these rival contentions were supported were drawn from precisely the same sources as those from which Richard de Haldingham filled his map with visionary shapes and imaginary names. They were arguments from the Scriptures, from the Fathers, from classical mythology, from supposed natural history. They turned upon the story of the Creation; upon the relation of the sun to the moon; of the soul to the body, of eternity to time; upon Samuel's attitude to Saul; upon the offerings of the Magi to the infant Lord; upon the sufficiency of the two swords possessed by Peter in the garden; upon the Saviour's parting command to the Apostles, and upon a multitude of other similar irrelevancies. They were, indeed, scholastic exercises almost wholly devoid of any relation to the actual politics of their age. For at the very moment when Richard de Haldingham was moving with his map to Hereford, and while Dante was still in his prime, the Papal Monarchy, which St Thomas had exalted to the sky, passed from the humiliation of Anagni to the debasement of the "Babylonish Captivity" at Avignon. Similarly, the Holy Roman Empire, to which Dante looked for the unification and pacification of mankind, sank to the condition of a mere German overlordship, and even in that limited sphere ceased to function, since it failed to give even to Germany either unity or peace.

In short, while mediæval champions of Papacy and Empire were contending in the academic empyrean for the prize of a visionary world-dominion, actual authority over the men of a distracted and disrupted Christendom was being divided among a number of secular princes, out of whose mortal conflicts and diabolical intrigues the modern state-system was being evolved. Unchecked by either papal or imperial authority, regardless of both canon and civil law, emancipated alike from the restraints of religion and of ethics, the "new monarchs" of the political jungle were displaying in a desperate struggle for existence those qualities of the lion and the fox which in the earlier ages of the cosmic process of biological evolution had enabled the animal possessors of these qualities to survive and prevail. The weapons in this fierce political struggle for existence were war and diplomacy. On the one hand, new armies, new means of offence and defence, new tactics and strategy, and, above all, a new ferocity, completely changed the military art from what it had been during the Middle Ages. On the other hand, missions, embassies, royal visits, supplemented by dispatches, memoranda, and reports, instituted a new science of diplomacy in which craft and guile found a limitless field for exercise. The princes who had to defend themselves in arms against a circle of powerful, alert, and merciless foes, and to protect themselves diplomatically against the conspiracies and intrigues of countless malignant rivals both within and without their states, had no use for the lofty speculations of Aquinas or Dante respecting the two powers, the two lights, the two swords, and the general duality of things. What they required was not a *Mappa Mundi* giving them sanctified information respecting the imaginary situation of the Garden of Eden, the Tower of Babel, and the kingdom of Prester John; it was a *portolano* providing, in the form of a precise chart, the data indispensable for the navigation of the stormy and rock-infested seas on which their frail barques were tossing. It was such a *portolano* that Machiavelli professed to provide. His prime achievement, indeed, was to change the method of political speculation; to make it once again, as it had been in Aristotle's day, inductive and historical; to bring it back from the heavens to the earth; to render it (so he hoped) practical and useful. He converted an abstract political philosophy, subordinate to ethics and theology, into an independent art of government divorced from both morals and religion.

II

Nicolo Machiavelli was born at Florence in 1469. This was the year in which Lorenzo the Magnificent began that period of uncrowned principality (1469–92) wherein the splendid city of Machiavelli's birth attained the summit of its glory and assumed the undisputed leadership in the scholarship, the thought, and the art of the Renaissance. It was also, by a coincidence, the year in which occurred the marriage of Ferdinand of Aragon and Isabella of Castile— an event which some historians speak of as marking the beginning of modern history, since it led to the unification of the Christian powers of the Peninsula, the conquest of Granada, the discovery of America, and the establishment of a century of Spanish ascendancy in Europe. It was signifi- cant that Machiavelli should thus have been born in the heyday of the Renaissance, and that he should have spent his youth amid the vast and rapid changes which inaugur- ated the era of the modern national states. For no one since the days of Marsilio and Wycliffe so completely divested himself of the Middle Ages, or displayed himself so nakedly to his contemporaries, as the "New Man."

Of his early life we know little. His family was Tuscan, old and noble. His father, Bernardo, followed the law, and occasionally held public appointments in Florence: he was also a landowner in a small way, drawing rents which were sufficient to relieve him—and his son Nicolo after him—from the fear of extreme poverty. Nicolo, although he soon showed an acuteness of mind which raised him above the level of his family and his neighbours, did not receive a very elaborate education: he learned to write Latin, but appar- ently not to read Greek. "The comparative restriction of his culture," says Villari, in words which should cheer and console modern undergraduates, "had the inestimable advantage of preserving the spontaneous originality of his genius and his style, and preventing them from being suffo- cated beneath a dead weight of erudition." So long as the rule of the Medici endured in Florence Machiavelli had, it would seem, no regular occupation. But the expulsion of Lorenzo's unworthy son, Piero, by the French in 1494, and the establishment of the republic, opened to him the way of civic employment. His study of Livy and Polybius had made him convincedly republican in sentiment. He looked with enthusiasm to the renewal in Florence of the great days of antique Rome, and he held the fervent hope that through the Florence of his day, as through the Rome of two thousand years earlier, Italy would attain to unity and peace.

At first, it would appear, Machiavelli attached himself to Savonarola, who, then in the flood-tide of his influence, was preaching the salvation of Italy through moral reform and religious revival, under French domination. But Machiavelli lacked moral sense, was entirely devoid of religious faith, and was filled with a loathing for foreigners. Hence he soon drew away from the agitating friar, and viewed with approval the means that were employed to extinguish him (1498). In both the *Discourses* and *The Prince* he examines with cold precision the cause of Savonarola's collapse: it was, he decided, that he was unarmed, and that behind the fury of his empty words, and the passing frenzy which he roused in the fickle populace, there was no *force* on which he could rely for the realisation of his ideals. Machiavelli came to the conclusion, which all his subsequent experience confirmed, that *force* directed by craft is the only thing that counts in politics.

This subsequent experience of his was varied and important. In 1498 he was appointed secretary to the so-called Second Chancery, otherwise known as "The Ten"—an administrative body specially concerned with the conduct of diplomacy and war. This office he held for fourteen years, that is, until 1512, when the republican constitution under which he served was overthrown and the Medicean tyranny restored. He performed his duties as a Secretary of State with conspicuous zeal, ability, fidelity, and success. In 1502, when his friend Piero Soderini—to whom he refers in many passages of his writings—was appointed perpetual Gonfalonier, he became, as his confidential adviser and

55

trusted agent, one of the most influential men not only in Florence, but in Italy as a whole. His high position and the growing recognition of his exceptional powers of mind caused him to be sent by the Florentine Signory on a number of important military and political missions. On the one hand, he had to raise troops, hire mercenaries, make alliances, secure auxiliaries, and even conduct operations in the long-drawn war with Pisa. On the other hand, he had to visit many courts and camps, in order that he might counter conspiracies against his beloved city, break up hostile confederations, secure the withdrawal of unreasonable demands, and cement doubtful friendships.

His task was a far from enviable one. Since the death of Lorenzo de' Medici in 1492 a new and critical condition of things had arisen in Italy. The foreigners had begun to pour their armies into the peninsula. The French invasion of 1494 had been followed by incursions of Spaniards, Germans, and Swiss, until Italy had become the battle-ground of the ferocious monarchs and marauders of the New Europe. It was the French with whom Florence, and Machiavelli as its representative, had most to do. The French had driven out the Medici in 1494; the French were the nominal allies of the Florentines in their efforts to conquer the intractable city of Pisa (which was supported by Spain and the Empire); the French were their main bulwark against the machinations of Cæsar Borgia and the exiled Piero de' Medici. The Florentine Republic, in short, existed only by sufferance of the French, and the French king, Louis XII, was entirely aware of the fact. Hence neither he nor his subordinates felt it at all necessary to conceal their contempt for Florence, their indifference to Machiavelli, or their complete unconcern as to what anyone in Tuscany said or did. They mulcted the Florentines of money; they subjected them to the grossest insults; they deserted them in critical emergencies; they finally left them naked to the vengeance of their foes. Four times was Machiavelli sent to Louis XII to plead for better treatment, and the humiliations which he was compelled impotently to suffer ate like a red-hot iron into his soul. How was it, he asked, that the French were so much stronger than the Italians that they could do with them what they liked? How was it that they could march from end to end of their peninsula without opposition; could sack their cities, overthrow their governments, plunder their treasures, slay their men, and violate their women, with complete impunity? How was it that the representative of an Italian state, such as Florence—a state eminent throughout Christendom in commerce, finance, art, and learning—could be treated with a contempt reserved in other lands for serfs and dogs? The answer, to Machiavelli, was plain: the Italians lacked political unity, and the small states among which they were divided lacked, whether singly or in combination, military power.

III

The two obvious weaknesses of Italy in Machiavelli's day were, indeed, political disunion and military incapacity.

The outstanding political phenomenon of the period was the formation of strong national states in the west of Europe. First, England had attained to unity and self-consciousness during the long and fiery process of the Hundred Years War. The subsequent Wars of the Roses, by eliminating the feudal nobility, had completed her consolidation. Under the firm and patriotic rule of the Tudor kings she had begun to enjoy peace, prosperity, power. Secondly, France had grown from a distracted collection of ungovernable fiefs into a mighty monarchy. One by one the great lordships had been subordinated to the Crown, until, with the acquisition of Burgundy and Brittany in Machiavelli's own time, the direct royal authority had been established over all the vast territory of the realm. Thirdly, Spain had arisen, as if by miracle, from the chaos and confusion of eight centuries of religious conflict and civil war. The Christian states of Leon, Castile, Navarre, Aragon, Catalonia, had all been brought under the rule of the joint monarchs Ferdinand and Isabelle. The last Moorish enclave, Granada, had been

SOME GREAT POLITICAL IDEALISTS

absorbed. A vigorous religious unity had been impressed upon a newly created and proudly conscious Spanish nation.

Even in Germany a national spirit was moving—a spirit which was destined, ere the end of Machiavelli's life, to manifest itself in the upheaval of the Reformation. The Emperor Maximilian, moreover, amid the distractions of his diversions and dissipations, was striving to re-establish some sort of central government, with courts and councils, military forces, and calculable revenue. Machiavelli anticipated the speedy unification of Germany, in spite of Maximilian's ineffectiveness, because it already had a titular head, because it possessed racial homogeneity, because it was peopled by men accustomed to war, but above all because it was the home in a special degree of such virtue as still remained upon the earth.[1]

The case of Italy, however, was very different. Intellectually and æsthetically in the van of all European peoples, morally and politically she lagged far in the rear. Her people, widely diverse in race and culture, were utterly degenerate and corrupt; she had lost all military capacity; her princes were craven and criminal; her Church was secularized and incredibly depraved; she was torn by violent schisms and incessant intrigues. No bond of any sort of unity held together her struggling atoms. The task of consolidating her, and making a nation of her, seemed to be beyond the reach of any normal means. And yet consolidated, nationalised, re-created, she must be, if she were to hold her own with the New Monarchs, if she were to be able to expel the foreign invaders, if she were to succeed in restoring order and in suppressing the orgy of villainy by which she was degraded and disgraced.

Five main states divided the peninsula between them. In the north the duchy of Milan and the republic of Venice contended for dominance in the Lombard Plain and for control of the eastern passes of the Alps. In the south the kingdom of Naples, under a line of illegitimate and treach-

[1] Cf. *Discourses on Livy*, I, 55.

erous Aragonese rulers, contended for power and dominion against a resistant and fulminating Papacy. Between the two pairs of combatants Tuscany, under the hegemony of Florence, held a fluctuating balance. Normally, the Papacy and Venice were allied against Milan and Naples; but departures from the norm were frequent and bewildering. Hence the study of Italian politics in the fifteenth and sixteenth centuries is like an attempt to solve a complicated puzzle. One dominant fact, however, emerges from the study. It is that in the game of politics as played in Italy at that time no rules of honour or morality whatsoever were observed. Treasons, betrayals, poisonings, assassinations, perjuries, hypocrisies, sacrileges, infidelities—all kinds of base and hateful villainies—were employed without scruple or remorse. The Papacy, in particular under such Popes as Sixtus IV, Alexander VI, and Julius II, forgetting its sacred nature, and ignoring its international responsibilities, made itself notorious for its violence, selfishness, treachery, and mendacity. Machiavelli came to regard it as the root cause of Italy's disunion and debasement.

Another cause, however, the importance of which profoundly impressed him, was the military weakness of the Italians. Individual Italians, such as Castruccio Castracani of Lucca (whose life he made the basis of a notable romance), showed, it is true, both bravery and capacity. But the people of the peninsula, as a whole, were soft and effeminate, cowardly and unwarlike, engrossed in commerce and finance, distracted from virtue by philosophy and art, debilitated by sensuality, depraved by scepticism. They were, indeed, extremely quarrelsome, and they were experts in the use of poison and the dagger; but they preferred to wage their wars by proxy—that is, by means of companies of hired mercenaries, or by means of armies of auxiliaries drawn from foreign lands. So long as Italy's quarrels were merely domestic this did not matter much. Her wars became little more than bloodless games, wherein treachery and bribery played a more decisive part than force or military skill. But it was another matter when she had to deal with the hosts of the new nations who came across the mountains or the seas to slay, to plunder, and to subjugate.

Northern Europe had been undergoing a military revolution. The days of feudal levies, armour-clad knights, battlemented castles, and picturesque chivalry were over. Everywhere national armies—large forces of foot-soldiers drawn mainly from the third estate—equipped with new weapons, and supported by that satanic novelty, artillery, were making havoc of old military conventions, transforming the art of war, and reconstructing the political framework of the Continent. First France, by the famous Ordonnance of Orleans, in 1439, had established the force which had finally cleared both Normandy and Aquitaine of the English, and brought the exhausting Hundred Years War to a victorious end. Spain, Switzerland, the states of Germany, all had followed suit. Even England was reorganising her national militia, and was building the Royal Navy, which was destined to enable her from time to time to determine the balance of power in Europe. Only Italy remained inept, her coasts unprotected, her passes unguarded, her rich cities a prey to any invader, her fruitful plains open to every spoiler. What, to Machiavelli, appeared the remedy for this deplorable condition of affairs?

IV

For the salvation of Italy from internal disorder and external oppression Machiavelli looked principally to the military regeneration of the people. The "Nation in Arms" was his ideal. "All able-bodied men between the ages of seventeen and forty should be drilled so as to be always ready to defend their country."[1] The treacherous and ineffective mercenaries should be dismissed. The dangerous and doubtful aid of alien auxiliaries should be refused. Machiavelli was speaking of what he knew. He himself, in the course of the protracted struggle between Florence and Pisa, had had agonising experience of both the violent perfidy of the Italian *condottieri* and the perfidious violence

[1] *The Art of War*, Book I.

of the French men-at-arms whom Louis XII had sent to the nominal aid of the republic. The net result of their operations had been the humiliation of Florence, the failure of all her schemes, and the exhaustion of her treasury.

In all his great political works Machiavelli gives this supreme military problem a prominent place. To take the works in the order of their composition: (1) In *The Prince* he devotes a whole section (chapters xii–xiv)—about one-eighth of the entire book—to the question. First he exposes, with numerous examples, the evils of the *condottieri* system: "If Italy," he says, "had not trusted so many years to mercenary troops she would not now be ruined." He blames "the ecclesiastical princes, strangers to the art of war," for introducing the vicious practice, the final consequence of which is that "Italy has been overrun by Charles, pillaged by Louis, forced by Ferdinand, and disgraced by the Switzers." Secondly, he treats of the perils which flow from the acceptance of the aid of foreign auxiliaries, and he illustrates his thesis by the disasters which accrued to Julius II from his Spanish allies, to Florence from its French levies, to the Byzantines from the Turkish stipendiaries, to Louis XI from the hired Swiss, and to the later Roman Emperors from their Gothic *fœderati*. Finally, he emphasises the prime importance of military skill to princes, and of military training to their people: "Princes," he asserts, "ought to make the art of war their sole duty and occupation, for it is peculiarly the science of those who govern. War and the several sorts of discipline and institutions relative to it should be their only pursuits, the only profession they should follow, and the object they ought always to have in view." Moreover, they "must above all things, as the very foundation of the whole business, be furnished with soldiers of their own natives."

(2) In the *Discourses on Livy*, using the Romans as examples, he shows why "mercenary soldiers were unprofitable" and contends that "it is necessary in the maintaining of a state, whether it be a republic or a kingdom, to arm the native

subjects, as we see all those have done who with their armies have made any great conquests."[1] But if the mercenaries are unprofitable, foreign auxiliaries are much worse: "Of all kinds of soldiers the auxiliaries are the most dangerous—therefore a prince or a republic should rather take any other course than seek to bring auxiliary soldiers into his country."[2] The decadence of the Roman Empire began, he considers, when the Imperial armies ceased to be native and were recruited from Parthians and Germans.[3]

(3) *The Art of War*, one of Machiavelli's most noteworthy and original works, is, as its title implies, wholly devoted to this cardinal theme. Its seven books are cast in the form of dialogues, in which the successful Italian commander, Fabrizio Calonna, expresses the views that may be regarded as Machiavelli's own. "The fundamental idea of *The Art of War*," says Villari, "is that the best militia can be formed by arming the people, and that at all periods the infantry constitutes the backbone of an army."[4] Or, in the words put into the mouth of Fabrizio, "We are taught by history and experience, that all states must be based upon national arms, and that by these alone can they be securely defended." Machiavelli regards the Roman legion as the supreme model for imitation, but he considers that improvements in matters of detail are suggested by examination of the military systems of the Swiss, Germans, and Spanish foot-soldiers of his own day. He describes his resultant ideal for an Italian national army. It is curious—and it suggests the limitations of the literary man when he is dealing with practical affairs—that he would not equip his national force with firearms, but would revert to javelins, pikes, swords, and bows and arrows! Even artillery—which in his own day had played a decisive part in the battles of Ravenna, Novara, and Marignano—he regards as of little account. "Cannon are so difficult of management that if you aim ever so little too high their shots pass over the enemy's head, and if you lower them in the least they fire into the ground. They are altogether useless

---

[1] *Discourses*, I, 44.   [2] *Ibid.*, II, 20.   [3] *Ibid.*, II, 30.
[4] Villari, *The Life and Times of Machiavelli*, ii, 292.

in a general engagement."[1] Into Machiavelli's detailed discussions of the methods of training a militia, the conduct of armies in the field, the principles of strategy and tactics, the manner of quartering troops, and finally the theories of fortification, it is unnecessary for us to enter. Suffice it to say that *The Art of War*, as a whole, is a pioneer treatise: it holds the same eminent place in military science as *The Prince* does in political science. Moreover, the purpose of the two works is the same: it is the emancipation and unification of Italy. Just as Machiavelli concludes *The Prince* with the declaration, "The first Italian who will follow my councils shall, to his immortal honour, succeed in the magnanimous enterprise of freeing his country," so does he end *The Art of War* with the words, "I declare to you that whichsoever of the princes now holding states in Italy shall first enter upon this road, he will be the first to become lord of this country."

(4) In the *History of Florence*, written towards the close of his life, Machiavelli once more reverts to this dominant military matter. Again and again he emphasises his conviction that the *condottieri* have been the cause of Italy's undoing, and his belief that her redemption can come only by means of a return to the patriotic ways of the antique legionaries of Rome.

Machiavelli did not limit himself to words. During the republican period of his life, in his official capacity, he was able to secure authority from the Florentine Signory to organise and equip a militia. For six years (1506–12) he toiled unremittingly at the task, persevering amid the most disheartening difficulties. In 1512, when the French—the chief allies of the republic—were driven from Italy by the Spaniards, Germans, and Swiss; when the hostile Pope, Julius II, supported the exiled Medici in their efforts to return; when all extraneous aid failed them—in 1512 the militia was put to the test of war. At the first puff of gunpowder it turned tail and fled! The product of Machiavelli's six years of devoted labour vanished into thin air. Florence

[1] *The Art of War*, Book III.

fell; the Medici resumed their tyranny; Machiavelli, having suffered imprisonment and torture, passed into banishment. He realised that Italy needed not only arms, but a man.

V

Machiavelli's banishment to his country estate at San Casciano provided him with leisure and opportunity to ponder his past career, to consider the lessons of his experience, and to reinforce his conclusions by parallels drawn from Roman history. But for the ruin of his political prospects in 1512 we should have had none of his great literary works, and save for his official documents he would have passed almost inarticulate into oblivion. As it was, he relieved the boredom of his enforced retirement from affairs by diligent reading, hard thinking, and voluminous writing; seeking, moreover, by means of his pen, to win his way back into the service of the state which he loved with the purest devotion of his life.

He wrote primarily of the things which he himself had seen and known. True, he discoursed largely on Livy. Nevertheless, he was a student of current politics rather than of history. His method was that of observation more than of research. He was, indeed, devoid of the historic spirit, and, if he drew extensively upon history in his works, he did so uncritically and unscrupulously, being concerned merely to find examples to support conclusions already reached. Legend suited him quite as well as fact. The source of his science of politics was, in truth, his own diplomatic experience. As secretary of the Ten he had gone, as we have remarked, during the fourteen years of his service, on many important missions to Italian and other Courts. Of these numerous missions the four of outstanding significance were those to Louis XII in 1500, to Cæsar Borgia in 1502, to Pope Julius II in 1506, and to the Emperor Maximilian in 1507. The first and the last of these four had taken him beyond the Alps; had revealed to him peoples vaster and more virile than the Italians; had opened his eyes to the meaning of nationality, patriotism, and civic virtue; had filled him with speculations as to the means by which the heterogeneous populations of his own country—cultivated but corrupt, intellectually renascent but morally decadent, individually quick but politically dead—could be welded together and vitalised with a spirit of unity. His speculations had taken rough shape in the dispatches which he had sent from time to time to the Ten, and so gradually in his official writings an art of government had begun to formulate itself. Thus a series of political *portolani* had come into existence, specially constructed to enable the statesmen of the Florentine republic to steer the frail barque of their defenceless city amid the storms of the tempestuous dawn of the modern era, and among the shifting quicksands of the peculiarly treacherous diplomacy of the time. A state which had no native army, but was at the mercy of hired *condottieri* and alien auxiliaries, had to depend for the continuance of its precarious existence upon the craft and subtlety of its politicians. Machiavelli had sought in his masterly dispatches to guide the helpless and distracted Signory along ways of security.

His mission to the camp of the warlike Pope Julius II had been important in that it had confirmed him in his opinion that the prime cause of Italy's disruption was the existence of the States of the Church, and that the most formidable obstacle to the unification of the peninsula was the temporal power of the Papacy. This conviction remained with him to the end of his days. His last work, his unfinished *History of Florence*, although it was written by order of a cardinal and was dedicated to a Pope, is inspired throughout by a fierce and freely avowed detestation of clerical rule. Having in the introductory book portrayed the sad condition of Italy, Machiavelli concludes—to quote Villari's summary—"The sole remedy for these evils is the institution of a national army under the rule of a prince able to organise and command his troops, and to use them for the defence and unity of the country, by abasing the power of the Papacy, emancipating and fortifying the State, and leaving at his death a

E

legacy of good laws and civil institutions towards the establishment of liberty."[1]

The abasement of the power of the Papacy, however, requires, he perceives, the effective existence of a national army; and the effective existence of a national army necessitates the rule of an autocratic and capable prince. What sort of a person must the prince be who, in the desperate circumstances of the time, can carry through this titanic project of unification? The answer to this question had been provided by the experience which Machiavelli had gained on the most remarkable of all his diplomatic missions, namely, that to the moving camp of Cæsar Borgia in 1502—at Urbino, Imola, Cesena, Sinigaglia.

In 1502 Cæsar Borgia, son of Pope Alexander VI, had been engaged in his father's name, but on his own behalf, in reducing the Romagna. Nominally a portion of the States of the Church, the Romagna had, during the eclipse of the Papacy in the Captivity and the Schism, passed into the hands of a number of petty tyrants, whom it had proved impossible to dispossess or control. Cæsar, having procured from the papal Curia the cession of the Romagna as a dukedom, had been employed in expelling the tyrants and establishing an orderly government. Having few forces of his own, he had been compelled to operate with mercenaries under such leaders, then noted, as Paolo Orsini, Vitellozzo Vitelli, and Oliverotto of Fermo. But he had been mainly dependent on Gascon and Swiss auxiliaries provided under treaty by Louis XII of France. His little war had raged within a few miles of the Tuscan frontier, and Florence had been perturbed both by raids into her territories and also by pressing demands on Cæsar's part for men and money. Machiavelli had been sent—at first nominally under Bishop Francesco Soderini—to Cæsar's headquarters to ward off the Duke's hostility, mitigate his demands, and, if possible, safeguard Florence from injury and spoliation. On the whole he had succeeded in his purpose, and he had secured the cordial commendation of the Signory. The fifty-two

[1] Villari, *The Life and Times of Machiavelli*, ii, 394.

letters, still extant, which he had penned from the Borgian base contain not only the most vivid and authentic of all existing pictures of Duke Cæsar at the height of his fortune, but also a clear forecast of that science of statecraft which ten years later Machiavelli was to embody in *The Prince*.

For some six months in 1502 Machiavelli had had the formidable Cæsar under close and almost constant observation. Although his diplomatic enemy, engaged with him in an incessant contest of subtlety and wit, yet he had acquired for him an immense admiration. His quickness, his courage, his secrecy, his terrific vigour, his iron resolution, his remorseless severity, his amazing success, had filled Machiavelli with wonder and envy. He had contrasted his mode of procedure with the slow, vacillating, inept feebleness of the Florentine Signory. In particular, he had watched with the most profound interest and appreciation the way in which he had succeeded in emancipating himself from his faithless mercenaries, and in rendering himself independent of his dangerous French auxiliaries, by winning the confidence of his new subjects and building up a native army. In Cæsar Borgia Machiavelli had found a prince who might, if fortune had continued to favour him, have accomplished the desire of his heart. In Cæsar Borgia's methods he had seen what appeared to him to be the only means by which the revivification of Italy could be effected, the foreigner expelled, and unity achieved.

VI

Machiavelli's sympathies were wholly republican; one of the finer traits in his cynical and repellent character is his faith in the people—a faith, we may remark, not very easy to reconcile with his pessimistic estimate of individual human nature. If ever the clarity of his style begins to glow with the warmth of generous emotion it is when he speaks of the virtues of the Roman commonwealth or the liberties of his native city. His *Discourses on Livy* are eloquent of democratic enthusiasm, and it was the reading of them to the select assembly which used to meet in the Oricellarii Gardens which inspired the Soderini conspiracy against the Medicean tyranny in 1522.[1] But he was entirely aware that republican institutions are possible only to a virtuous people—that is to say, to a people courageous, simple and pure in life, self-sacrificing, devoted to the service of the State and zealous for the common weal. Such a people were the ancient Romans of whom he read credulously in the First Decade of Livy and in the voluminous eulogies of Polybius. Such too, he thought, were the Swiss and the Germans of his own day. But such were *not* the contemporary Italians. His experiences in Florence, especially in relation to his militia, coupled with his observations in the Papal States, Venice, Milan, and Naples, all filled him with the conviction that, although Italy might be ready for republicanism when she should have been disciplined, united, regenerated, yet in her existing condition her only hope lay in the stern and strong autocracy of a militant and politic prince—such a prince as Cæsar Borgia had been in his prime, such a prince as Giuliano or Lorenzo de' Medici might conceivably be.

By what means should a prince seek to attain to ascendancy in such an Italy as that of Machiavelli's day, and, having attained to it, by what means should he seek to keep it? That is the question which Machiavelli set himself to answer in the most famous—or infamous—of all his works, the treatise entitled *Il Principe*. This brief but pungent treatise, written in the latter half of the year 1513, was composed for, dedicated to, and intended for the exclusive perusal of the Medicean tyrant who had overthrown the Florentine republic the year before. It is imperative that those who read it should realise that they were not meant to do so. It was not written for them. It was a paper of private and confidential instructions prepared for the personal and peculiar use of a particular individual. It was not a general dissertation on the science of politics or the art of government. It was not compiled for publication, nor was it in fact published until five years after Machiavelli's death (1532), when an injudicious Pope—Clement VII, cousin of the man to whom

[1] Villari, *The Life and Times of Machiavelli*, ii, 333.

it had been dedicated—imprudently let it loose upon the world. Its whole efficacy depended upon its *not* being published: for in vain is the snare set in the sight of any bird! The very success of such craft and guile as Machiavelli commends hangs upon the faith in the honesty and sincerity of the deceiver. To proclaim to the world that you are going to tell lies renders it useless for you to do so. Your very truth is not believed.

The Prince, then, is a *vade mecum* dedicated to the use of the Medici—first Giuliano; secondly, after Giuliano's death in 1516, Lorenzo. That Machiavelli should have sought to serve the Medici is, indeed, at first sight, surprising; for the whole of his public life had been spent in trying to prevent their return to Florence; and when, in spite of him, they had come back he had suffered much inconvenience at their hands—including dismissal from office, exile, imprisonment, and torture on the rack. When, in fact, *The Prince* passed into circulation it was its dedication to the Medici rather than its surrender to the devil that caused astonishment and adverse criticism in Italy. It was not its obvious abandonment of morality, but its apparent desertion of the republican cause which excited scandal and demanded explanation. To us the explanation is fairly clear: Italy, in Machiavelli's opinion, needed a despot; and Machiavelli quite obviously needed and desired employment. Hence he addressed the Medici, who at the moment were doubly powerful in the possession of both Tuscany and the Papacy. On the one hand: "May your illustrious house, strong in all the hopes which justice gives our cause, deign to undertake this noble enterprise," *i.e.*, the deliverance and consolidation of Italy.[1] On the other hand: "If from your elevated position you should condescend to look down on a person in my lowly station, you will see how long and how unworthily I have been persecuted by the extreme and unrelenting malevolence of fortune."[2]

Apart from the Dedication, the twenty-six chapters of *The Prince* fall into five groups. The first group (i–xi) treats

[1] *The Prince*, ch. xxvii.   [2] *Ibid.*, Dedication.

of generalities, the greater part being devoted to the classification of principalities in respect of their nature and mode
of acquisition. In this section by far the most noteworthy
chapter is that (vii) which contains Machiavelli's account
of the meteoric career of Cæsar Borgia, whom he idealises,
under the name of Valentino, until he becomes a mytho-
logical being, the embodiment of sheer, unmitigated statecraft. He holds him up as a perfect model for a new prince
who would secure himself in his principality. He does this
with his eyes open, knowing intimately well the appalling
crimes—murders, assassinations, treacheries, duplicities, de-
baucheries, sacrileges—of which this terrible adventurer
had been guilty. In one of his earlier writings, the so-called
first *Decennale* (1504), he had truly and frankly described
him as "a man without compassion, rebellious to Christ,
the Hydra, the basilisk, deserving of the most wretched end."
But in spite of this he exalts him in *The Prince* as a model,
because he sees in his methods, frightful and immoral as they
are, the only hope of success in the task which the New
Prince has to face in the Italy of his day. What these methods
are he reserves for explicit treatment in the third section of
his work.

The second group of chapters (xii-xiv) is, as we have
already remarked, devoted to military matters. Machiavelli
writes with an obvious intensity of conviction. His purpose
in writing is eminently practical: "My aim," he says, "is to
write for the advantage of him who understands me." He
descants on the curse of mercenary armies, his argument
being pointed by the stories of how Sforza betrayed Naples,
Vitelli Florence, and Carmagnola Venice. He passes on to
treat of the peril of trusting to foreign auxiliaries, with
instances drawn from the disasters which Italy has suffered
at the hands of French and Spanish allies. Finally, he
emphasises the importance of military skill to princes, and
shows how they can acquire it—practically, by exercises and
by the pursuit of the chase; theoretically, by the study of
history and the lives of great commanders.

The third group of chapters (xv–xviii) brings us to the

heart of the treatise, and displays to us the essence of what is called Machiavellism—that is to say, politics divorced from ethics. The keynote is struck in the sentence: "That man who will profess honesty in all his actions must needs go to ruin among so many that are dishonest; therefore it is necessary for a prince who desires to preserve himself to be able to make use of that honesty and to lay it aside as need shall require." And, as with honesty, so with mercy and compassion. Then follows a detailed examination of the circumstances in which—quite irrespective of moral considerations—a prince should be liberal or parsimonious, cruel or merciful, faithful to his word or perfidious. The illustrations by means of which Machiavelli points his narrative throw a lurid light into the abysses of Italian politics in the Renaissance period, especially when, as his supreme example of successful mendacity and merciless treachery, Machiavelli selects Pope Alexander VI. To the problems raised by Machiavellism we must return in a moment. They are living and burning problems, and it is by reason of their continuing urgency that the present-day study of Machiavelli is worth while.

The fourth group of chapters (xix–xxv) sinks from the giddy heights of political non-morality attained in the preceding group down to a rather dull level of commonplace maxims of prudence. The prince is instructed how to avoid contempt and hatred, how to secure popularity, how to acquire respect and reputation, how to steer a happy mean between excessive *hauteur* and undue familiarity, and so on. The unhappy examples of Ferrante of Naples and Ludovico of Milan point the moral and adorn the tale.

The fifth and final division of *The Prince* consists of the solitary and magnificent twenty-sixth chapter, in which the Medici are exhorted to rise to the height of the great opportunity which lies before them, to establish their authority, to call the Italians to arms, to expel the barbarians, and to reign as saviours of their country. How does this splendid and stirring appeal—the herald cry of Italian national unity—accord with the diabolical devices described in chapters

71

xv–xviii as appropriate for the realisation of the ideal? Neither to Machiavelli nor to his contemporaries did there appear anything incongruous between a noble political end and grossly immoral means. How does the case seem to us?

VII

Machiavelli was above and beyond all else a prophet and a preacher of the principle of patriotism and the idea of the national state. Now, on the one hand, the principle of patriotism seems to be a lower ideal than the cosmopolitan conception which had dominated the Middle Ages; and the idea of the national state appears to be a less lofty one than the mediæval idea of a Universal Christendom based upon religion and ruled by a Vicegerent of God. But, on the other hand, it must be borne in mind that the mediæval principle of Christian brotherhood, and the mediæval ideal of an œcumenical Church-State, had never been even approximately realised in fact. The horrid actuality of the thousand years which separated Machiavelli from the deposition of Romulus Augustulus had been a weltering chaos of conflicting clans, struggling tribes, anarchic fiefs, and encroaching kingships, stirred up incessantly by rebellious bishops, and kept at the boil by fulminating Popes. Never had there been a more marked contrast between theory and practice; never had the *Mappa Mundi* been more entirely unrelated to the facts of human geography. Hence, if in the realm of abstract doctrine the national state suggested a decline from the unity of Christendom, in the realm of concrete politics it stood for an immense and incalculably beneficial advance upon the parochialism, localism, tribalism, and feudalism which had been the actual condition of the Dark Ages. Machiavelli clearly perceived the enormous advantages which France had gained by the absorption of the great fiefs, and by the centralisation of the government of the country under the Capetian and Valois kings. Not less clearly did he see the benefits which had accrued to Spain through her unification under the Catholic kings. From his observations he concluded that it was vitally necessary for Italy to pass through the same process of consolidation, and to attain to the same condition of unity.

The ideal form of national state which Machiavelli projected for Italy was undoubtedly a republic modelled upon the Roman commonwealth as portrayed by Livy. But he realised that the conditions which had rendered possible the unification of the peninsula under the old city-state were absent in his own day. If the consolidation of France and Spain had been effected only by means of the force and craft of exceptionally able monarchs, how much more did the disorder of Italy demand the exercise of the vigour, the subtlety, the swiftness, and the secrecy which an autocratic prince alone could provide! The all-important thing was the establishment of the national state. Both the form which it should take and the means by which it should be established were secondary concerns.

This question of means brings us to the heart of the Machiavelli problem. For the essence of Machiavellism is the doctrine that the end justifies the means. It implies the deliberate dissociation of politics from ethics, and the assertion that the plea of 'reasons of state' is a sufficient answer to any and every accusation of cruelty or deceit. Perhaps the two clearest summaries of the doctrine presented by Machiavelli himself are the following, the first from the *Discourses*, the second from *The Prince*: "Where the deliberation is wholly touching the safety of the fatherland there ought to be no consideration of just or unjust, pitiful or cruel, honourable or dishonourable, but rather, all other respect being laid aside, that course ought to be taken which may preserve the life and maintain the liberty thereof";[1] and, "Let a prince, therefore, take the surest courses he can to maintain his life and state; the means shall always be thought honourable"[2]—the means specially alluded to by Machiavelli being those which he has just been describing as analogous to the merciless ferocity of the lion and the unscrupulous craftiness of the fox. The statesman, in Machiavelli's view, is

[1] *Discourses*, III, xli.   [2] *The Prince*, ch. xxviii.

73

emancipated from the ordinary restraints of morality. In the interests of his country he is entitled, nay, is on occasion required, to commit acts of violence and to perpetrate frauds which if performed on his own account in private life would brand him as a criminal and a scoundrel. He must not shrink, if reasons of state demand it, from any cruelty however great, or from any perfidy however base.

That is Machiavellism. It is the doctrine that terrorism and treachery are legitimate instruments in politics. Machiavelli does not urge their indiscriminate use. He recognises the fact that they are dangerous instruments, prefers the normal employment of the safer implements of ethics, blames such operators as Agathocles of Syracuse and Oliverotto of Fermo for employing them too freely.[1] But, all the same, he regards them as essential elements in the statesman's equipment, and he severely condemns those who have failed to employ them when emergency has demanded their use. Romulus, he considers, was justified in slaying his brother Remus, for unity of control was necessary for the successful founding of Rome; hence "though the act accuse him, the effect excuses him—for though he that uses violence to waste is blameworthy, not he that uses it for redress and order."[2] Similarly he defends the sanguinary severity of Brutus after his overthrow of the Tarquinian monarchy, in words which might have been employed by Lenin in 1917 or by Hitler in 1937: "This is always well known to those who read ancient stories, how that after the change of a state, either from a republic into a tyranny or from a tyranny into a republic, some memorable execution upon the enemies of the present condition is needful."[3] Conversely he contemptuously condemns Gian Paolo Baglioni of Perugia, who, when he was resisting the papal claims to overlordship over his city, failed through squeamishness and "base cowardice" to avail himself of a golden opportunity of decisive victory and everlasting renown which Fortune offered to him. Pope Julius II having rashly visited Perugia, unguarded, together with twenty-four cardinals, Gian Paolo omitted to

[1] *The Prince*, ch. viii.   [2] *Discourses*, I, ix.   [3] *Ibid.*, III, iii.

exterminate the lot of them. "He had not the courage," says Machiavelli, "to do an exploit that every one would have admired, a deed that would have given him an everlasting memory, an act whose greatness would have surpassed all infamy."[1] His weakness was aggravated by the fact that the cardinals "had the best of all their jewels with them!" Hence, when some time afterward Pope Julius overthrew him and strung him up on a gibbet, he paid a fitting penalty for his indecision and lack of enterprise.

As with violence, so with craft and fraud: "How commendable it is in a prince to keep his word and live with integrity, not making use of cunning and subtlety, every one knows well; yet we see by experience in these our days that those princes have effected great matters who have made small reckoning of keeping their words and have known by their craft to turn and wind men about and in the end have overcome those who have grounded upon the truth."[2] And again, "It is necessary for a prince that will achieve great matters to learn to be a cunning deceiver,"[3] for "that man who will profess honesty in all his actions must needs go to ruin amongst so many that are dishonest. Wherefore it is necessary for a prince who desires to preserve himself to be able to make use of honesty or to lay it aside as need shall require."[4] Machiavelli in both *The Prince* and the *Discourses* gives many examples, drawn from history and his own observation, of what he regards as successful chicanery. But he reserves his highest eulogies for Pope Alexander VI, who, he says, "never did anything else than deceive men, and never meant otherwise, and always found whom to work upon." "Yet," he adds, "never was there a man who would protest more effectually, or aver anything with more solemn oaths and observe less than he; nevertheless, his deceptions all succeeded, for he knew how to play his part cunningly."[5]

If, however, Machiavelli admires one ruler for his consummate mendacity and another for his remorseless ferocity,

---

[1] *Discourses*, I, xxvii. [2] *The Prince*, ch. xviii. [3] *Discourses*, II, xiii.
[4] *The Prince*, ch. xx. [5] *Ibid.*, ch. xviii.

75

he sees the perfect combination of the qualities of the lion and the fox—terrorism and treachery—in Cæsar Borgia, to whose baleful career he again and again recurs, as though irresistibly fascinated. Cæsar Borgia in 1502—the year of his highest power and luckiest fortune—supplies the perfect model of the methods by which alone, Machiavelli thinks, the overthrow of the *condottieri*, the expulsion of the foreigners, and the salvation of Italy can be secured.

VIII

What is the verdict of history upon Machiavellism—that is to say, upon the doctrine that the end justifies the means, that ethics have no relevance to politics, that reasons of state excuse all deviations from the moral law, and that Satan may properly be called in to cast out Satan? The verdict of history is, it seems to me, one of decisive condemnation and emphatic rejection. And yet the doctrine has persisted, and still persists, with a strange vitality. In the sixteenth century, in spite of the denunciation of both Catholic and Protestant theologians, *The Prince* became the text-book of monarchs; while the unscrupulous practices which it recognised established themselves as the common devices of politicians. The massacre of St Bartholomew's Day 1572, for instance, was regarded as a perfect exposition of Machiavellian craft and violence. In the seventeenth and eighteenth centuries, when the furies of the wars of religion had died down, the more sanguinary aspects of Machiavellism ceased to display themselves so conspicuously as before, and its prime manifestations had to be sought in the dark intricacies of diplomacy. Napoleon I, however, was a Machiavellian in both senses of the term: he believed equally in violence and in fraud as legitimate, and at times necessary, instruments of policy. His sinister influence dominated many of the makers of nineteenth-century history, and his Machiavellian principles found disciples and exemplars in such men as Metternich, Louis Phillippe, Napoleon III, Bismarck, and Cavour.

In the Italy of Cavour, indeed, a formal revival of the Machiavellian cult took place in the middle of the nineteenth century. Machiavelli was recognised and exalted as a pioneer of the unification of the peninsula, and the methods which he had suggested as necessary for the realisation of his ideal in the sixteenth century were accepted as appropriate and inevitable in the later age. But it was in Germany that the most formidable recrudescence of Machiavellism took place. The philosophy of Hegel prepared the Teutonic mind for an exaltation of the State. The disintegration of the Fatherland after the Napoleonic wars made its reconstruction on a national basis imperative. The task of reconstruction was one of almost superhuman difficulty, and it seemed to call for methods of "blood and iron," and methods of craft and guile, similar to those which Machiavelli had expounded and Cæsar Borgia had exemplified. Hence men like Bismarck adopted and applied them, and men like Treitschke defended and glorified them. The apparent success of Machiavellian methods in the making of the German Empire caused the principles of *The Prince* to establish themselves as fundamental postulates of Prussian politics. In 1914 they received their perfect exposition in the shameless perfidy which violated the solemn guarantees of Belgian neutrality, and in the diabolical cruelty which sought to extinguish Belgian independence in agony and blood. From Germany, as part of the heritage of Karl Marx, Machiavellism spread to Russia, where in 1917 it displayed itself in the appalling terrorism and abysmal treachery of Bolshevism. Hence we see now, even more clearly than Lord Morley could see when in 1897 he delivered his Romanes Lecture, that Machiavelli "represents certain living forces in our actual world," and that, as Lord Acton remarked, "he is a contemporary influence."

Nevertheless, I hold that both the conscience of mankind and the verdict of history have declared themselves decisively against Machiavellism. The one says that it is theoretically indefensible, the other that it is practically unsound. (1) *It is theoretically indefensible.* The State is not, as Machiavelli and his disciples regard it, an end in itself. It is merely a means to the good life of its members individually and collectively. It is a moral institution whose supreme purpose is the definition and maintenance of justice. *Justitia remota, quid aliud est regnum quam grande latrocinium:* in the absence of justice what is the state but organised brigandage on a large scale? A state established for any other end than the realisation of the moral law had better not exist at all. And this ethical end cannot be dissociated from the means by which its attainment is sought. There must be congruity between the two. As well might you expect to gather figs from thistles as look for the fruit of justice from a root of violence and deceit. (2) *It is practically a failure.* The verdict of history is that Machiavellism has not in fact succeeded. In the long run the lion and the fox do not prevail; the cruelty of the one and the craft of the other not only do not save them, but are the very causes of their destruction. As Talleyrand might have said, Machiavellism is worse than a crime; it is a mistake. In the sixteenth century Gentillet condemned it because of the ruin which it brought to those who practised it; in the seventeenth century Richelieu, who had no moral objection to it, warned his king against it because of its fatal consequences.[1] In the eighteenth century Voltaire, who will not be suspected of Puritanism, in a famous letter to Frederick the Great of Prussia—one of the most consummate practitioners of the Machiavellian politic —condemned the art of *The Prince*: "Cet art," he said, "que l'on doit mettre à côté de celui des Locustes et des Brinvilliers, a pu donner à quelques tyrans une puissance passagère, comme le poison peut procurer un héritage; mais il n'a jamais fait ni de grands hommes ni des hommes heureux, cela est bien certain." In the nineteenth century Lord Morley concluded his Romanes Lecture in the same strain. After expounding and denouncing the Machiavellian principle he says, "The effect was fatal even for his own purpose, for what he put aside, whether for the sake of argument, or because he thought them in substance irrelevant,

[1] Richelieu, *Testament Politique*, ii, 6.

78

were nothing less than the living forces by which societies subsist and governments are strong."

These weighty opinions are borne out by the chronicle of events. Machiavelli made shipwreck of his own life because with excessive subtlety and with shameless lack of principle he sought to run with the republican hare and hunt with the Medicean hounds; when in 1527 the Medici fell and the republic was restored he found that he had succeeded in earning the ineradicable distrust of both parties. Hence he was left to die in dishonour, disillusionment, destitution, and disgust. Similarly his hero, Cæsar Borgia, excited so unutterable a loathing and dread by his ferocity and perfidy that, wholly apart from ill-fortune, he was hounded out of Italy and sent to perish in the Pyrenees. The record of the Machiavellians in all ages is the same—a brief and unsubstantial triumph due to terror and surprise, followed by permanent and irretrievable ruin when the conscience and the courage of mankind have revived.

To sum up the matter in a nutshell: Machiavelli with all his acuteness of observation had a singular faculty for failing to see factors of the first importance. Loudly as he professed to see things as they really were, he saw them as they really were not. Just as he depicted an art of war in which artillery played no part, so he depicted an art of government in which neither morals nor religion had any place. His estimate of human nature, on which his whole political system was based, was radically mistaken. He regarded man as entirely bad, and founded his system on that false assumption. He ignored goodness in man just as he ignored gunpowder in war. Goodness and gunpowder! Could a man of the early sixteenth century who professed to be practical have made two more colossal errors of omission? In the art of war the development of firearms has swept the Machiavellian precepts into ridicule and oblivion. In the art of politics the conscience of mankind has repudiated the Machiavellian maxims, and the experience of the human race has demonstrated their folly. The records of history tend to show that Socrates and Plato were right when they said that in the

79

long run the knave and the fool are one and the same. For human society is established on moral foundations, and righteousness must in the end prevail.

BOOK LIST

A. PRIMARY SOURCES

Tutte le Opere di Nicolo Machiavelli. 1550.

Il Principe, edited by L. A. Burd, with an Introduction by Lord Acton. 1891.

The Prince, translated by N. H. Thomson. 1882.

Discourses on Livy, translated by N. H. Thomson. 1883.

Historical, Political, and Diplomatic Writings of Machiavelli, translated by C. E. Detmold. 4 vols. 1882.

B. SECONDARY SOURCES

BURD, L. A.: " Machiavelli," in *The Cambridge Modern History,* vol. i. 1902.

DUNNING, W. A.: *History of Political Theories, Ancient and Mediæval.* 1910.

DYER, L.: *Machiavelli and the Modern State.* 1904.

FEUERLEIN, E.: " Zur Machiavelli-Frage," in *Historische Zeitschrift.* 1868.

FRANCK, A.: *Réformateurs et publicistes de l'Europe,* vol. i. 1864.

JANNI, E.: *Machiavelli* (translated by M. Enthoven). 1930.

MACAULAY, LORD: " Machiavelli," in *Critical and Historical Essays.* 1827.

MANCINI, P. S.: *Prelezioni con un Saggio sul Machiavelli.* 1876.

MORLEY, LORD: *Machiavelli.* The Romanes Lecture, 1897.

MUIR, D. E.: *Machiavelli and his Times.* 1936.

MUNDT, T.: *Nicolo Machiavelli und das System der modernen Politik.* 1867.

NITTI, F.: *Machiavelli nella Vita e nelle Opere.* 1876.

OWEN, J.: *Skeptics of the Italian Renaissance.* 1893.

PREZZOLINI, G.: *Nicolo Machiavelli the Florentine* (translated by R. Roeder). 1927.

SYMONDS, J. A.: *The Renaissance in Italy,* vol. i, Chapters V and VI. 1875.

TOMASINO, O.: *La Vita e gli Scritti di Nicolo Machiavelli.* 1883.

VILLARI, P.: *The Life and Times of Machiavelli* (translated by L. Villari). 1878.

IV

GROTIUS AND THE REIGN OF LAW[1]

THE perennial conflict between 'direct action' and
constitutional procedure, which to-day agitates the
world of Labour, in the sixteenth and seventeenth
centuries rent in twain the world of Religion. Not trade-
union leaders and academic syndicalists, but the heads of
churches and dogmatic theologians were the persons who
had to debate the question whether or not obedience should
be paid to the civil authority, and whether or not opposition
to policy should be carried to the length of privy conspiracy
and rebellion. The particular form of direct action round
which controversy raged was tyrannicide. At a time when
autocracy was dominant, when individuality was resurgent,
when personality counted more largely than it had done
since the days of Cæsar, if not of Pericles, the short and
simple way to change a government was to assassinate a
king; the straight and effective device to frustrate a plan
of campaign was to remove its leader by means of sedative
or stiletto. The blow which slew Henry of Navarre in
1610 had a more profound and far-reaching effect on the
destiny of Europe than a score of Parliamentary debates or a
hundred political treatises. So obviously and immediately
operative were accomplished tyrannicides that even wise and
good men—blinded by the passion of the moment, and oblivious of the awful implications of such deeds—gloried in them,

---

[1] From *The Social and Political Ideas of Some Great Thinkers of the Sixteenth
and Seventeenth Centuries* (Harrap, 1926). The other studies in this volume
are: "Introductory: The Social and Political Problems of the Sixteenth
and Seventeenth Centuries," by the editor; "Jean Bodin," by J. W.
Allen; "Richard Hooker," by Norman Sykes; "Francisco Suarez," by
A. L. Lilley; "King James I," by Miss H. M. Chew; "Thomas Hobbes,"
by E. L. Woodward; "James Harrington," by Miss A. E. Levett; "Benedict
Spinoza," by A. D. Lindsay.

thanked God for them, and vindicated their perpetrators. The murder of Cardinal Beaton in 1546 was justified by John Knox; the assassination of Francis of Guise in 1563 was defended by Theodore Beza; the Spanish Jesuits maintained that the slaying of William of Orange in 1584 was a pious and praiseworthy deed; while Pope Sixtus V himself commended the monk who took the life of Henry III of France.

Moreover, not only were isolated acts of homicide vindicated, but a general theory of tyrannicide was formulated in which with extreme precision the term 'tyrant' was defined, and in which with elaborate care the proper agents of assassination were specified. Perhaps the most advanced exponent of this sanctified form of direct action was the Spanish Jesuit Juan de Mariana, to whom every heretical ruler was a tyrant, and to whom every devout heretic-slayer was a Christian hero.

The appearance of Mariana's *De Rege et Regis Institutione* in 1599 coincided with a formidable recrudescence of violence. The aggressive forces of the Counter-Reformation came into more and more ferocious conflict with the resistant but retreating forces of the Reformation. In 1605 the Gunpowder Plot portended the murder of the Protestant James VI and I and the recovery of Scotland and England for Catholicism; in 1608 a Catholic League was formed in Germany for the sanguinary restoration of the Empire to the unity of the Faith; in 1610 the great coalition of Henry IV of France against those main bulwarks of the Papacy, the Hapsburg rulers of Spain and Austria, was broken up by the dagger of Ravaillac. For the next eight years the furies roused by plot and counterplot, by assassination and counter-assassination on the part of Catholic League and answering Calvinistic Confederation, seethed and raged until at last they found issue in the unparalleled horrors of the Thirty Years War.

Through the major portion of this period of battle, murder, and sudden death Grotius lived (1583–1645). He was one year old when, in the country of his birth, William of Orange was shot by Balthazar; he was six when the dagger of Clément extinguished the Valois house; he was only thirty-five when the conflicts of religion reached their climax in the Thirty Years War, and he survived to witness all but three of the destructive campaigns of this last and worst of the sectarian struggles. Grotius was a man of large and tolerant spirit. Sincerely pious, he had none of the fanaticism of the sectary or the fury of the partisan. He felt that the great truths of Christianity which Catholic and Calvinist, Lutheran and Arminian, held in common were immeasurably more important than were the details concerning which they differed. His remarkable apologetic, *De Veritate Christianæ Religionis* (1627), was devoted to the defence of a creed which was accepted by all the combatants in the suicidal wars of the sects. In many respects he resembled Bodin, *e.g.*, in his encyclopædic learning, in his legal outlook, in his desire for peace, in his belief in the principle of religious toleration. But he had none of Bodin's cynical indifference to religion, none of Bodin's fundamental scepticism. He desired tranquillity not merely in the political interest of his own state; he wished for it in the interest of both the Church Universal and also the whole family of the nations of Christendom. He had a wide cosmopolitan and catholic purview. It was to further the well-being of humanity as a whole that he composed and in 1625 issued his *magnum opus*, his famous *De Jure Belli et Pacis*, the basal treatise of modern International Law.

II

The early life of Grotius had well fitted him for the fulfilment of this supreme task of his life. Born on April 10, 1583, at Delft in the province of Holland, Huig van Groot (Hugo Grotius) was the son of an eminent and wealthy lawyer who had not only been four times burgomaster of the important town of Leyden, but was also curator of its famous university, the headquarters of the Arminian revolt against strict Calvinism, and a centre of Republican resistance to the ambitious house of Orange. The Groot family was of French origin; it claimed descent from the aristocratic Cornets, one of whom had migrated to the Netherlands in the fifteenth century. The family had become thoroughly naturalised in Holland, had prospered greatly, and had risen to a position of general esteem. Hugo was thus born in circumstances eminently favourable to the fostering of his talents, if he had any, and if he cared to foster them; or, alternatively, to the suffocation of his talents in *bourgeois* luxury and civic respectability. Fortunately, he was endowed with a quick and eager mind, avid for learning and tireless in industry. Hence he used his advantages to the full, and at a remarkably early age attained a wide reputation for scholarship. He was, in fact, an infant prodigy. When he was but eight years old his Latin verses were passed from hand to hand among schoolmasters and professors as models of subtle thought and graceful style. At twelve he entered the university, bringing with him an almost complete mastery of the Greek and Roman classics. At sixteen he emerged as a fully fledged Doctor of Law. During the period of his pupillarity, moreover, he had published a critical edition of Martianus Capella's famous pre-mediæval text-book of the seven liberal arts, and had further been chosen to accompany Olden Barneveldt on a diplomatic mission to Paris. At the age of twenty (1603) he was appointed official Historiographer of his native province; four years later he was made Advocate-General of the Fisc for Holland and Zeeland; finally in 1613 he became Pensionary of Rotterdam. By that time he was recognised as one of the ablest scholars and most learned lawyers in Europe, and was looked upon as a leader in the Arminian and Republican party which was struggling to check the intolerance of Calvinism and to prevent the dangerous aggrandisement of the house of Orange.

Soon after his appointment as Historiographer, Grotius had been called upon to turn his attention to the problem of International Law. The Dutch East India Company had become involved in a controversy with the Peninsular Powers arising out of the seizure of a Portuguese galleon in the Straits of Malacca by a captain in the employ of the Company. The case was a complicated one because, first, Portugal had been annexed by Spain, and Spain still

84

nominally regarded the Dutch as her own rebellious subjects; secondly, the East India Company was a private mercantile organisation whose right to engage in war was in the circumstances doubtful. Grotius dealt with the whole matter in a masterly dissertation, *De Jure Prædæ*, 1604. Not only did he solve, in the Dutch interest, the specific problem raised; but he laid down general principles of International Law substantially the same as those which he afterwards expanded and illustrated in his classical *De Jure Belli et Pacis*. The treatise *De Jure Prædæ* was not published at the time of its composition, and by some strange freak of fortune it was completely forgotten for two and a half centuries. Then, in the middle of the nineteenth century, it was rediscovered, and first issued in 1868. Its publication threw floods of light on the process of the formation of Grotius's opinions, and it solved for ever the mystery of how Grotius, a stranger in a strange land, had apparently been able to compose his great work on War and Peace, without previous preparation, in a little over a year (1624–25). A vast amount of preliminary work and preparatory thought had as a matter of fact been achieved in 1604. The critically important attitude of Grotius towards both the *Jus Naturæ* and the *Jus Gentium* had already been determined. Much of the material necessary for the construction of a systematic code of international morality and custom had been collected.

Although the *De Jure Prædæ* was not, as a whole, published during the lifetime of Grotius, nor for long centuries after his death, nevertheless one of its chapters (xii) found its way into print—probably without the consent or knowledge of Grotius —in connexion with another controversy which the Dutch were maintaining with their old Iberian enemies. This controversy related to the freedom of the seas. Could the high seas—the Indian Ocean, the Atlantic, the Pacific—become State property, in the same manner as islands and continents could become such? Might the Spaniards and Portuguese, in virtue of prior discovery and first occupation, claim the right to exclude the Dutch, together with all other nations, from the great waters of the world? No, said Grotius in his

Mare Liberum (1609). Twenty years later the same emphatic negative was presented to England's claim to exclusive control of the North Sea and the Channel. In vain did the English antiquary and lawyer John Selden attempt to rebut the arguments of Grotius in his *Mare Clausum* (1632). The issue had ultimately to be decided by the three Anglo-Dutch wars of the later seventeenth century.

Long, however, before the English and Dutch came to blows respecting the lordship of the narrow seas, the connexion between Grotius and his native land had been violently terminated. In 1618 the smouldering antagonism between the Republican party—*bourgeois*, commercial, maritime, Francophile, Arminian—and the Orange party—aristocratic, agrarian, military, Anglophile, Calvinistic—burst into open flame. Maurice of Nassau effected a successful *coup d'état* on July 31, routed the Republicans, and captured and executed their leader, Olden Barneveldt. Grotius was sufficiently important to become involved in his leader's fall, but not personally so obnoxious to Maurice as to incur the fate of Barneveldt. He was condemned to lifelong incarceration, and in June 1619 was placed in the prison of Louvestein, near Gorcum, whence he expected never to emerge. Fortunately, however, for himself and for the world he had in 1608 married a wife, Marie Reigersberg by name, who was a woman not only of complete devotion, but also of unusual resource. Taking advantage of a concession which allowed books to be sent to her husband in his imprisonment, and taken away when read, she concealed the adventurous philosopher in a packing-case and had him conveyed from his cell as a cargo of Arminian theology. After agonies not unlike those suffered by victims of premature burial, he was released by friends and enabled to escape, first to Antwerp and then to Paris, where he was welcomed by Louis XIII and provided with a pension (seldom actually paid). This was in 1621.

It was soon after his arrival in France that he began seriously to turn his attention to the Law of War and of Peace. The Thirty Years conflict had broken out in Bohemia during the course of 1618; the decisive battle of the White Mountain had been fought in 1620; the defeated Elector Palatine was in a flight that was destined to terminate only with his life; his territories were in process of devastation by exasperated and merciless enemies. The spectacle horrified Grotius. "I saw prevailing," he said, "throughout the Christian world a licence in making war of which even barbarous nations would have been ashamed; recourse being had to arms for slight reasons or for no reason; and when arms were once taken up all reverence for divine and human law was thrown away, just as if men were thenceforth authorised to commit all crimes without restraint." In these circumstances of unmitigated militancy some of the more extreme theorists, following the lead of Erasmus, tended towards an absolute pacificism. Grotius entirely dissociated himself from them. Some wars, he admitted, were just, were necessary, were divinely imperative. His problem was to find a law according to which righteous wars could be distinguished from unrighteous; a law potent enough to set a humane limit to the violence by belligerents; a law sufficiently evident and universal to be recognised as binding by men of all races, ranks, and religions.

III

Grotius, in setting himself to compose his great treatise *De Jure Belli et Pacis*, was faced by all the difficulties which naturally confront a man who is exiled from his home, cut off from his books, and in straitened circumstances. He had, however, a copy of his earlier work *De Jure Prædæ*; he was assisted by a large collection of apposite quotations selected for him during the reading of many years by his laborious, if uninspired, brother, William; he was, moreover, endowed with a prodigious memory which enabled him to carry a dictionary of reference in his mind. Finally, he was assisted by a number of French friends, one of whom lodged him comfortably in the Château de Balagni near Senlis, another of whom supplied him with books from an ample library.

So well, in fact, was he equipped that he was able to achieve his enormous and erudite work within the brief period already noted (1624–25).

What were the books which Grotius read? To what extent was he indebted to them for his ideas? How far was he original? As to his sources, he himself gives us a list in his Prolegomena, but the list is obviously incomplete. He mentions Victoria, Ayala, and Gentilis, to all of whom his debt is evident. But he does not name Suarez, with whose masterly treatment of the types and varieties of law he must have been familiar; nor does he refer to his Protestant fore-runners, Oldendorf, Hemming, and Winckler, from whom even more conspicuously some of his leading conceptions were borrowed. Grotius, indeed, has little claim to origin-ality. Although he said of International Law, with some truth, that before him "no one had treated it as a whole and in an orderly manner," the novelty which he professes is to be found only in the completeness and orderliness of his work. All its elements were pre-existent. He combined them, co-ordinated them, arranged them, harmonised them, displayed them with considerable lucidity and grace. Hallam goes too far when, in his *Literary History*, he says that the *De Jure Belli* "may be considered as nearly original in its general platform as any work of man in an advanced state of civilisation and learning can be." Hallam, with all his erudition, was insufficiently informed respecting the fruitful labours of the forerunners of Grotius, and he suffered from the curious illusion (so soon to be dispelled by the writings of Darwin) that the limits of human knowledge had been almost reached. Dr T. A. Walker in his careful and scholarly *History of the Laws of Nations*[1] judges more accurately, when he says, "There was little novel in the legal system of Grotius, and there was equally but little original in either the arrangement or the matter of his work." He proceeds to show in detail Grotius's indebtedness to Gentilis for arrangement and to Victoria, Ayala, Winckler, Bodin, and many others for his subject-matter.

[1] Vol. i, p. 333.

If, however, the mind of Grotius was accumulative rather than creative; if it excelled in classifying and co-ordinating rather than in discovering and inventing; if it was more skilled in giving lucid expression to the old than in propounding the new, nevertheless the work of Grotius was of cardinal importance. The very fact that it contained no startling novelties commended it to the conscience of the age. It summed up the accepted wisdom of the ancients and applied it to the unprecedented conditions of the Renaissance and Reformation world; it epitomised all that had been written by Stoic philosophers, Roman lawyers, scholastic theologians, and Jesuitical casuists concerning the Law of Nature and the Law of Nations, and combined it into a solid foundation for an incalculably valuable superstructure of international morality and custom. The *De Jure Belli et Pacis* won instant recognition not only by reason of its vast learning, its methodical arrangement, and its admirable style, but also because of the European reputation of its author, and because of its own amazing appositeness to the circumstances of the age in which it appeared. The urgent need of the day was the formulation of a code of laws of war which should be accepted as obligatory alike by Catholic and Protestant, by Christian and infidel, by theist and atheist. The conscience of mankind was in revolt against the limitless atrocities of the Wars of Religion—against, for example, the assassination of leaders, the slaying of prisoners, the violation of women, the massacre of children, the pillaging of defenceless towns, the poisoning of wells, the wanton spoliation of peaceful populations. What principles could be found which should condemn these barbarities? On what basis could an authoritative body of rules be framed which the public opinion of the civilised world would require to be observed? On what foundation could be erected a stable structure of recognised international morality and custom?

The need of such a code had been felt as early as the Crusades, which had been a truceless war just because there had been no common authority to which the combatants could appeal for the consecration of oaths or commendation to mercy. Still more had there been necessity for some universally established ethic of war when the supra-national authority of the Middle Ages—the Papacy—was itself engaged as a belligerent in the task of exterminating the Albigenses with fire and sword. The want had been emphasised when the New World was discovered, and when Christian adventurers, devoid of all compassion, went to conquer and to rule in regions east of Suez and west of Panama, where "there ain't no Ten Commandments."

Since we are not concerned with International Law, but are limited in our consideration to social and political ideas, we are exempted from the necessity of summarising the *De Jure Belli et Pacis* of Grotius. Those who wish to find such a summary will get what they want in Hallam's *Literary History*, or, better still, in Dr T. A. Walker's *History of the Law of Nations*. Best of all, however, would it be for them to read the abridged translation of the book—a masterpiece of selection and condensation—issued by Dr Whewell of Trinity College, Cambridge, in 1853. Suffice it here to say that the work consists of a Dedication to Louis XIII, a Prolegomena, and three Books. Book I treats of war in general, and particularly with the problem whether among so-called Christian nations war can ever be just. Grotius convincingly maintains, against the pacificists, that it can. That being his conclusion, in Book II he goes on to treat, at great length, of the possible just grounds of war—that is to say, he deals with rights which it is allowable to defend, and duties which it is imperative to perform. Book III, towards which the whole argument of the work majestically tends, discusses the laws of war—that is to say, the limits, moral and customary, beyond which belligerents must not go in maintaining even their just cause by armed force.

Books II and III are almost wholly legal; the Prolegomena and Book I, however, are rich in political ideas. Grotius is compelled to lay a foundation for his juristic system on a deep and wide basis of general theory. Incidentally, some of his tacit assumptions are as interesting as his explicit assertions. His political generalisations focus round two main themes, viz., (1) the State and (2) law. They do so because the aim and purpose of his work is, as we have already noted, to find some sort of law which is capable of binding and restraining that great Leviathan, the sovereign national state.

IV

(1) THE STATE

One of the most significant of the tacit assumptions of Grotius is that of the non-existence of the mediæval *Respublica Christiana*, which was the dominant conception of such papal theorists as St Thomas Aquinas, or such imperial dreamers as Dante. The idea of a united Christendom has completely passed away, and has given place to that of a Family of Nations, or group of sovereign national states, who have no common superior, and acknowledge no allegiance to any extraneous authority whatsoever, whether civil or ecclesiastical. As to the origin of the state, Grotius is in accord with Aristotle, who regarded man as by nature social and political. "Man," says Grotius in his Prolegomena, "is an animal indeed, but an animal of an excellent kind, differing much more from all other tribes of animals than they differ from one another . . . and among those properties which are peculiar to man is a desire for society, that is, a desire for a life spent in common with fellow-men, and not merely spent somehow, but spent tranquilly and in a manner corresponding to the character of his intellect. This desire the Stoics call οἰκείωσις, the domestic instinct, or feeling of kindred." It may be remarked that Grotius is here much nearer to the truth as revealed by modern psychology than is Hobbes, who regarded society as a contractual arrangement made by men naturally solitary and anti-social, or even than is Bentham, who conceived society as based merely on an intellectual recognition on the part of isolated individuals that they would gain by association and co-operation. Society, then, according to Grotius, comes into existence naturally and instinctively as the result of the operation of man's gregarious impulse. The state, however, is not quite the same as society. It is both less and more. It is less numerically: it consists of but a fragment of the whole community of mankind, the great society. Functionally it is more: it exists for defence against external foes, for the maintenance of law and order against internal disorders, and for the promotion of the general welfare of its constituent members. It is *cœtus perfectus liberorum hominum juris fruendi et communis utilitatis causa sociatus*, i.e., the perfect union of a body of free men joined together for the purpose of enjoying the protection of the law and of promoting the common interest. The state, in short, is a section of society organised for a specific purpose. It is, therefore, not a product of nature in the same sense as is society. It involves a perception of utility, and also an element of mutual consent or even contract. Though Grotius clearly recognises the existence of an agreement of wills beneath the structure of the state, he does not emphasise or develop the Contract Theory, as it is emphasised by his contemporaries, the Monarchomachs, or by his successors, the Republicans. His conception of the contract is derived from Roman Law rather than from Old Testament Scripture or feudal practice. It is the Social Contract of Hobbes and Rousseau which he envisages rather than the Governmental Contract of Duplessis-Mornay, Hooker, and Locke.

Government he does not regard as based on a contract, but as of the nature of a transfer of property. He looks upon it as human in origin and legal in its character: he knows nothing of any Divine Right of Kings. Neither, however, does he know anything of any inalienable sovereignty of the people. Even though primordially the source of sovereignty resided in the peoples, yet when once they have formed their state and established their government they have divested themselves for ever of their pristine powers.[1] He seems to regard sovereignty as a sort of dominion which, once having been alienated for valuable consideration, cannot be revoked.

---

[1] " Quidni ergo populo sui juris liceat se unicuipiam aut pluribus ita addicere ut regendi sui jus in eum plane transcribat, nulla ejus parte retenta " (*De Jure Belli*, i, 3).

Hence he takes a view of the relation between sovereign and subjects not unlike that which Hobbes developed a quarter of a century later in his *Leviathan*: a people having chosen its ruler and having conferred authority upon him has no right to rebel against him or in any way to resist his will. Republican though he had been in Holland, at the time when he wrote the *De Jure Belli et Pacis* his monarchic preferences were pronounced. The dedication of the work to Louis XIII shows its strong inclination and tendency. When some years later his opinion was asked concerning the quarrel which was developing in England between Charles I and his Parliament, he wrote without hesitation, *Regi Angliæ opto prosperiora, tum quia est rex, tum quia bonus rex.*[1]

Monarchy, however, to Grotius is by no means identical with despotism. He follows Bodin and many others of his contemporaries in distinguishing kings from tyrants. The fourth chapter of the first book of the *De Jure Belli* is full of subtle discriminations between kings who may not be resisted and tyrants who may not only be resisted, but even slain. Pre-eminently tyrants are those who have usurped a throne, or those who, having acquired it legitimately, nevertheless govern in violation of the fundamental laws of their realm. For to Grotius, as to Bodin, to Hooker, and to Suarez, the ultimate supremacy in the world and in the universe at large resides in Law. Even sovereignty, to him, is a dominion held under Law, and in especial the Law of Nature. And since sovereignty is of the nature of property he sees no difficulty in regarding it as limited in several directions. Just as an estate can be held subject to any number of easements, so can the *summa potestas* or *jus imperandi* be possessed under a large variety of restrictions—restrictions of time, as in the case of the Roman dictators; restrictions due to pledges given at coronation; restrictions established by immemorial constitutional connexions, such as the Salic Law. Grotius's conception of sovereignty is not, as has sometimes been said, a confused and inconsistent one. But it is one so radically different from that of Hobbes, Bentham,

[1] *Grotii Epistolæ*, No. 946.

93

and Austin, that any attempt to state it in terms of the more modern theory of these great jurists is bound to generate confusion. If it is realised that to Grotius sovereignty is merely a limited right of property held under Natural Law, all his reservations and restrictions fall into their proper and logical places.

Among the possible and conceivable limitations of sovereignty, however, is *not* limitation by another human will. The sovereign may and must obey Natural Law, Divine Law, Constitutional Law, and even the Law of Nations, and he may do so without any derogation from his sovereignty. For even God Himself is subject to the laws which He has instituted. But if any *civil* law can supersede the command of a ruler, if any *human* will can override his will, then he is not sovereign: he does not hold the title-deeds which confer dominion. Hence Grotius defines sovereignty as "the supreme political power vested in him whose acts cannot be rendered void by any other human volition."

The principle of Grotius that—subject to the superiority of Law Natural, Divine, Constitutional, and International, and except in so far as bound by pledges given—the will of the sovereign is supreme in the State enables him to set forth without any ambiguity both the duties and the rights of the individual in respect of the ruler. Active resistance is always wrong. "Even if we receive injury from the will of the Supreme Power, we are to bear it rather than resist by force." For "civil society being instituted to secure public tranquillity, the State acquires a superior right over us and ours, so far as is necessary for that end." On the other hand, however, not even the sovereign can require active obedience to fiats which, in the opinion of the subject, contravene the dictates of the higher laws. "It is beyond controversy among all good men, that, if the persons in authority command anything contrary to Natural Law or the Divine Precepts, it is not to be done." Those who thus passively resist the will of the sovereign must, of course, be prepared to stand the racket. The sovereign has his duty to perform to society, and that duty involves the enforcement of his

94

authority. Here, then, is a real conflict of loyalties—the clash of an irresistible force and an immovable obstacle. What will result? The passive resister and conscientious objector must be prepared to perish from the community—whether by death, or loss of liberty, or deprivation of civil rights, as the sovereign may decree. He must, without demur, face the inconveniences of martyrdom. Then all will be well. He will, on his part, have saved his soul alive, and, on the other part, the sovereign will have vindicated that authority which is both his proprietary right under Natural Law and also his public duty under the Law of the Constitution.

Grotius is concerned in describing the State and defining its sovereignty not as a political philosopher, but as an international lawyer. His task is to frame a code of rules applicable to the relations between states and between the Governments of states. Therefore it is imperative for him to classify his ideas and to give the precise connotation of his terms. All this work of definition and classification is, however, preliminary in its nature. It is, for the most part, contained in his Prolegomena and in the opening chapters of Book I. From that he passes on to his real business—which, however, is *not* our prime concern—the relation of states to one another in that condition of masterless nature wherein the disintegration of mediæval Christendom has left them. He postulates, first, their complete independence, both of one another and of any supra-national authority such as Empire or Papacy. Each and every sovereign is within the territory under his control supreme in all causes, whether temporal or ecclesiastical, and over all persons. No extraneous power can interfere with any claim to superior jurisdiction. A second postulate—one of far-reaching significance and importance—is that of the formal equality of states. The Law of Nature knows no distinction between great and small in the Family of Nations. Legally and for the purposes of diplomacy all are on a par, whether strong or weak, whether rich or poor, whether monarchic or republican, whether venerable with antiquity or newly admitted. In order, however, to share in the advantages of this legal and diplomatic equality, membership of the Family of Nations is essential. And membership is not without its qualifications. No community, however powerful and independent, can be recognised as a full subject of International Law unless it shows the marks of (1) a civilisation akin to that of the Christian polities of the West; (2) an organised Government capable of entering into and observing treaties and conventions; (3) a fixed territory within which its sovereignty is complete; and (4) a stability which seems likely to offer a guarantee of permanence.

Among communities thus qualified for admission into the Family of Nations three different relations are possible. These are, first, *peace*, which includes both friendly intercourse of the active kind between specific states and also benevolent non-interference with similar friendly intercourse between other states; secondly, *war*—that is, armed conflict between states; and thirdly, intermediate betwixt the two and the most difficult to define and maintain, *neutrality*, a relation which arises when war breaks out between two states or groups of states, and non-belligerents wish to continue in peaceful intercourse with both the combatants. Although Grotius included *et Pacis* in the title of his great work, he says, as a matter of fact, very little concerning the laws of peace. The most important matters that come under that head are the various pacific modes of acquiring property, the occasional deviations from the principle of territorial jurisdiction, the numerous formal rules for the conduct of legation and negotiation, and the general regulations for the making and the ratifying of treaties. Where Grotius discusses these questions at all, he does so not because they are sections of the laws of peace, but because they give rise to rights, the defence of which may become just occasion for the waging of wars. Concerning neutrality he says still less. International commerce was not very highly developed in his day, and consequently the problems of neutrality were not either so complex or so pressing as they became later. It was left to Bynkershoek in the eighteenth century—when trade had expanded, when chartered companies had established gigantic interests all over the world, and when colonies had been planted by all the leading European peoples—to formulate in detail the fundamental principles of a rational law of neutrality. In Grotius's day, as we have had occasion to notice more than once, the critical questions related to the laws of war. Grotius as official Historiographer of Holland had acquired an intimate knowledge of the limitless barbarities perpetrated by the Spaniards under Alva and his successors in their attempts to suppress the revolt of the Netherlands from 1572 onward. He lived and wrote amid the still more appalling horrors of the Thirty Years War. His main concern was to discover and formulate such principles of law as should appeal to the reason and the conscience of combatants, and should command such universal consent and such general obedience as to render a continuance or repetition of these abominations impossible.

The guiding motive of Grotius would seem to have been the determination to secure the recognition of the principle that war is an armed conflict carried on, under conditions fixed by morality and custom, between the *public* forces of responsible states, and not an unrestricted struggle of a whole people against a whole people, without any distinction between combatants and non-combatants, or between legitimate and illegitimate modes of violence. It marked an immense mitigation of the terrors of war when he and his successors secured the recognition of the existence of a noncombatant class among enemies, and established the rule that, in general, non-combatants should be exempt from injury in person and in property. It marked a still more notable advance when, largely through the influence of the *De Jure Belli et Pacis*, it came to be acknowledged, both in theory and in practice, that even as against combatant enemies there are certain forms of violence which cannot be allowed, and that, in general, no superfluous cruelty is permissible, but only such an amount of force as shall prove to be necessary to overcome the enemies' armed resistance.

These were great achievements. By what means was Grotius able to aid in their accomplishment? To what did he appeal as the sanction of his revised and meliorative law of war? He appealed to the Law of Nature and the Law of Nations. In doing so he had to define and explain these exalted and authoritative codes.

V

(2) LAW

The conception of 'law' is one which has been much canvassed by both philosophers and jurists from the days of the Stoics onward. It connotes the correlation of two distinct ideas, viz., on the one hand, a causal intelligence and will, and, on the other hand, a resultant conformity and uniformity of behaviour. The conception arose in primitive pre-scientific times, when the phenomena of human conduct and the phenomena of irrational and inanimate nature were regarded as of one and the same order; when the sun was looked upon as a chariot driven in a race, and when men were envisaged as automata moved in their predestined circles by inexorable fate. Hence no distinction was attempted between 'law' in the scientific sense of the term and 'law' in the juristic sense of the term. Thus Demosthenes spoke of "the whole world, and things divine, and what we call the seasons" as "regulated by law and order." So Cicero talked at large of law astronomical and law imperial as equally *ratio recta summi Jovis*. The confusion continued throughout the Middle Ages. St Thomas Aquinas, for instance, discoursed of a *lex æterna* which is *nihil aliud quam summa ratio divinæ sapientiæ, secundum quod est directiva omnium actuum et motionum*. From St Thomas the confusion between law scientific and law juristic entered the modern world; it is seen in the works of Suarez, Hooker, and many others. Becoming even less excusable, it reached the eighteenth century, and was glaringly exhibited in the opening sentences of Montesquieu's *Esprit des Lois*: "Les lois, dans la signification la plus étendue, sont les rapports nécessaires qui dérivent de la nature des choses; et, dans ce sens, tous les êtres ont leurs lois; la divinité a ses lois, le monde matériel a ses lois, les intelligences supérieures à l'homme ont leurs lois, les bêtes ont leurs lois, l'homme a ses lois." Quite unpardonably, Blackstone, the English lawyer, perpetuated the muddle when he advanced to his proper study, viz., the Laws of England, by way of (1) the laws of inanimate matter, (2) the laws of animal nutrition, (3) the laws of nature, and (4) the laws of Divine revelation. It was, indeed, left for Bentham in his *Fragment on Government* (1776) and Austin in his *Jurisprudence* (1832) to clear up the ambiguity of the term 'law,' and to render it impossible for any serious thinker any more, by reason of a twofold connotation, to "deluge the field of jurisprudence and morals with muddy speculation."[1] In spite of Austin, however, one still hears (especially from pulpits and platforms) such purely nonsensical expressions as "the violation of physical law" or "obedience to the laws of political economy."

The two original ideas included in the term 'law,' viz., (1) causal intelligence and will, and (2) resultant uniformity and order, have now been entirely separated from one another. 'Law' in the *scientific* sense of the word merely connotes an unvarying sequence of phenomena; it is a general statement in the indicative mood, an abstract idea of observed relations, a theoretical principle, a provisional hypothesis. For example, one of the 'laws of motion' runs: "Action and reaction are equal and opposite"; while Newton's famous 'law of gravitation' commences with the words "Every particle of matter in the universe attracts every other particle." Nothing here is said or implied respecting either the forces whose operation is described or the causes by whose impulse they operate. 'Law' in the *juristic* sense of the word, on the other hand, connotes command; its mood is imperative; it is a general rule of human conduct; it is addressed to the will of man by the will of superior authority. "Thou shalt not steal": this law is intended to secure uniformity of behaviour on the part of all the members of the human race. But it remains 'law' even if no member of the human race obeys it.

Grotius lived and wrote at a time when the confusion

[1] J. Austin, *Jurisprudence*, fifth edition, p. 88.

between law juristic and law scientific was at its height.
Hence his work, like that of his contemporaries already mentioned, is to some extent vitiated by the ambiguity attaching
to his fundamental term, viz., *jus*. It sometimes connotes a
rule of conduct; but it also at other times connotes the
necessary relation of things. For instance, Grotius, early in
his first chapter, says, "Natural Law is so immutable that it
cannot be changed by God Himself . . . thus God Himself
cannot make twice two not to be four." Did he really sup-
pose that it is owing to a Divine command that two and two
make four? Can he indeed have imagined that a mere
mathematical postulate, a provisional hypothesis, an assumption of logic—concerning the truth of which, by the way,
Einstein has recently thrown grave doubt—has anything
whatsoever in common with a command addressed to the
human will? Apparently he did in very fact suffer from this
appalling confusion of ideas. Fortunately, however, it did
not affect much of his writing. For he soon left the realm of
science, in which he was an alien wanderer, and turned to
the world of human behaviour, wherein he was at home and
a master.

In treating of Grotius's conception of law, the first point
to be noted is that he consistently prefers the term *jus* to the
term *lex*. In other words, he selects a term which connotes
'right' irrespective of its origin, and rejects a term which
suggests statutory enactment. This choice was of special
significance in respect of Natural Law; for whereas Suarez,
who called it *Lex Naturalis*, had treated it as the unrevealed
Law of God—as truly statutory as the law revealed in the
Scriptures, or as the law promulgated by the canons of the
Church—Grotius under the name of *Jus Naturale* regards it
merely as the dictate of right reason, which would have
weight even if (to quote the Prolegomena) "we were to
grant that there is no God, or that He bestows no regard on
human affairs." But perhaps I ought not to say "*merely* as
the dictate of right reason"; for the word 'merely' suggests
inferiority. So far, however, from regarding Natural Law as
inferior to Divine Law—that is, to Law promulgated by the

direct will and voice of God—Grotius regards it as the basis of that Law, and as determining the limits within which the Divine Will itself must move. "Natural Law," he says in Book I, Chapter I, "is so immutable that it cannot be changed by God Himself. For, though the power of God be immense, there are some things to which it does not extend; because, if we speak of those things being done, the words are mere words, and have no meaning, being self-contradictory." Thus Natural Law stands in a class by itself. It is the δίκαιον φυσικόν of Aristotle. It is "the dictate of right reason, indicating that any act, from its agreement or disagreement with the rational nature, has its moral turpitude or moral necessity."[1] Hence it is of universal authority, supreme over angels and men alike, determining the modes and motions of all creatures both animate and inanimate, fixing the bounds of even the divine operations. As regards men, it existed in its pure form—*Jus Naturale Merum*—before the Fall. Since the Fall it has had to be somewhat modified, not in its principles but in its application, to suit the new circumstances: it is *Jus quod pro certo statu est Naturale.*

How may this sovereign Law of Nature be known and recognised? First, it is perceived instinctively by the conscience of the normal individual; secondly, it is proclaimed by general agreement among the best minds: thirdly, it is confirmed by the practice of all the most civilised peoples (*omnes moratiores populi*). But who shall decide what individuals are normal, what minds are best, what peoples are the most civilised? Grotius gives us no criterion; but it is obvious that he alone is normal; that minds which accord with his own mind are the best; and that the most civilised peoples are those who behave themselves as he thinks they ought to behave. In other words *Jus Naturale* is nothing more or less than the common dictates of conscience.

Similarly, *Jus Gentium* is nothing more than the precepts

---

[1] " Jus Naturale est dictatum rectæ rationis, indicans actui alicui, ex ejus convenientia aut disconvenientia cum ipsa natura rationali, inesse moralem turpitudinem aut necessitatem moralem " (*De Jure Belli et Pacis*, i, 1).

of common sense. Grotius, however, spends much time and energy in giving it an objective existence, and in placing it in its proper position in the category of laws. Over against the great body of *Jus Naturale*, consisting of the dictates of reason, he sets the *Jus Voluntarium*, or body of positive commands, which are the dictates of will. The whole of this class of laws is subordinate to the *Jus Naturale* and conditioned by it. It is subdivided into the *Jus Divinum*, or Law of God; the *Jus Civile*, or law of the State; and the *Jus Gentium*. But what is the *Jus Gentium*? The term is an expression of Roman Law, and in its original sense it meant law common to the peoples with whom the Romans had dealings. It was in Roman times private law, that is to say, law between subject and subject, a sort of highest common factor of the codes of the Italian tribes. It embodied dictates of common sense so obvious that, quite independently of one another, both the Romans and their neighbours had given expression to them in their legal systems. So closely did they in general accord with those dictates of conscience to which the name *Jus Naturale* had been given that some thinkers tended to identify the two entirely. The fact, however, that they differed on one or two matters—of which slavery was the most important—prevented their complete fusion.

The *Jus Gentium*, then, presented itself to Grotius as a code of precepts distinct from the *Jus Naturale* and of lower authority, yet immensely valuable. It provided a body of international custom which in a most serviceable way could supplement the universal morality of the Law of Nature. In order, however, that it might fulfil his purpose, he had to effect a complete change in the connotation of the term. He had to transmute it from private law, establishing relations between subject and subject; into public law, establishing relations between state and state. This was an immense and momentous transformation, and it has been warmly debated whether he effected it deliberately, or whether he perpetrated it by a happy accident out of sheer muddle-headedness and inability to distinguish between elementary differences. It may be admitted that the expression *Jus*

Gentium is an ambiguous one; it may well stand for the law common to the peoples of all nations, or for the law which regulates the mutual relations of states. It may also be admitted that Grotius was not careful to indicate that he was using the expression in the second sense, whereas the Roman lawyers from whom he derived it had used it in the first sense. But it is incredible that a man of his erudition should have made a mistake which would to-day cause an undergraduate to be ploughed in a preliminary examination. It is possible that he did not wish to call attention to the fact that he was using the *Jus Gentium* in a manner unknown to the great civilians; it is probable that he considered that the validity of the principles of the *Jus Gentium* was not in the least affected by the fact that their application was extended from the sphere of private law to the sphere of public International Law. Be that as it may, he was not the first to make the extension : it had already been done by Benedict Winckler in his *Principiorum Juris Libri Quinque,* which had appeared in 1615. Thus, just as Grotius followed Bodin in regarding the *Jus Naturale* as the dictate of human reason rather than as the unrevealed Law of God, so did he follow Winckler in treating the *Jus Gentium* as a rudimentary code of International Law rather than as a body of private law. If, however, neither of these great conceptions was original to Grotius, it was his work which gave them currency and established them as the basis of modern international morality and custom.

How may the principles of the *Jus Gentium* be known and recognised? They are displayed, first, in the usages of the best nations, and secondly in the testimony of the wisest men. But which are the best nations, and who are the wisest men? There again, as in the case of the *Jus Naturale,* the best are those who act as Grotius himself thinks they should, and the wisest are such as agree with his opinions. Hence the distinction between *Jus Naturale* and *Jus Gentium* tends to vanish away. The standard of international morality and the criterion of international custom become one and the same, viz., the conscience and the common sense of Grotius himself. Thus the *De Jure Belli et Pacis* is essentially the judgment of Grotius concerning what is allowable in war and proper in peace. The numerous opinions quoted are those of which Grotius approved; the rest he rejects. The frequent examples cited are those which support his plea for mercy and moderation; those which do not support it are either ignored or are condemned as the barbarities of nations other than the best. Thus the argument travels in a circle, and it ultimately returns to the point whence it started, viz., the conscience and the common sense of Grotius.

The weakness of so-called International Law has always been the absence of any extraneous standard. The *Jus Naturale* has no objective existence, and the *Jus Gentium* is a mere code of custom devoid of moral quality. Thus International Law lacks determinate source, lacks precise formulation, lacks sanction, lacks effective tribunals. Hence in times of severe stress, as for example in the autumn of 1914 and increasingly during the course of the Great War, it breaks down, and shows itself powerless to prevent a recurrence of precisely those barbarities which stirred Grotius to attempt his great task. To say that, however, is not to say that Grotius and his successors laboured in vain. It is not for nothing that a general set of rules has been framed, even though the force necessary to ensure their observance has hitherto been wanting. For gradually but certainly there is coming into being an International Authority—a Concert of Europe; a Council of Great Powers; a Hague Tribunal; a Geneva Court; a League of Nations—which in due time will give to the moral precepts and the customary practices which the conscience and the common sense of the great jurists have formulated the force and the majesty of a genuine and operative International Law.

BOOK LIST

A. PRIMARY SOURCES

GROTIUS, HUGO: *De Jure Belli et Pacis Libri Tres,* accompanied by an abridged translation by William Whewell. 3 vols. 1853.

B. SECONDARY SOURCES

CARMICHAEL, C. H. E.: " Grotius and the Literary History of the Law of Nations " (*Transactions of the Royal Society of Literature,* Second Series, vol. xiv).

FRANCK, A.: *Réformateurs et publicistes de l'Europe.* 1864.

HÉLY, D.: *Étude sur le droit de la guerre de Grotius.* 1875.

HOLLAND, T. E.: *Studies in International Law.* 1898.

KALKENBORN, K.: *Die Vorläufer des Hugo Grotius.* 1848.

PRADIER-FODÉRÉ, P. L. E.: *Essai sur Grotius et son temps.* 1865.

VREELAND, H.: *Hugo Grotius.* 1917.

WALKER, T. A.: *History of the Law of Nations.* 1899.

WHITE, A. D.: *Seven Great Statesmen.* 1910.

BOLINGBROKE AND PROGRESSIVE CONSERVATISM[1]

O F all the political thinkers of the Augustan Age none was so eminent or so highly applauded during his life, none so profoundly despised or generally rejected after his death, as Henry St John, the Lord Viscount Bolingbroke. To his contemporaries, in the days of his magnificent prime, he seemed to be the embodiment of all that was splendid and effective among men. High in rank, handsome in person, stately in deportment, polished in manners, cultivated in mind, quick in wit, fascinating in conversation, unrivalled in oratorical power, a scholar, a linguist, a bold and original speculator, a capable administrator, a skilled diplomatist, a dæmonic actor, a finished courtier and man of the world—he appeared to be almost superhuman in his gifts and graces, or, at the very least, "not one, but all mankind's epitome." Jonathan Swift, who was not too well disposed towards the human race at large, said of him when he was still youthful (in a letter to Stella, November 3, 1711) that he was the greatest young man he ever knew, marked by wit, capacity, beauty, quickness of apprehension, good learning, and excellent taste; the best orator in the House of Commons, admirable conversation, good nature and good manners, generous, and a despiser of money. A quarter of a century later Alexander Pope, also inclined to general misanthropy, writing to Swift, said (March 25, 1736):

---

[1] From *The Social and Political Ideas of Some English Thinkers of the Augustan Age*, A.D. 1650–1750 (Harrap, 1928). The other studies in this volume are: "Introductory: The Augustan Age," by G. N. Clarke; "Sir Robert Filmer," by J. W. Allen; "George Savile, Marquis of Halifax," by A. W. Reed; "John Locke," by C. H. Driver; "Jacobites and Non-jurors," by H. Broxap; "Benjamin Hoadly, Bishop of Bangor," by Norman Sykes; "Daniel Defoe," by Miss A. E. Levett; "Jonathan Swift," by G. B. Harrison.

I have lately seen some writings of Lord B's, since he went to France. Nothing can depress his genius. Whatever befalls him, he will still be the greatest man in the world, either in his own time, or with posterity.

Shortly afterwards, in a letter to Bolingbroke himself (September 3, 1740), he exclaimed, with an amusing play upon his own name, "I would, if I were Pope, canonize you, whatever all the advocates for the devil could say to the contrary." Chesterfield's eulogy is well known. In a letter to his son he wrote:

I have sent you Lord Bolingbroke's *Letters on Patriotism* and *The Idea of a Patriot King*, which he published about a year ago. I desire that you will read these letters over and over again, with particular attention to the style, and to all those beauties of oratory with which they are adorned. Till I read that book, I confess I did not know all the extent and powers of the English language. Lord Bolingbroke has both a tongue and a pen to persuade; his manner of speaking in private conversation is full as elegant as his writings. Whatever subject he either speaks or writes upon, he adorns it with the most splendid eloquence; not in studied or laboured eloquence, but such a flowing happiness of diction as—perhaps from care at first—is become so habitual to him that even his most familiar conversations, if taken down in writing, would bear the press, without the least correction either as to method or style.

After some remarks on the vicissitudes of his career he continued:

He has an infinite fund of various and almost universal knowledge which, from the clearest and quickest conception and happiest memory that ever man was blessed with, he always carries about him. . . . He engaged young, and distinguished himself in business; and his penetration was almost intuition. I am old enough to have heard him speak in Parliament,[1] and I remember that, though prejudiced against him by party, I felt all the force and charms of his eloquence. . . . All the internal and external advantages and talents of an orator are undoubtedly his. Figure, voice, elocution, knowledge, and above all the purest and most florid

---

[1] Bolingbroke's last speech in Parliament was delivered on March 17, 1715.

diction, with the justest metaphors and happiest images, had raised him to the post of Secretary at War at four-and-twenty years old, an age at which others are hardly thought fit for the smallest employments.

Bolingbroke himself deliberately and avowedly wrote for posterity, and his editors confidently predicted for him a literary immortality. For instance, the anonymous author of his *Memoirs*, published the year after his decease, said, "Death, in removing him out of the reach of envy and the rage of jealousy, has extended the utility and fixed the immortality of his writings," adding, "His writings are the monuments which he consecrated to posterity; and, though he is now no more, these will last for ever."

II

The spell, however, which Bolingbroke cast over his contemporaries by the charm of his person, the graces of his behaviour, and the brilliance of his gifts did not long survive him. Nay, for some years before his death, when he lived retired in his ancestral home at Battersea (1744–51), he himself realised, with deep chagrin, that he was becoming isolated and impotent in an alien world. Young men, like William Pitt, who had been attracted to him by the magic of his reputation, drifted away as they found that he had no further contribution to make either to the political and social, or to the philosophical and religious, problems of their age. The spell of Bolingbroke's unquestionable genius was, in fact, broken while he was yet alive, by, first, the notorious depravity of his private conduct; secondly, his obvious lack of political principle; thirdly, the violence and factiousness of his restless and relentless antagonism to Walpole and the Whigs; fourthly, the palpable impracticability of his constitutional proposals; and, finally, his doubtful attitude towards the Christian religion. The publication of his posthumous writings, under the injudicious editorship of David Mallet, in 1754, completed the ruin of his reputation. The first two volumes showed that where he was not an unscrupulous party politician, seeking by all means to justify himself and inculpate his enemies, he was a mere empty rhetorician, propounding with pompous prolixity the emptiest platitudes. The remaining three volumes displayed him fully, for the first time, as the inveterate and envenomed foe of Christianity; as the repudiator of both revelation and immortality; as the vehement rejector of most of the articles of the creed of the Church on whose behalf he had in the days of his power persecuted and proscribed Dissenters. What the Whig bishops thought of him may best be seen in William Warburton's *View of Lord Bolingbroke's Philosophy* (1756). What even the pious Tories, who had at one time looked up to him as their champion, came to think of him is shown by Dr Johnson's severe judgment: "Sir," he said to Boswell, "he was a scoundrel and a coward: a scoundrel, for charging a blunderbuss against religion and morality; a coward, because he had no resolution to fire it off himself, but left half a crown to a beggarly Scotchman to draw the trigger after his death." Thus Bolingbroke became the shadow of an evil name, condemned for his immorality, hated for his irreligion, rejected for his political impossibility, despised for his rhetorical superficiality. Only forty years after his death, Edmund Burke asked, respecting those very works whose immortality had been so confidently predicted, "Who now reads Bolingbroke? Who ever read him through?" adding, "I do not often quote Bolingbroke, nor have his works in general left any permanent impression on my mind. He is a presumptuous and a superficial writer."

The note thus struck in the late eighteenth century by Warburton, Johnson, Burke, and their fellows was reiterated in the nineteenth century, particularly by the Whig historians. To Macaulay Bolingbroke appeared to be merely "a brilliant knave." Carlyle described his works as "lacquered brass." Sir Leslie Stephen characterised them as "a mass of insincere platitudes," and their writer as "a showy actor." Lord Morley condemned him as "a charlatan—a bankrupt politician—a shipwrecked adventurer—a consummate posture-maker." Mr Walter Bagehot regarded insincerity and speciousness as the outstanding features of his works. Mr J. M. Robertson speaks of him as "a *condottiere*—without fixed principle or aim—unscrupulous—an adroit parliamentary swordsman, a forensic debater, but not a true thinker."

III

Such was the chorus of late Hanoverian and Victorian detraction. There can be no doubt that its note of condemnation was as much exaggerated and over-emphasised as had been the uncritical adulation of the Tories of the days of Swift, or the 'Patriots' of the days of Pope. Bolingbroke unquestionably had the defects of his qualities; but he also had the qualities of his defects. That is to say, if he was immoral, he was also strikingly free from debilitating convention—fresh, original, emancipated: no Puritan, even when inebriated, would have run, as Bolingbroke is said to have done, naked through St James's Park. Again, if he lacked political principle, he was prolific in political ideas and fruitful in political expedients. If he was violent and factious, he was at any rate alive and active. If he talked and wrote much mere rhetoric, he was a master of the oratorical style, with an incomparable command of the music of words. If he was vehemently anti-Christian, he was not simply destructive in the sphere of religion. On the one hand he was a pioneer in the imperatively necessary application of historical and literary criticism to the Bible; on the other hand he developed a positive theism, a "natural religion," based on what appeared to him to be the secure inductions of science, and on the irrefragable precepts of natural law. That he is not universally recognised as one of the first and foremost of the rationalists—the veritable harbinger of the eighteenth-century Age of Reason—is primarily due to the fact that the publication of his philosophical and religious opinions was postponed until he was in his grave, whereas through Voltaire and other disciples they had for thirty years or more been moulding the thought of the *intelligenzia* of the West.

IV

Efforts to rehabilitate Bolingbroke have from time to time been made by those who have refused to believe that men so critical and discerning as Swift and Pope and Chesterfield were wholly mistaken in the character of the hero whom they knew and adored. In particular Disraeli and the Young England group of the thirties and forties of the last century looked to Bolingbroke as their prophet, and took his writings as gospel. Rarely has a more splendid and impressive appreciation of one politician by another been written than Disraeli's eulogy of Bolingbroke in his *Vindication of the English Constitution*. He exalts him as the founder of Tory democracy—the union of Crown and nation—as against the Whig oligarchy—the corrupt coalition of feudal nobles with fraudulent financiers. He praises him to the skies because, he says, he

> eradicated from Toryism all those absurd and odious doctrines that Toryism had adventitiously adopted; clearly developed its essential and permanent character; discarded the dogma of divine right, demolished passive obedience, threw to the winds the doctrine of non-resistance; placed the deposition of James and the accession of George on their right basis; and in the complete reorganisation of the public mind laid the foundation for the future accession of the Tory party to power.

The same tendency to exalt Bolingbroke, extol his influence, and claim him as founder appears in the utterances of the Tory democrats of the generation of Lord Randolph Churchill.

Similarly the Young Tories of the present day, restless under the reactionary incubus of the "old gang," cry, "Back to Bolingbroke!" For Bolingbroke, like Disraeli, like Randolph Churchill, like Birkenhead, like—but I must not mention the names of living men—stood for the curious and rare combination of Conservatism with Radicalism; of a strenuous maintenance of old institutions with a vigorous infusion into them of a new spirit; of a careful preservation of vital continuity with a constant modification of structure;

of a union of order with progress; of stability with necessary change; of antiquity with modernity. Lord Birkenhead, it is true, is critical; but perhaps he speaks for the "old gang": "The Whigs," he says, "went bathing, and Bolingbroke stole their clothes."[1] He, apparently, does not approve of the way in which Bolingbroke in his later writings, "meets his opponents upon the pure ground of Whiggism, tries them, and finds them wanting." It certainly is a method extremely perplexing to the still-surviving Toryism of the seventeenth century. Sir Geoffrey Butler, however, perceived the greatness and importance of Bolingbroke's work in weaning the Tory party from Jacobitism and from all its implications.

> In every age Tory thinkers must perceive that the Jacobitism against which Bolingbroke fought has its counterpart in many theories dear to the Old Guard. That, for the Tory, possibly for the Radical too, is the abiding lesson of Bolingbroke's career.[2]

Similarly Maurice Wood, in his vivacious *History of the Tory Party*, describing Bolingbroke as "one of the two great men of practical capacity joined to intellectual genius which Toryism has produced," recognises the great and enduring influence of his ideas. They did much, he says, to determine the character and career of the elder Pitt; they were operative in the overthrow of Walpole in 1742; they inspired George III and the King's Friends to shatter the Whig oligarchy between 1760 and 1770; they guided the genius of the younger Pitt in the critical days of the Revolutionary War; they illuminated the path of Canning; above all they became the source of the prevailing power of Disraeli in his great task of educating the Victorian Tories out of Protection and into Parliamentary reform. Churton Collins says:

> To the influence of Bolingbroke's writings is to be attributed in no small degree that remarkable transformation which converted the Toryism of Rochester and Nottingham into the

---

[1] F. E. Smith, *Toryism*, p. xxxv.
[2] G. G. Butler, *The Tory Tradition*, pp. 26–27.

Toryism of Pitt and Mansfield. . . . He inaugurated a new
era in the annals of Party. He made Jacobitism contemptible.
He reconstructed the Tory creed.[1]

V

The education of the Tory party: that was Bolingbroke's
great achievement in the eighteenth century. It strikingly
resembled Disraeli's great achievement in the nineteenth
century: it was indeed, as we have just remarked, the model
upon which Disraeli avowedly and deliberately framed his
policy and his programme. Now, few tasks can be so difficult
as the education of the Tory party; perhaps the only task
obviously more difficult is the education of a religious sect.
For the Tory party—under whichever of its countless names
it may be known—is the party that venerates antiquity, that
maintains tradition, that supports old institutions just
because they are old, that reverences customs, that worships
ancestors, that obeys without question the authority of the
dead. Its main sources of strength—the veterans and stal-
warts of the 'Old Guard'—are men of emotion rather than
men of reason; men of passionate devotion to causes inexpres-
sibly dear, rather than men of intellect with minds open to
new conceptions. Thus the education of the Tory party is
an education in the difficult art of forgetting, the education
of steadfast and resolute men out of convictions sincerely
and strenuously held; nay, more, it is the education of
zealous and consecrated devotees out of loyalties to which
they cling with a passion that is stronger than love of life
itself.

Just as Disraeli in the middle of the nineteenth century
had to draw the followers of Lord George Bentinck away
from devotion to the Corn Laws, and train the regiments of
Wellington's political army to march in the direction of
household suffrage, so, a hundred years earlier, had Bolingbroke to lure the Jacobites of Shippen's rout from the
obsolete advocacy of divine right and passive obedience, and

[1] J. Churton Collins, *Bolingbroke: an Historical Study*, pp. 7, 94.

persuade the High Church clergy of Atterbury's way of thinking to cease from the hunting and harrying of Dissenters.

There is another resemblance, too, between Bolingbroke and Disraeli. It is this: Each of them had qualified for his post of instructor by a period of apprenticeship during which he had vigorously propounded the antiquated fallacies from which he subsequently purged his party. Just as Disraeli, before he took up his educative task, had distinguished himself by his defence of the Corn Laws in 1846, and by his destructive criticism of every Parliamentary Reform Bill introduced into the House of Commons between 1837 and 1867, so had Bolingbroke, before he assumed the work of emancipating the Tory party from Jacobitism and religious exclusiveness, rendered himself notorious by his advocacy of the Occasional Conformity and Schism Acts, and by his term of conspicuous service as Secretary of State to the Pretender. The parallel may be carried still farther. For just as Disraeli when most he defended the Corn Laws was never a Protectionist, and when most he opposed Reform Bills was always a reformer, so Bolingbroke, even when serving the Pretender, was never a Jacobite, and even when persecuting Dissenters was always a free thinker. In truth, neither Bolingbroke nor Disraeli, although each of them joined the Tory party, worked with it, and for a time led it —neither of them was ever really of it. They advocated Tory measures with perfect sincerity and with strong conviction, but for reasons wholly different from those which actuated the Tory party—reasons which the average members of the Tory party were totally incapable of comprehending. Hence they were able to abandon Tory measures—such as the eighteenth-century Penal Laws, or the nineteenth-century Corn Laws—without any abandonment of principle, or any change of policy. They were working for ends which transcended mere measures; they were labouring to realise ideals which were capable of attainment by many routes; they were educating their followers in the art of distinguishing essentials from accidents; they were moulding their reluctant and resistant pupils to the shape of their own masterful wills.

VI

It is now time to examine a little more in detail the life, the writings, the social and political ideas of Bolingbroke. Of the life not much need here be said. Those who are unfamiliar with its particulars will find them set forth with discriminating brevity in Mr Arthur Hassall's *Life of Viscount Bolingbroke* (1889, new edition, 1915), and with undiscriminating fullness in Mr Walter Sichel's erudite but excessively eulogistic *Bolingbroke and his Times* (two volumes, 1901–2). Suffice it here to note a few outstanding facts. Henry St John was born at the beginning of October 1678 in the manor-house at Battersea—the house in which he was destined to die seventy-three years later. His parents, Sir Henry (later Viscount) St John, a worthless reprobate, and his mother, the Lady Mary, a colourless and inert daughter of the Earl of Warwick, did not at that time own the manor. They were living as guests or dependents of the old Sir Walter St John (founder of the Free School still flourishing in Battersea) and his formidable wife, the Lady Joanna, herself a St John by birth—daughter of Oliver St John, one of the leading opponents of Charles I, and later Cromwell's Chief Justice of the Common Pleas. The ancient Joanna was the dominant personality of the household. Of Roundhead descent and of strong Puritan leanings, she controlled her grandson's early education. Hence while Sir Henry haunted taverns and gained notoriety by sanguinary brawls,[1] and while the Lady Mary sat passive with her hands in her lap, the old lady saw to it that the infant Harry was nourished on the parables of Daniel Burgess, and was fortified by Dr Manton's hundred and nineteen sermons on the hundred-and-nineteenth Psalm.

After such a preparatory school, entry into Eton was to Harry St John what the Restoration was to the Cavaliers after the rigidities of the Commonwealth. It emancipated

---

[1] He killed a man in 1684, and with difficulty escaped execution.

him from Puritanism and opened the way to that extreme reaction into scepticism and licentiousness which marked his manhood. At Eton he acquired a good working knowledge of Latin, and laid the foundation of that extensive acquaintance with Roman literature which characterises all his writings. He displayed, in particular, a marvellous memory, which enabled him to store his mind with historical precedents and illustrative passages, so that later he was able to compose without the aid of books works of considerable elaboration. On leaving Eton he travelled in France and Italy, and showed his mental alertness and natural capacity by gaining an almost perfect mastery of the two great Romance languages. In after-years Voltaire professed that Bolingbroke had been able to give him valuable lessons in French! In France and Italy, too, it would appear, Bolingbroke learned what little his father's example had not already imparted to him of the art and craft of the debauchery then prevalent in the fashionable world. Certainly Harry St John came back to England in 1700 an accomplished *roué* and man of pleasure. London soon echoed with the report of his drunken and licentious orgies. In the hope of reforming or at any rate restraining him, his grandfather found him a wife worth £40,000, and a seat in the House of Commons for the pocket-borough of Wootton Bassett in Wiltshire. Thus auspiciously, in February 1701, Henry St John the younger entered upon his public career.

VII

It may be said at once that the immediate object at which the old Sir Walter aimed in securing for his grandson a consort and a constituency was not achieved. Henry St John remained a rake and a reprobate. There can be little doubt, indeed, that the ultimate failure which marked his career was primarily due to his personal vices. His drunkenness not only weakened his will and incapacitated him on occasions when deliberate and decisive action was necessary; it also in at least two critical junctures betrayed him into indiscretions of speech which raised up against him powerful and implacable enemies. His gross sexual excesses not only shattered his fine constitution, rendering him prematurely old when little over forty, and decrepit when he ought to have been in his prime; they also made him an object of disgust to Queen Anne, to the Anglican clergy, and to the bulk of the great party which he aspired to lead; they were indeed the main cause of his failure to secure the White Staff at the crisis of his fate (July 27–30, 1714), when to have secured it, and thereby to have become Prime Minister, would have been to alter the whole course of subsequent English history, and probably to have established for himself a political ascendancy as enduring as that actually achieved by his great rival, Sir Robert Walpole. As a contemporary observer remarked, "his character was too bad and his bottom too narrow to carry the great ensign." Nay, more, we may confidently assert that the life of lawless dissipation that he led during the period of his power—the condition of feverish and unnatural excitement in which he constantly moved and had his being—was largely responsible for the wildness of speech, the recklessness of action, the unscrupulousness of policy, the disregard of consequences, which characterised him as a Minister of the Crown.

In the matter of morals, then, the contrast between Bolingbroke and Disraeli is striking. In another respect also it is remarkable. Disraeli, beginning life with the heavy handicap of alien race, *bourgeois* rank, imperfect education, and harassing poverty, attained political power only at the end of his life, when he was too old, too weary, too forlorn, to use it to full effect. Bolingbroke, on the other hand, beginning life with every advantage of race, rank, education, and wealth, reached all but the summit of his ambition while still he was a very young man—Member of Parliament at twenty-two; War Secretary at twenty-six; chief Secretary of State at thirty-one; virtual Prime Minister (although but for three days) ere he was thirty-six. It was his (and his country's) misfortune that he was placed in high and responsible office before he was morally mature enough

to perform his duties with a proper sense of their serious-
ness.

VIII

When he entered Parliament in 1701 he attached himself
to Robert Harley, and joined the Tory party. This party,
after some ten years of embittered opposition, had recently
recovered power. In 1701 it was out to humiliate William
of Orange; to limit the prerogative of the presumptive
monarchs of the house of Hanover; to punish and proscribe
the Whig leaders; to penalise Dissenters; to disband the
standing army; to withdraw from Continental politics; to
re-establish the ascendancy of land over money, and of
country over town; and to place the Tories in permanent
possession of office. It was a party large and passionate, but
bucolic and inarticulate; capable of roaring and raging, but
incapable of expressing its emotions in intelligible language.
Henry St John gave it a voice. Without sharing, or even
professing to share, its prepossessions and prejudices, he
propounded with an eloquence such as the House of
Commons had never before heard the extremest tenets of its
most reactionary die-hards. He denounced the Partition
Treaties of 1698 and 1700; he supported the impeachment
of Somers and his colleagues; he assailed the Kentish
petitioners; he strove to deprive the Aylesbury electors of
their common law right to vote; he defended the malignant
Occasional Conformity Bill. Never had there been a more
conspicuous example of the mere party politician, devoid of
either conscience or moderation, struggling for leadership by
following the most violent section of his faction. By the
almost unanimous judgment of posterity in every one of the
causes which he advocated he was in the wrong.

His conspicuous abilities, however, soon procured for him
place and power. Before he had been twelve months in the
House of Commons he was chosen by ballot (March 1702)
to be a Commissioner for taking the public accounts, with a
salary of £500 a year, besides lavish allowances for expenses.
Two years later he was taken into the Ministry by Godolphin

and Marlborough as Secretary at War. Now, the Ministry was a mixed one, containing a good many Whigs; so that St John as a member of the Government had to modify his extreme Toryism. The War of the Spanish Succession, more-over, which in 1704 reached its climax in the decisive battle of Blenheim, was a Whig war, started by William of Orange in defence of those very Partition Treaties which St John had hitherto denounced. The Secretary at War, therefore, had to change his tone respecting foreign affairs, and had to devote such administrative abilities as he possessed to the active furtherance of the great struggle which he had hitherto condemned. He seems to have performed his official duties efficiently and well, if somewhat spasmodically. The performance of his official duties, however, while it alienated his old allies, the wildly pacific Tories, did not wholly satisfy his new associates, the belligerent Whigs. He, together with his colleague Harley, fell into suspicion of lukewarmness and intrigue, so that in 1708 he was con-strained not only to resign office, but also to withdraw from Parliament for a season. He spent two years (1708–10) in retirement, watching the course of events, and spending his time in fruitful study.

The General Election of 1705, fought amid the delirious excitement caused by the victory of Blenheim and the cap-ture of Gibraltar the preceding year, re-established the Whig party in power. The vigorous prosecution of the war became the cardinal principle of the Government's policy. The triumphs of Ramillies and Turin in 1706 gave rise to hopes that the power of France might finally be broken, and Europe freed for ever from the menace which had hung over her for nearly a century. Hence almost abject offers of peace from Louis XIV were contemptuously rejected in 1706, 1709, and again in 1710, by the allied British, Dutch, and Germans. They were resolved to be content with nothing short of the annihilation of the Bourbon power. From the British Ministry were expelled all who did not accept the full Whig programme. Thus, for the first time in our history (1708–10) a true 'Cabinet' was brought into existence—that is to say, a body of ministers drawn entirely from one political party, and dependent for its position and power not upon the monarch, but upon a majority in the House of Commons.

Queen Anne, indeed, was notoriously hostile to her Ministry during the two years of the Whig monopoly. She disliked Godolphin, the First Lord of the Treasury; she was jealous of the fame of Marlborough; she hated the house of Hanover with which the Whigs were in the closest alliance; she loathed the Dissenters who constituted the strength of the Whigs in the corporate towns; she longed for peace, so that she might discuss with her half-brother, the Pretender, and with Louis XIV, his patron and protector, the conditions of a new Stuart Restoration. The errors of the Whigs in flouting the Queen, in irritating the Church, in prolonging the war, in rejecting the terms offered by the French, in piling up taxation, in perpetrating jobs, and finally in impeaching Dr Sacheverell for a Tory sermon, enabled the angry Anne (under the inspiration of Harley and St John) to dismiss the Whig Ministry with ignominy, dissolve Parliament, appeal to the country, and secure an overwhelming Tory majority.

IX

Thus, in 1710, Harley (soon to be created Earl of Oxford) found himself First Lord of the Treasury, with Henry St John as his principal Secretary of State. For the four remaining years of Queen Anne's reign the Tories retained their ascendancy. Their main concern during this period was to make such arrangements as would ensure their continuance in power after the Queen's decease. To this end they desired (1) to bring the war to a close; (2) to sever England's connexion with the Dutch and the Germans; (3) to secure guarantees on the one hand from the Pretender for Protestantism and on the other hand from the Hanoverians for Toryism; (4) to break the power of the Dissenters and restore the authority of the Church of England; (5) to overthrow the might of the new moneyed magnates and re-establish the ascendancy of the old landed gentry; (6) to abolish or at any rate reduce the standing army and revive the glories of the Militia and the Navy.

It was unfortunate for the carrying out of their programme that Harley and St John soon ceased to agree concerning ways and means. Harley, in spite of certain prudent parleyings with the Pretender, was entirely devoted to the Hanoverian succession; St John, contemptuous of the Electoral Court when sober, and insolently hostile to it when inebriated, pursued a policy which inevitably led him to the Pretender. Harley was sincerely devoted to the Church of England; St John cared for it only in so far as it represented the Tory party at prayer. Harley was anxious for peace with honour; St John was resolved to secure peace at any price. Above all, Harley was willing to work with the Whigs, and was continually making overtures to them (and to Robert Walpole in particular); St John, on the other hand, was filled with an implacable rage against them (and against Robert Walpole in particular), and was determined to leave no stone unturned to accomplish their complete annihilation. These profound differences made continued co-operation between the two men impossible. Early in 1711 their old alliance was dissolved, and each began to go his several way. The Tory party became split into divergent factions, the moderates following the Treasurer, the wild men the Secretary. St John, especially when in his cups, declaimed violently and vehemently against his chief—the echoes of his declamations still reverberate through the sonorous passages of his *Letter to Sir William Wyndham*, his last *Remarks on the History of England*, and his dissertation on *The State of Parties at the Accession of George I*. Harley, for his part, intrigued against St John; told the scandalised Queen the secrets of his private life; whispered to the bishops the worst respecting his horrible infidelities; hinted to the Hanoverians that St John's ascendancy would be fatal alike to the Elector and to Protestantism. In vain did Jonathan Swift, their common friend, mediate between the two rivals; in vain did their colleagues in the Ministry seek to heal the breach; in vain

121

did the Queen herself, alarmed at the magnitude of the brawl, command accommodation. The struggle became a mortal combat, without parallel in the annals of Parliamentary history. That St John with his violent and clear-cut measures commanded the majority of the party soon became evident: Harley, in order to retain his nominal leadership, was compelled to acquiesce in measures of which he thoroughly disapproved. St John took entire charge of the peace negotiations, and concluded the Treaties of Utrecht (1713) on terms which threw away the fruits of a hundred victories, dissolved the Grand Alliance, and left in the minds of Dutch, Imperialists, and Catalans a sense of gross desertion and betrayal. He carried through Parliament a Property Qualifications Bill which made the possession of large landed estates an indispensable condition of membership of the House of Commons. He secured the passage of the Occasional Conformity Bill—a blow to the Dissenters and therefore to the Whigs—which had been a matter of furious conflict in Parliament for ten years. He added an incredible Schism Act, intended to exclude Dissenters from the teaching profession, which went beyond the extremest expectations of the High Anglican clergy. He attacked his quondam colleagues of the Godolphin Ministry on the ground of peculation, and got his enemy Walpole condemned, expelled from the House of Commons, and sent to the Tower. He began to clear Whigs out of offices in the Army, out of lord-lieutenancies in the counties, out of all administrative posts where their influence might jeopardise the complete Tory control of the machinery of government. Never had party fury raged so ferociously as it did during these four hectic years; never had a party politician shown a more complete disregard of all save party considerations than did Henry St John.

But though St John thus, as he expressed it, "gave the view-halloo" to the pack that followed him, "showed the Tories game," and established a masterly ascendancy over the majority in both Houses of Parliament, his position was insecure and his triumph incomplete so long as he was out of favour at Court. The English monarch still ruled as well as reigned; still presided at Councils; still determined policies; still appointed and dismissed ministers; still vetoed legislation. In order to oust Harley and obtain supreme power it was necessary to win Anne. This was no easy matter; for Anne had been thoroughly poisoned against St John by well-authenticated reports of his evil life and his heterodox opinions. The difficult task, however was achieved by the instrumentality of the dominant serving-woman, Abigail Hill (Mrs Masham).[1] Hence on July 27, 1714, Harley (since 1711 Earl of Oxford) was dismissed, and St John (who in 1712 had been made Viscount Bolingbroke) found himself in undisputed headship of the Tory party, and virtually Prime Minister.

X

Bolingbroke's triumph was short-lived. It rested on an extremely insecure basis, viz., the life of Queen Anne. Now Anne had been in failing health for many months. The agitations incident to the expulsion of Oxford (who did not retire gracefully) were more than her constitution could stand. She had an apoplectic fit on July 30, and on August 1 she died. If Anne had really liked and trusted Bolingbroke she would on July 27 have made him Lord Treasurer in succession to Oxford, and he would then have controlled the administration during the crisis of the next five days and after the Queen's decease. She steadily refused, however, to confer this commanding office upon him; his character was too bad, his principles were too loose, his partisanship was too violent and unscrupulous, to render it possible to place the kingdom in his charge. Above all, she felt that the Church would be unsafe in his keeping. If Bolingbroke had during the four years of his power shown himself less reckless in his pursuit of the Whigs, less outrageous in his persecution of Dissenters, less perfidious in his diplomacy, less malignant in his hostility to Harley, less devoid of all the qualities

---

[1] She persuaded the Queen not so much to like St John as to dislike Harley more.

required for statesmanship except brilliance and audacity, he still might have controlled the situation through his leadership of the Tory party. But not even the Tory party could trust him. For if he had always subordinated the interests of his country to the interests of his party, he had, equally obviously, invariably subordinated the interests of his party to his own ambitions, and even to his own lusts. The Tory party, therefore, in the crisis of the summer of 1714 was paralysed by dissension and distrust. Finally, if Bolingbroke had even been sure of himself he might have seized the reins of power and have prevailed. For three days, indeed, the reins were actually in his hands. But at the crucial moment his nerve and his courage failed him. The brilliance and the audacity which had been his outstanding characteristics deserted him: he fumbled for a policy, hesitating between George and James; he played for safety, groping for lines of retreat. Through sheer ineptness, indecision, cowardice, and incompetence he let the Whigs secure control of affairs. George was proclaimed; a Council of Regency was established; the seals of office were taken from him, and he was relegated to private life.

Rarely has there been a more sudden change of fortune than that which befell Bolingbroke in 1714, between July 27, when he secured the dismissal of Oxford at the hands of Anne, and August 28, when he received his own formal and emphatic expulsion from George I. He, of course, like most ambitious men who have spectacularly failed, attributed his disaster to circumstances: if only Anne had lived another six weeks, he said, all would have been well both for himself and for the Tories. But no amount of specious argument could conceal from himself, from his disillusioned followers, or from the world at large, the fact that his failure and the ruin in which he involved his party were attributable to himself alone. His vices had alienated Anne; his impiety had alarmed the Church; his violence and fierce invective had turned the Earl of Oxford from friendship to embittered antagonism, and had split the Tory party in hopeless schism; his malignant persecution of Whigs and Dissenters had roused against him the disapproval of most moderate and reasonable men; his unscrupulous and short-sighted conduct of foreign affairs had left Britain without a friend in Europe. Finally, his resourcelessness, nervelessness, feebleness, and inefficiency in the cardinal week of Queen Anne's illness and death showed alike to Whigs and Tories, Jacobites and Hanoverians, Britons and interested peoples on the Continent that, clever as Bolingbroke might be in debate, and crafty as he undoubtedly was in diplomacy, he was but a broken reed in the day when decisive and courageous action was called for. His reputation never recovered from the shock of the fiasco of August 1714.

If any things remained to be done to complete his political damnation, these things he proceeded incontinently to do. In March 1715, at a threat of impeachment, he fled to France; in July he joined the Pretender at Commercy, accepted office as Secretary of State in his shadow Ministry, and helped to organise the Jacobite rebellion in England and Scotland which marked the autumn of that fateful year. Quite naturally and properly, therefore, he was, in September 1715, attainted of high treason, deprived of his property, degraded from the peerage, and condemned to death. Comedy followed tragedy. He soon mortally offended his new master, the Pretender, by what he said in his cups concerning him and his tinsel Court; he outraged the Catholic priesthood which surrounded and sustained the Pretender by his contemptuous attitude towards their religion and by his frank insistence that they were the main obstacles to the Pretender's restoration to his ancestors' throne; he exasperated the Irish and the Scottish Jacobites by his refusal to approve of the rash and ridiculous schemes with which their imaginations teemed. The failure of the '15 was attributed to him. In February 1716 he was summarily and ignominiously dismissed by the Pretender, and his dismissal was followed by an impeachment on the alleged grounds of treachery, incapacity, and neglect. By Jacobite writers in France he was attacked with a ferocity not less intense than that with which he was attacked by Whig writers in England.

XI

Thus in 1716 Bolingbroke's political damnation was complete. He was regarded both by the Tories in England and by the Jacobites in France as the main cause of the disasters which had overwhelmed them. By the dominant Whigs, headed by George I himself and by Robert Walpole, he was looked upon as a malicious and unscrupulous arch-enemy to be kept at all costs from any restoration to place or power. His official career was, in fact, at an end. He was but thirty-eight years old, and he had thirty-five more years to live. In vain, however, did he toil, intrigue, and bribe with a view to securing the removal of his attainder and his readmission to Parliament. In 1723, it is true, he obtained a cancellation of the sentence of death and permission to return to England. Two years later, by Act of Parliament, his property was restored to him. But that was all. He remained till the end of his days a peer merely by courtesy, an exile from the House of Lords, and an alien ineligible for office under the Crown. Such was the Nemesis of Bolingbroke's application of the principles of Machiavelli to British politics.

The thirty-five years of his outlawry were, however—precisely because he was shut out from public life—the all-fruitful years of his literary and philosophical activity. The written remains of the earlier portion of his career are negligible. We have a few worthless poems; an anonymous attack on Marlborough and Godolphin contributed to the *Examiner* in 1710; numbers of diplomatic dispatches in English and in French penned during the peace negotiations of 1711–13; and a mass of private correspondence, much of which lies yet unpublished in the archives of Petworth and Hemel Hempstead. After 1716, however, Bolingbroke's literary output was extensive: in the first collected edition of his works, issued by David Mallet in 1754, it fills five large folio volumes. Four periods in his later career can be distinguished: (1) from 1716 to 1723 he was a proscribed exile in France; (2) from 1723 to 1735 he was mainly in England working with the energy of mortal hatred to overthrow the Ministry of his implacable enemy, Sir Robert Walpole; (3) from 1735 to 1744, disappointed by his complete failure either to destroy the Whig ascendancy or to recover his own position, he was for the most part back in France; (4) from 1744 to his death in 1751, having inherited the family manor of Battersea (on the removal of that "monument of extinct profligacy," his aged and disreputable father, in 1742), he returned finally to England, and there in failing health, gathering obscurity, and depressing impotence finished his distressful career.

Each of these four periods has its own peculiar literary memorials. During the first of them, viz., 1716–23, Bolingbroke, in order to distract his mind from contemplation of the appalling mess which he had made of things, dabbled in philosophy and theology. He compiled some vapid and platitudinous *Reflections upon Exile*, in which he plagiarised from Seneca a number of inane truisms which one virtuous fool might think capable of consoling another virtuous fool under the buffetings of inexorable fate, but which can assuredly have afforded no solace to a highly intelligent knave suffering the consequences of his own moral delinquencies. He composed, in French, a series of brilliant letters to the philosophic M. de Pouilly, arguing for a theistic, as against an atheistic, interpretation of the universe. He indited, also in French, a vehement and powerful criticism of one of Archbishop Tillotson's sermons, in which he assailed with merciless logic and much asperity the Mosaic cosmogony. In these two theological works he took up the religious position which he occupied for the remainder of his life. That is to say, he maintained the cause of deism against materialistic philosophy on the one side and against Christian divinity on the other. If these works had been published when they were written—about 1720—they would have created a sensation. They would have established Bolingbroke's reputation as a pioneer of free thought, or more exactly anti-Christian thought; for he was much more passionate and much more effective in his attacks upon the Anglican divines and the Old Testament patriarchs than he was in his defence of theism against atheism. But in establishing his reputation as a free thinker they would have seriously impeded his chances of restoration to the leadership of the Tory party in England. And that leadership he was at this time eager to recover. Hence his theological dissertations of 1720 remained unpublished—although known in manuscript to the elect—until they were printed posthumously by David Mallet in 1754, by which time they were obsolete. Their substance had been made known to the world by Voltaire and others who had sat at Bolingbroke's feet in his French house at La Source, near Orleans. A corrective to such serious argument as they contained had been provided by Butler's *Analogy* and kindred works.

Bolingbroke, however, as we have just noted, while he employed his excessive leisure at La Source in privately pleading with atheists and in pounding divines, was primarily concerned in his working hours with laborious endeavours, on the one hand, to secure from the Hanoverian Government of England a reversal of his attainder, and, on the other hand, to rehabilitate his reputation with the English Tories, who now regarded the noble and disinterested Sir William Wyndham as their chief. In order to achieve the reversal of his attainder, he condescended to abject petitions to George I; he made futile attempts to conciliate his inveterate enemy Sir Robert Walpole; he tried to win the favour of the dominant Duchess of Kendal; he finally secured the effective advocacy of the influential lords Stanhope, Sunderland, and Stair, and by their aid gained in 1723 a partial pardon under the Great Seal. To rehabilitate his reputation with the deserted, disillusioned, and desperate Tories was a less easy task. In fact, we may say that he never fully achieved it. The Tories as a party, in spite of Wyndham's whole-hearted endeavours to persuade them, were never able either to forgive or again to trust the man who, by identifying the reigning house of Hanover with Whiggism and the impossible house of the exiled Stuarts with Toryism, had condemned his misguided followers to half a century of impotence and contumely. Bolingbroke's famous *Letter to Sir William Wynd-*

ham (1717) is his *apologia pro vita sua.* It is, on the whole, the ablest, the best written, the most powerful of all his works. It contains a masterly survey from his own point of view of the events of the critical six years 1710 to 1716. It attempts to justify and defend every one of his important measures and significant acts during that fateful period, including his persecution of the Dissenters, his desertion of the Allies at Utrecht, his behaviour at the death of Anne, his flight, his adherence to the Pretender, his support of the '15 rebellion, his procedure subsequent to his dismissal from the Pretender's service. He tries to show that from first to last he was actuated by one motive, and one alone, viz., zeal for the Tory cause. On the one hand he protests that he was never moved by personal ambition, personal fear, or personal resentment. On the other hand he confesses that the interests of his country were entirely subordinated to the interests of his party. His vivid description of the Pretender's Court and his lurid story of the Jacobite proceedings in 1715–16 are magnificent as literature. In the world of affairs they sufficed to sweep Jacobitism out of the sphere of practical politics. The concluding sections of this inimitable pamphlet are devoted to a passionate appeal to the Tories to free themselves from all thought of recalling the exiled Stuarts. The Pretender little dreamed when in sudden fury he insolently dismissed Bolingbroke from his service in 1716 that he was doing a deed which would render the restoration of himself and his house for ever impossible. Yet so it was. The one great and successful task accomplished by Bolingbroke during the course of his long and generally unsuccessful life was to purge Toryism of Jacobitism with its concomitant superstitions of divine right and passive obedience. He re-established Toryism on the surer foundation of the Revolutionary Settlement of 1688–89.

XII

In 1723, as we have seen, Bolingbroke received a pardon under the Great Seal, and in 1725 he definitely came back to

England to reside, soon taking up his abode on a fine estate which he bought at Dawley, near Uxbridge. He brought with him his second wife, the French Marquise de Villette, whom he had formally married in 1722, four years after the death of his unhappy first wife, whom he had treated with unpardonable faithlessness and neglect. The years 1723–25 had been primarily occupied in efforts to obtain the complete reversal of the attainder of 1715, and complete readmission into English public life—on the one side humiliating, rather discreditable, and wholly unsuccessful efforts to win the favour of Walpole and the Whigs; on the other side extremely expensive, most disreputable, but partially successful efforts to win the favour of the King, by means of his German mistress, the recently exalted Duchess of Kendal. The Duchess detested Walpole, and naturally fostered any influence opposed to his; the King was dissatisfied with Walpole's foreign policy (which paid no regard to the interests of Hanover), and was wishful to draw upon Bolingbroke's unique knowledge of Continental politics. Walpole became seriously alarmed for his ascendancy. In 1725 he was strong enough to prevent the Act of Parliament which restored Bolingbroke's private rights as a citizen from being extended to include his public rights. In 1727, however, it appeared probable that the King and the Duchess would insist on complete rehabilitation, and that Bolingbroke would at last triumph over his arch-antagonist. But just as in 1714 Bolingbroke's Tory hopes were shattered by the death of Anne, and just as in 1715 his Jacobite designs were ruined by the death of Louis XIV, so in 1727 the sudden demise of George I at Osnabrück destroyed his dreams of restoration, and left him for ever excluded from Parliament and office. It is true that he tried to win the favour of George II by means of his mistress, Mrs Howard (later Countess of Suffolk); but in doing so he 'put his money on the wrong horse.' His intrigues with Mrs Howard merely won for him the mortal enmity of Queen Caroline, the real controller of the King's policy, who threw the whole weight of her influence on to the side of Walpole. It is also true that when Frederick, Prince of Wales, quarrelled violently and publicly with his parents and was excluded from the Court, Bolingbroke cultivated his company, and hoped that when he should become King he might come back in his train as 'patriotic' minister. But Frederick—well described by Mr J. M. Robertson as "the one thorough fool and rascal in the Hanoverian line"—died before his father, and Bolingbroke's last illusive vision of his rehabilitation and his earldom was dispelled. Bolingbroke's 'patriotic' ideas of government were left to be realised by George III with, not Bolingbroke, but Bute as his minister. This, however, was all in the far future.

In 1725 Bolingbroke, seeing that Walpole and the Whig magnates were his implacable enemies, determined to do what in him lay to secure their overthrow. For ten years he toiled enormously at this engrossing task—and toiled in vain. Nevertheless he made much stir in the world, and he left a permanent impress upon British politics. He organised the first persistent and avowed 'opposition' to the King's Government; he inspired it with the conviction that the one and only function of an opposition is to oppose; he conducted, in the Press and through his allies in Parliament, a virulent and sustained attack both upon the men who constituted the Ministry and upon their measures; he did much to rouse the power of that latent public opinion in England which under Chatham and Pitt was destined to assert its claim to sovereignty in the State. He found three groups of men hostile to Walpole, viz., the Jacobites led by Shippen, the Hanoverian Tories led by his friend Wyndham, and a number of Dissentient Whigs led by the two Pulteneys and Carteret. He tried to weld these disparate factions into a coherent whole, and soon found that the only thing on which they were all agreed was desire for the degradation of Walpole. Hence he started an organ for his crazy coalition, the single and simple theme of which was the iniquities of the Prime Minister and his fellow-conspirators. It first appeared as *The Country Gentleman* in July 1726; in December of that year it changed its name to *The Craftsman*, and under that name continued to appear—at first twice a week, later

131

once a week—until April 1736. Much of the writing was done by Bolingbroke himself; no one loathed Walpole so much as he, and no one had so rich a vocabulary of virulent abuse. He poured forth without restraint the vials of his detestation upon his hated foe. He found able coadjutors, however, in Swift and Pope, Arbuthnot and Gay, the two Pulteneys, Chesterfield and Lyttelton, Amherst and Akenside. Never had a periodical excited so much interest in the political world; it was read and discussed in every club and *salon*; the secret of the authorship of its anonymous tirades was eagerly debated. Bolingbroke's superior style and fiercer malignity made the identification of his articles easy. Even the pachydermatous Prime Minister writhed under some of his lashes. Once—unless, as some critics think, the composition has been fathered upon him—he was goaded to reply. The following extracts will give some conception of the tone of the political controversy of this Golden Age of peace and prosperity.

Though you have not signed your name, I know you. Because a man who is without all principle of honesty; who in no one thing can be relied upon; a betrayer of his friend [Oxford]; a traitor to his prince; an enemy to his country; a perjured, ungrateful unfaithful rascal, must be you. . . . You are an infamous fellow who makes a reputation of doing mischief. . . . You are of so profligate a character that in your prosperity nobody envied you, and in your disgrace nobody pities you. . . . You are a fellow who has no conscience at all. . . . You have no abilities. You are an emancipated slave, a proscribed criminal, and an insolvent debtor. . . . You have been a traitor and should be used like one. . . . I do not value what you or your company say of me. . . . You rail at me because you envy me, and I despise all that a man in the impotence of disgrace can do against me, who could never terrify me in the zenith of his power. . . . I would rather have you my enemy than my friend. Change your names, and be as scurrilous as you please. I shall find you out. I am Aristæus; you are Proteus. You may change to a flame, a lion, a bull, or a bear, I shall know you, baffle you, conquer you, and contemn you.[1]

[1] *The Occasional Writer*, Article No. III.

This style of controversy lacks delicacy, and it tends speedily to exhaust its freshness. Bolingbroke's retorts were much more skilful, sustained, and artistic productions. They were rapier-thrusts, not bludgeon-blows. Many of them dealt with topics of current concern, the interest of which has wholly vanished away—such, for example, as the fortification of Dunkirk, the restoration of Gibraltar to Spain, the levying of an excise, the terms of the Treaty of Hanover, the hiring of Hessian troops. Other subjects of discussion were of more enduring importance—such, for example, as the repeal of the Septennial Act, or the exclusion of placemen from Parliament. But first and foremost were the personal attacks upon Walpole, for his greed of power, his degradation of the monarchy, his supersession of the 'patriotic' Privy Council by the party Cabinet of submissive Whigs, his dictatorship over Parliament, his corruption of the constituencies, his tyranny over local administrators, his bribery, his jobbery, his sordid mercantilism, his peculation and dishonesty.

The most sustained, most brilliant, and most damaging of Bolingbroke's attacks upon his elephantine enemy were those which he delivered in the two series of articles entitled respectively *Remarks on the History of England* (twenty-four letters, published in *The Crafstman*, 1730–31) and *A Dissertation upon Parties* (nineteen letters prefaced by a mockdedication to Walpole, published in *The Craftsman*, 1733–34). The *Remarks on the History of England* are extremely clever and infinitely diverting, but of course entirely valueless as contributions to knowledge. The only thing that Bolingbroke is out to do is to find plausible parallels in English history to the political circumstances of his own time. He wants to strike Walpole—and to give an occasional poke at George II and Queen Caroline—without incurring the risk of prosecution for libel or sedition. He clearly hints at George in his account of every weak and woman-ridden king; he draws readily recognisable portraits of Queen Caroline in Isabella, wife of Edward II, Margaret of Anjou, wife of Henry VI, and Elizabeth Woodville, wife of Edward IV. But he

roused throughout the country a wild fury of opposition based on ignorance and prejudice. Bolingbroke and his colleagues of *The Craftsman*, with a total disregard of either political principle or national interest, fomented the outcry against the harassed minister, and hoped, in spite of the Court, to effect his ruin. At the same time they stirred up a considerable agitation against the Septennial Act, demanding, in the interests of popular control, a return to triennial elections. All their assaults, however, were vain. Walpole withdrew his Excise Bill, vindicated the Septennial Act, stuck to his post, and secured a new lease of office by his success in the General Election of 1734.

Bolingbroke was bitterly disappointed at the failure of all his plans and the frustration of all his labours. Walpole, who seems to have got on the track of some doubtful correspondence of Bolingbroke with foreigners, threatened prosecution; Pulteney hinted that the non-success of the anti-Walpole coalition was due to the unpopularity of Bolingbroke himself; Bolingbroke's health was breaking; his finances were in a tangle; he thought it best to depart. Hence in 1735 he vacated Dawley, said farewell to his fellow-craftsmen, and returned to France.

XIII

During the years 1735 to 1744 Bolingbroke was mainly abroad. He settled first at Chanteloup in Touraine, but soon moved to Argeville near Fontainebleau, where he had the privilege of hunting in the royal forest. During these nine years he visited England three times. The first visit was a long one, viz., June 1738 to May 1739. The death of Queen Caroline and the serious illness of George II caused him to hope that the day of Whig and Walpole supremacy was ending, and that the day of Frederick and 'patriotism' was dawning. It was during this visit that he wrote his famous *Patriot King*, a work which was intended to exalt its author in the eyes of Frederick; to make Walpole's Government odious in the eyes of the nation; and to furnish the 'patriots' with a programme. As a party pamphlet it is of supreme excellence; as a contribution to political thought or constitutional practice worse than worthless. George II recovered; Frederick lapsed into imbecility and vice; Bolingbroke returned to France and philosophy. His second visit, in 1742, was occasioned by the death of his father, and his succession to the ancestral manor of Battersea. The fall of Walpole which occurred the same year caused him to linger in England in the hope that 'patriotism' might get the better of party. But the Dissentient Whigs—Pulteney, Carteret, and company—who pulled down Walpole soon showed that all they desired was to succeed to his office and his power, and that they had not the slightest wish to obliterate party government, increase the royal prerogative, or purify Parliament. Bolingbroke's last hope of his own generation was dispelled. He could only look to posterity for the realisation of his ideals. His third visit, occasioned by the care of his estates, was paid in 1743. On this visit it became so clear that business matters would require his frequent presence in England that, after much hesitation, he decided finally to return. Accordingly, in June 1744 he took up his abode in his first and last home, the old manor-house of Battersea, on the south bank of the Thames.

His main activity during the nine years 1735 to 1744 was literary. His health was very bad: gout, rheumatism, low fever, haunted and harassed him, and he was able to keep going only by frequent pilgrimages to the waters of Aix, and by regular exercise in the forest of Fontainebleau and elsewhere. He was troubled, too, by the steady decline in the strength of his wife, the Marquise de Villette, to whom he had become devotedly attached. Nevertheless, in spite of anguish and anxiety, his intellect remained vigorous, and he produced some of his most important writings. He planned, and began to collect materials for, two large and impressive works, viz., a *History of Europe from 1659 to 1713*, which was to vindicate his official career, and a *Treatise on Metaphysics*, which was to define the limits of knowledge and extinguish the theologians. He was, however, incapable of the steady

137

application required for the production of large and systematic works. Neither of these *magna opera* was ever achieved. He could labour only by jerks and in spasms. He could compose nothing which could not be expressed in the form of a series of articles, a collection of letters, or a congeries of notes. He was essentially a journalist and a jotter.

He began his second sojourn in France as he had begun his first, twenty years earlier, by seeking to drown his chagrin in a flood of platitudes let loose from the inexhaustible reservoir of Seneca's inanity. In the form of a letter to Lord Bathurst he treated of *The True Use of Retirement and Study*. Churton Collins justly remarks of this production that in it "all that is new is false, and all that is true is trite." But Mr Macknight points out that, worthless as it is, it does serve to indicate the everlasting conflict which went on in Bolingbroke between his intellect and his emotions. By passion and by prejudice he was a thorough reactionary: in mind and soul he was a pronounced revolutionary. In this letter he insists that "we ought always to be unbelieving," and that "in religion, government, and philosophy we ought to distrust everything that is established."[1] Strange doctrine, this, for a Tory!

More important and interesting was the series of eight letters addressed to Lord Cornbury on *The Study and Use of History* (1735–36). The first seven merely lead up to the eighth, which is a vindication of Bolingbroke's conduct of the peace negotiations of 1713: he could never get far away from politics or from himself. The earlier letters, however, incidentally contain a number of arresting observations. First, as to the true end and object of the study of history: it is ethical, viz., the training of citizens in private and public virtue. Secondly, as to the scope of historical study: ancient history both sacred and profane is valueless as a civic educator; modern history, since the Renaissance and the Reformation, is alone useful. Finally, as to the content of this modern history: three periods can be distinguished— viz., 1500–1600, 1600–59, and from 1659 onward, of which

[1] T. Macknight, *Life of Bolingbroke*, p. 630.

there follows a summary account, culminating in a detailed study of the Utrecht negotiations.

This series of letters on history was followed by another long epistle, also addressed to Lord Cornbury, on *The Spirit of Patriotism* (1736). This brilliant disquisition is significant as marking a change in Bolingbroke's political programme. He was, throughout his career, always against the Whigs, even when he was attempting to destroy them by the appropriation and application of their own principles. He attacked them first (1701–15) as a Tory; secondly (1715–16) as a Jacobite; thirdly (1716–35) as a Coalitionist; finally (1735–51) as a 'Patriot,' the enemy of all parties, the prophet calling for, and predicting, the advent of a monarch who should sweep away the corrupt Whig oligarchy, appoint his own ministers, and rule an emancipated people by his own beneficent will. *The Spirit of Patriotism* is instinct with indignation at the defection of the malcontent Whigs in the crisis of 1734, and quick with the consciousness of the impotence of coalitions.

The Idea of a Patriot King (1738) was intended to be a study supplementary to that of *The Spirit of Patriotism*. The two were issued together in 1749 by Bolingbroke himself, when it seemed to him that, with the advent of Frederick, the day of the realisation of his dream was at hand. *The Spirit of Patriotism*, he tells us, was written to set forth "the duties which men owe to their country"; the *Patriot King* to delineate "the duties of a king to his country, of those kings particularly who are appointed by the people; for," he adds, "I know of none who are anointed by God to rule in limited monarchies." The duties of a "Patriot King," it appears, are, first, to admit that the monarch derives his authority from his people, and to abandon all nonsensical theories of divine right; secondly, to recognise that this authority is not absolute, but limited—limited by natural law, by the rights of his subjects, and by the customs of his realm; thirdly, to realise that his supreme task as monarch is to establish and maintain the "free Constitution" of his kingdom—that is to say, a Constitution marked by the two outstanding features of personal liberty and national unity; hence, fourthly, to suppress parties and factions, to reconcile antagonistic classes, and to make patriotism the dominant virtue throughout the land; fifthly, to expel from his councils corrupt partisans (such as Walpole) and call to his side pure patriots (such as Bolingbroke); sixthly, to reclaim the royal prerogatives, wrongly appropriated by the Whigs, and weakly yielded by "silly kings" (such as George II); and, finally, to rule Britannia with the help of a subjugated Parliament and a grateful people, on sound patriotic lines, by which is implied the fostering of sea-power, the reduction of the standing army, the avoidance of foreign entanglements, and the general reversal of the policy of the Whigs. The fundamental conception of the *Patriot King* may be said to be "Back to Elizabeth." The realisation of Bolingbroke's ideal would have meant the undoing of the Revolution Settlement, the repeal of the verdict of the Civil War, and the return to the Tudor autocracy. It might be attractive to antiquarians and sentimentalists, but in the middle of the eighteenth century it was not practical politics. To the *Patriot King* he added an appendix on "The State of Parties at the Accession of King George the First," in which he defended his own conduct during the closing years of Anne's reign; made another ferocious attack on his old *bête noire* Harley; and blamed the fury of the Whigs in 1714–15 for driving the Tories, including himself, into Jacobitism.

XIV

The closing years of Bolingbroke's life, 1744–51, spent in the old manor-house at Battersea, were marked by little activity. The health both of himself and his wife rapidly declined. The friends of his earlier days passed away, and he made few new ones. He found himself isolated and forlorn. He employed himself in preparing his writings for posthumous publication, devoting much time to the revision of some of them, especially his *Letter to Sir William Wyndham*. He secured the services of a certain David Mallet who commended himself to Bolingbroke as a deist, as an under-secretary to the Prince of Wales, as the prospective biographer of Marlborough, and as an enemy of Bishop Warburton—which eminent ecclesiastic was the successor of Harley and of Walpole as Bolingbroke's enemy-in-chief. Only two new works—neither of them of any importance— distinguished these closing years. One was a *Familiar Epistle* to Warburton, full of violence and abuse, occasioned by a controversy concerning some shady proceedings of Alexander Pope, revealed after his death in 1744. The other was entitled *Some Reflections on the Present State of the Nation*, written after the Peace of Aix-la-Chapelle, and left un-finished in 1749. It is an attack upon the Whig foreign policy. It takes a very gloomy view of the situation of Britain; expresses profound alarm at the magnitude of the National Debt, which has reached the enormous sum of £80,000,000; deplores the dominance of the moneyed over the landed interest in the country; and predicts catastrophe unless there is a reversion to peace, retrenchment, and reform. Bolingbroke was without an inkling of the fact that Britain was actually at the moment entering upon the most remarkable period of prosperity—colonial expansion, com-mercial advance, industrial supremacy, agricultural revival, military and naval victory—ever known in the whole course of her long annals.

It is not amazing, however, that to one situated as Boling-broke was the whole world should seem to be going to the bad. He had no prospect of health or happiness in this life, and he had no belief in any life beyond the grave. His domestic felicity perished with his beloved wife in March 1750; his last political hope vanished with the death of Frederick, Prince of Wales, in March 1751; he himself was seized by virulent cancer in the summer of the same year, and he died after six months of agony on December 12, 1751.

XV

We have noted cursorily most of Bolingbroke's leading social and political ideas. It remains now merely to summarise and systematise them.

To social and political theory Bolingbroke contributed nothing. He had not the profound philosophic mind of his great disciple Burke, who was never content until he had based the practical expedient of the moment upon the solid foundation of eternal principle. Bolingbroke invented his principles to suit the exigencies of the passing day. Hence they lack consistency, homogeneity, authority. As a Tory he should have had an organic conception of the State, and on one occasion at least he seems to have gained an inkling of it. In his short paper on *The Constitution of Great Britain* he says:

> Our constitution may, in some sense, be said to be a fleeting thing, which at different times hath differed from itself, as men differ from themselves in age and youth, or in sickness and health; but still it is the same, and it is our duty to preserve it, as far as we are able, in its full strength and vigour.

Burke might well have taken this as the text of his *Reflections*. As a rule, however, Bolingbroke accepted the contractual view of the State set forth by Locke and exemplified by the Revolution of 1688–89. Thus in his *Dissertation upon Parties* (Letter XIII) he emphasises the artificial origin of political institutions, and in particular maintains that "our Constitution is in the strictest sense a bargain, a conditional contract between the prince and the people, as it always hath been, and still is, between the representative and collective bodies of the nation." Again, he accepts Hobbes's doctrine of sovereignty in one passage of his *Patriot King*: "There must be an absolute, unlimited, and uncontrollable power lodged somewhere in every government"; but usually he is concerned to dissipate sovereignty among a group of coordinate powers so that individual liberty may remain unimpaired.

It is not then in the region of pure theory, but in the region of applied politics, that we must look for Bolingbroke's operative ideas. In his opposition to the Whigs he passed through four phases: he was successively Tory, Jacobite, Coalitionist, and 'Patriot.' Each phase, except perhaps the second, had its own conceptions and principles of action.

Of his Tory phase (1701-15) we have but scanty literary remains. It is remarkable that, although he was admitted to have been the most superb Parliamentary orator of his day, no report of a single one of his speeches has come down to posterity. William Pitt, once commenting upon this extraordinary circumstance, proclaimed that he would rather recover one of Bolingbroke's famous orations than all the lost works of Livy or of Tacitus. We have, however, the record of his deeds, and they are eloquent of the extremest partisanship. He provided Walpole with the model upon which he framed that purely party administration which Bolingbroke attacked with such ferocious vehemence during the third and fourth phases of his career. He sought to reassert the ascendancy of the landed interest over the moneyed interest; of the country over the city; of the Church of England over Dissent; of the navy over the army; of the policy of splendid isolation over that of interference in Continental politics; of the old England of the Tudors over the new England of Oliver Cromwell and William of Orange. With Machiavellian violence and unscrupulousness he did everything in his power to destroy the Whigs and to establish Toryism in perpetual possession of office.

His Jacobite phase (1715-16) was a mere aberration which—as his letter to Wyndham and all his later writings abundantly show—he never ceased to regret. His adherence to the Pretender was a false move due to the impulse of ungovernable passion—disgust at his failure and folly in 1714, resentment at his treatment by George I and the Whigs, fury at the triumph of Walpole and Townshend, Stanhope and Sunderland. The central doctrine of Jacobitism was the divine hereditary right of kings, with its corollary, the doctrine of the duty of passive obedience on the part of subjects. This doctrine Bolingbroke never so much as pretended to believe. Hence he was always an alien at the Court of the exiled Stuarts. As little did he sympathise with the mediæval theories of the relation between Church and State which were maintained by the ultramontane priests who dominated the Pretender's *entourage*. He was, in fact, wholly out of harmony with both the politics and the religion—to say nothing of the manners and the intellectual interests—of his motley associates during the tragic year 1715–16. It was a profound relief to him when the Pretender saved him from the odium of resignation by dismissing him.

The third phase of his career (1716–35) was that in which he made his appearance as a paper-politician. He had now two sets of virulent enemies to contend against—viz., Whigs and Jacobites—and he had no means of fighting them except his pen. With his pen, then, he waged a wordy battle on two fronts. As against the Jacobites he denounced the dogma of the divine right of kings, arguing that monarchs are mere magistrates deriving their authority from their subjects and having only a conditional claim to their allegiance and obedience; against them, too, he proclaimed (at the end of his letter to Wyndham) the impossibility of allowing a Catholic king to ascend the English throne. On the other hand, as against the Whigs, he maintained that the party distinctions of the days of Charles II and James II had become obsolete in 1688; that the Glorious Revolution had been effected by a coalition of Whigs and Tories; that the great object of the Revolution had been the vindication of English liberty; and that since 1714 the main peril to English liberty had come not from the royal prerogative, but from ministerial corruption. He therefore appealed for the formation of a new "Country" party, inspired by Elizabethan traditions, whose object should be to reunite the nation, emancipate the monarch, purify Parliament, dispossess place-men, purge the constituencies, and free the electorate from the spell of faction and the lure of lucre. In accordance with his appeal, he tried, as we have seen, to weld together Tories, Jacobites, and Dissentient Whigs into a coalition capable of overthrowing Walpole. By 1735 his failure was patent.

From 1735 to his death in 1751 'patriotism' was his watchword. Under cover of that term (of which Dr Johnson in his Dictionary spoke with great disrespect) he developed a theory of the English Constitution which had a profound influence upon George III and the King's friends in the late eighteenth century, and upon Benjamin Disraeli and the Young England group in the mid-nineteenth century. On the Continent it inspired the political writings of Montesquieu and Voltaire, and through them it helped to fix the principles of the American Constitution in 1789. The supreme good of man, said Bolingbroke, is personal liberty. Liberty can be retained and secured only under a Constitution in which the legislative, executive, and judiciary powers are separated from one another, and in which an accurate balance between them is established. In England, according to the spirit of its ancient polity, the supreme executive power should reside in the King in council, the supreme legislative power should be the function of the King in Parliament, and the supreme judicial power should be exercised by the King in his royal Court. The centre and bond of the Constitution is, or should be, the King. The King, too, is the head of the Church, and the Church (even though what it teaches is false) is the indispensable support of the State, and as such should be respected and maintained. In England since 1714 the balance of the Constitution has been destroyed, and consequently liberty endangered, by the decline of the royal authority. In the interest then of liberty it is necessary to revive the royal prerogative. Let the "Patriot King" once more choose his own ministers irrespective of party; let him determine the policy of the Government; let him nominate bishops; let him issue royal warrants; let him summon and dissolve Parliament at his will; let him freely dispose of the money voted for the conduct of the administration. The strength of Bolingbroke's 'patriotism' is its plea for personal freedom; for loyalty to the Crown; for reverence for the Church; for national unity; for the subordination of the interests of party, class, and *clique* to the interest of the people as a whole. Hence, haughty and exclusive as Bolingbroke was, he is rightly regarded as the founder of the modern Tory democracy.

BOOK LIST

A. PRIMARY SOURCES

BOLINGBROKE: *Works*, edited by David Mallet. 5 vols. 1754. In particular: *Letter to Sir William Wyndham* (1717); *Remarks on the History of England* (1730–31); *Dissertation upon Parties* (1733–34); *Study and Use of History* (1735–36); *The Spirit of Patriotism* (1738); *The Idea of a Patriot King* (1739).

B. SECONDARY SOURCES

BUTLER, G. G.: *The Tory Tradition.* 1914.
COLLINS, J. CHURTON: *Bolingbroke and Voltaire.* 1886.
COOKE, G. W.: *Memoirs of Lord Bolingbroke.* 2 vols. 1835.
HARROP, R.: *Bolingbroke: a Political Study.* 1884.
HASSALL, A.: *Life of Viscount Bolingbroke.* 1889; revised edition 1915.
MACKNIGHT, T.: *Life of Henry St John, Viscount Bolingbroke.* 1863.
ROBERTSON, J. M.: *Bolingbroke and Walpole.* 1919.
SICHEL, W.: *Bolingbroke and his Times.* 2 vols. 1901–2.
STEPHEN, L.: *History of English Thought*, vol. ii. 1881.

VI

ROUSSEAU AND THE SECULAR PLAN OF SALVATION[1]

THE most important event in modern history prior to the Great War of 1914-18 was without question the French Revolution of 1789. It marked the triumphant advent of that democracy which during the nineteenth century established its ascendancy throughout the Western world. Hence the prime interest of that varied and fascinating "Age of Reason" which preceded the Revolution consists in tracing the influences that were bringing the old *régime* to an end and instituting the new. The examination of these influences is all the more important because they were subtle influences whose operation was hidden from the eyes of almost all contemporary observers; even Mme de Pompadour's famous "Après nous le déluge" was merely the utterance of the perennial bankrupt in the presence of the eternal moneylender.[2] The eighteenth-century world went on smoothly with superficial gaiety, while beneath the surface seethed silently the gathering discontents.

The discontents in France, where they first came to a head, were of many and various kinds. There was political discontent, particularly on the part of the cultivated and prosperous middle class—the lawyers, the physicians, the financiers—on whose contributions the Government was entirely dependent for existence, but to whose interests and

[1] From *The Social and Political Ideas of Some Great French Thinkers of the Age of Reason* (Harrap, 1930). The other studies in this volume are: "Introductory: The Age of Reason," by Harold J. Laski; "Bossuet," by Norman Sykes; "Fénelon," by R. A. Jones; "The Abbé de Saint-Pierre," by Paul Vaucher; "Montesquieu," by A. J. Grant; "Voltaire," by J. B. Black; "Helvétius and Holbach," by William H. Wickwar; "Morelly and Mably," by C. H. Driver.

[2] *Cf.* the Greek Ἐμοῦ θανόντος γαῖα μιχθήτω πυρί, "When I am dead let the earth be consumed by fire."

opinions it paid not the slightest regard. There was social and economic discontent, shared by the whole of the third estate, middle class and lower class alike, as it contemplated, on the one hand, the magnitude of the burdens of State imposed upon itself, and, on the other hand, the iniquity of the exemptions and privileges conceded to the favoured estates of the nobles and the clergy. But, above all, there was intellectual discontent, the revolt of the emancipated mind of man against both the tyranny of an absolute monarchy claiming to rule by divine right and the inquisitorial oppression of a decadent and obscurantist Church which strove to maintain its ascendancy by persecution. Many other minor sources of discontent—racial, provincial, communal, personal—contributed to cause the great upheaval.

Into the vehemently controversial problem which of these various causes was the prime and controlling cause of the Revolution it is fortunately not necessary for us here to enter. It is sufficient for our present purpose, first, to note that the causes were numerous, separate, and distinct—not reducible to any one single category, whether economic or any other; and, secondly, to stress the importance of the intellectual causes and to point out how, among these, the influence of the writings of Rousseau stood pre-eminent.

Lord Acton in his epoch-making lectures on the French Revolution—which it was the privilege of the present writer to attend—laid dominant emphasis on the movements of ideas which marked this seminal pre-Revolutionary period, the Age of Reason. His opening discourse was wholly devoted to the thinkers whom he termed the "heralds of the Revolution." Among them he included a number of persons whose memory has now become dim, and the echoes of whose words have died away—e.g., Domat, Jurieu, and Maultrat. But besides and above these he placed such men of enduring eminence as Fénelon, Diderot, and Turgot; and, high over all, Montesquieu, Voltaire, and Rousseau. Montesquieu's *Esprit des lois*, with its fascinating examination of the connexion between climate and constitution, made havoc of the doctrine of the divine right of kings and the dogma of the universal validity of monarchy, teaching with unmistakable clarity the truth of the relativity of political institutions. Voltaire, with his devastating *Candide* and other works, poured destructive ridicule upon the pretensions of the corrupt and ignorant priesthood. But, more potent than either of the two, Rousseau, by means of his *Discours* and his *Contrat social*, undermined the whole social system of the old *régime*, and prepared the way for the new democratic order by promulgating his revelation of the primitive liberty, equality, and fraternity of mankind.

Montesquieu made a convincing appeal to constitutional lawyers, fostering in them that admiration for the separated powers and balanced functions of the English system of government, which ultimately engendered the French constitution of 1790. Voltaire, by his brilliant if scurrilous wit, won the ear of the literary world, and helped to disseminate in polite society that scorn of Catholic dogma which led in the opening months of the Revolution not only to the disestablishment and disendowment of the Church, but also to the formal repudiation of Christianity. The influence of both Montesquieu and Voltaire, however, was limited in scope and ephemeral in duration; the French constitution of 1790 lasted for but little more than a year; the effort to extirpate the Church and eliminate the Christian religion led to a revival of evangelical faith that culminated in a new *concordat* with Rome, the presence of the Pope at the coronation of Napoleon, and a general widespread Romantic reaction in the early nineteenth century. And the curious thing is that one of the main causes why the Revolution went, politically, far beyond the point to which Montesquieu's ideas carried it, and why it returned, in the region of religion, to a point far short of that to which Voltaire's ribaldry for a time succeeded in luring it, was the influence of Rousseau. For Rousseau's passionate assertion of the sovereignty of the people and the supreme authority of its general will indicated an advance in the direction of democracy incomparably more rapid and complete than any movement which up to that time had taken place in England;

while his sublime proclamation of the worship of *l'Être Suprême*, with its appendant dogma of personal immortality, marked an extreme emotional revulsion from the arid deism of Voltaire and the blatant atheism of Holbach.

The influence of Rousseau, as the event proved, was far more potent, far wider in its scope, and far more persistent than that of either Montesquieu or Voltaire. Who at the present day, apart from the professed student of political ideas, reads the 595 chapters of the *Esprit des lois*? Who, except specialists in literature, wades through the seventy volumes which Voltaire bequeathed to posterity, or peruses for either profit or pleasure anything that he wrote beyond a few of his inimitable tales? Both Montesquieu and Voltaire belonged, and belonged exclusively, to the eighteenth century. They influenced their own age profoundly, and in doing so, no doubt, indirectly influenced all subsequent ages; but directly and immediately they made no appeal to generations that had ceased to be afflicted by a despotic monarchy and a persecuting Church. Rousseau, on the other hand, not only reached and moved an immeasurably larger multitude in his own day, he continued to exercise a powerful sway long after he himself and all his contemporaries had passed away. Nay, even at the present moment his *Discours*, his *Contrat social*, his *Nouvelle Héloïse*, and his *Émile* are among the active forces that move the minds of living men and determine the course of current politics.

If we ask what was the secret of his power it may be replied, first, that he made his appeal not, as did Montesquieu and Voltaire, to the small select circles of the lawyers or the literary men, but to the masses of the common folk; that he brought political theory and social speculation down from the study into the street, and propounded doctrines that profoundly moved the mind and will of the hitherto unregarded proletarians; that he voiced, as never before, the sentiments and emotions of the long-inarticulate multitudes of the peasants, the artisans, and the lower middle class. Secondly, it may be remarked that, though he lacked the learning of Montesquieu and the logic of Voltaire, he was possessed of a passion such as neither of them ever knew; he wrote in a white heat of emotion, and he displayed a magnetic capacity to rouse his readers to the same pitch of fervour as himself; he had a deep well of pity for the poor and a volcanic fury of hatred for the rich, and he succeeded by effortless instinct in conveying his sentiments to others. For—and this is the third secret of his power—he was gifted with a superb literary style. It was a natural endowment. As a youth he had no ambition to write; he received no training in the art and craft of letters; until he was nearly forty he published nothing, and even then he was turned to composition by the merest accident. He wrote because he had something to say, and his style was determined by his passionate desire to deliver his message in language that should be intelligible to all. Hence his words were perfectly adjusted to his subject; he said plain things plainly, and fine things finely; his utterances were the lucid expressions of his many-sided personality; with him more than with most writers the style was the man.

So intimately, indeed, were Rousseau's writings associated with his life that it is impossible to comprehend them without a detailed knowledge of his curious and remarkable career. And, fortunately, a knowledge of his career is extremely easy to acquire. It has, in fact, been said that we have more information about Rousseau than about any other human being whatsoever; and if we include under 'information' what is false as well as what is true the statement is probably correct. For, to begin with, he himself has left us in his *Confessions* so full and confidential a record of his early escapades that only in extensively expurgated editions is it considered proper to allow the book to be promiscuously circulated. His later vagaries, characterised by lunacy rather than lubricity, are recorded with equal candour in his *Dialogues* and his *Reveries*. Besides his own amazing revelations, moreover, we have countless supplementary sources of information—of varying degrees of trustworthiness—in the diaries and correspondence of his few friends, such as Le Bègue du Presle, and of his many enemies, among whom Grimm, Diderot, and Mme d'Epinay stand pre-eminent.

From numerous and varied sources we get the impression of a man of high originality and undoubted genius; an intense individualist, impatient of any sort of restraint; a man inordinately vain, yet shy, self-conscious, timid, awkward in society, happy only when alone; a man devoid of will-power, deficient in moral fibre, a slave to sensual passion, the plaything of circumstance; yet a man sensitive to noble impulses, full of kindly sympathies, pitiful towards weakness and suffering, full of fury against tyranny and injustice, capable of copious weeping on any convenient occasion. He loved the human race, although he quarrelled with every specimen of it with which he was brought into any but the most transient contact.

II

The sixty-six years of Rousseau's life can be divided for the purposes of our brief survey into five periods which we will distinguish as follows: first, the undisciplined boy, 1712–28; second, the super-tramp, 1728–42; third, the would-be man of the world, 1742–49; fourth, the inspired maniac, 1749–62; fifth and last, the hunted fugitive, 1762–78.

1. *The Undisciplined Boy* (1712–28). Jean-Jacques Rousseau, as is well known, was born in Geneva, the great autonomous city-state of Switzerland, the headquarters of militant Calvinism. His birth and early training in that city are cardinal facts of his career; for his political ideals always remained municipal, and his religion, even when it took the mould of Catholicism or of deism, never lost its Calvinistic character. But though he was Genevan to the bone his ancestry carried him back to a French stock on the one side and a Savoyard stock on the other; and he seemed to combine in his own person the Genevan *solennité* with the *légèreté* of his Gallic great-grandfather and the *vivacité* of his Savoyard great-grandmother. His mother died in giving him birth, and the task of educating and bringing him up thus remained in the sole hands of his father, Isaac Rousseau, a watchmaker

by profession, but a dancing-master by preference whenever the vigilance of the Calvinistic elders was relaxed. He could hardly have had a worse instructor; for, we are told, Isaac Rousseau "was absolutely without any feeling of responsibility; he lacked character; he allowed himself to be driven as circumstances dictated." Certainly he neither gave, nor was capable of giving, any systematic training to his son; still less did he subject him to any moral discipline. On the contrary, he made him as he grew up the companion of his less desirable pursuits. In particular, as the boy approached adolescence he helped to inflame his nascent passions by reading with him far into the night the erotic romances of such writers as La Calprenède and Mme de Scudéry.

When, however, Jean-Jacques was ten years old (1722) the parental demoralisation was suddenly ended; for his excitable father got involved in a brawl which caused him to flee from Geneva into the Duchy of Savoy, leaving his son, totally unprovided for, to be looked after by whomsoever among his relatives cared to undertake the task. An uncle took charge of him and sent him for two years to a school at Bossey, whence he departed (1724) without having learned or attempted to learn anything. He was then placed in a clerk's office with a view to the profession of the law, but a very few months of unpunctuality, laziness, indiscipline, and incompetence secured his decisive dismissal (1725). Next he was apprenticed to an engraver, under whom, within three years, he became an accomplished liar and thief. His complete moral *débâcle*, which he acknowledges and describes with engaging frankness in his *Confessions*, he attributes entirely to the brutality and tyranny of his master. Throughout the whole of his life, indeed, no matter how descreditable his deeds, he regards himself as the innocent and helpless victim of circumstances. He was almost devoid of conscience or sense of shame; only once or twice—as when by a deliberate and repeated falsehood he secured the dismissal of a fellow-servant for a theft which he himself had committed—did a slight compunction seize him. His wholehearted acceptance of the one-sided psychology which regards the mind of man as entirely determined by environment is one of the keys not only to his ethics, but also to his sociology.

The merest accident brought his undisciplined and disgusting infancy to a close. On Sunday evening, March 14, 1728, he went with two companions for a walk in the outskirts of Geneva. They were late in returning, and they found the city gates shut for the night. Twice had this happened before, and Rousseau's master had threatened condign punishment if it should occur again. Rousseau decided not to face the music. The one perfect consistency in his career, indeed, is his unvarying observance of the rule: When in trouble run away! In his opinion, if presence of mind is good, absence of body is better.

Hence at the age of sixteen, with nothing but the clothes he stood up in, without money, without friends, without plans, without aim or object in life, without education, without skill, without any capacity to render any but the most menial services to his fellows, he set himself adrift, compassless, upon the ocean of circumstance. He had, however, the true vagabond spirit. That is to say, he lived wholly in the present. He was free from all regrets for the past and all anxieties for the future. He revelled in the sunshine while it lasted; he took shelter from the rain when it came; he helped himself, so far as he could, to everything he wanted; he availed himself of the assistance of every one whom he met; he begged, he stole, he told lies, he professed piety, he changed his religion; he did anything, in short, which his interests seemed to indicate, or circumstances to suggest as expedient.

2. *The Super-tramp* (1728–42). Into the details of the fourteen years of his vagabondage it is, of course, as impossible as it is unnecessary for us here to enter. If there are any of my readers who are not acquainted with the amazing narrative of Books II–VI of the *Confessions* they should hasten to peruse it. The most astonishing of the many marvels which it displays is the extraordinary way in which this aimless and unprincipled drifter found friend after friend to assist him on his erratic course and to maintain him in complete or partial idleness. The two impressions that one

gets as one reads what he tells us of M. de Pontverre, Mme de Warens, Mme Basile, the Countess Vercelli, the Count Gouvon, the Abbé Gaime, M. Godard, M. de Mably, and the rest of his many benefactors are, first, a realisation of the immense wealth of kindness and compassion that exists in the world; and, secondly, a sense that there must have been something unusually attractive about this super-tramp—some hint of genius, some breath of distinction, some premonition of greatness, that served to mark him out as different from the common vagrant. He was never able, however, to retain any friendship permanently. His vanity, his egoism, his bad manners, his loose morals, his incapacity for any continuous employment, his sensitiveness, his quarrel-someness, his irresponsibility—these and other kindred defects of character ultimately wore out the patience of all his bene-factors, and they had to shake him off. Mme de Warens stood him longer than anyone else: no fewer than five times did she receive him into her ambiguous home. But at last even she grew cold and hostile, and then (1742) Rousseau, at the age of thirty, was at last compelled to fend for himself.

His various residences under the roof of Mme de Warens, however, had been decisive of the course of his career. From her he had learned something of the ways of the world, and something of the manners of polite society. She had provided him with opportunities to develop a natural talent for music which he had unexpectedly displayed. Above all, she had supplied him with books, and had so directed his reading that he to some extent had been able to make up for the gross defects of his early education. It was at Mme de Warens' country villa, Les Charmettes, near Chambéry, that (1738–40) his mind effectively awoke, that his imagination was quickened, and that his speculations respecting religion and politics began to take shape. Les Charmettes was, indeed, the birthplace both of modern democracy and of *l'Être Suprême* of the French Revolution. When, however, after a year's absence Rousseau returned to Les Charmettes, in 1741, his reception was such as to cause him finally to pack up and depart (spring 1742).

3. *The Would-be Man of the World* (1742–49). One reason why Rousseau was the more ready to leave Les Charmettes in 1742 was that he had invented a new form of musical notation which he was anxious to demonstrate before the Academy in Paris. He accordingly secured letters of introduction and made his way to the French capital in July 1742. His musical notation was speedily and decisively rejected by the Academy; but his introductions secured his admission to several of the *salons* of the great, where at first he was welcomed as a curiosity, but where soon he became dreaded as a boor and a bore. Hence, in order to get rid of him, influence was brought to bear to secure him a position in the French Embassy at Venice. To Venice he went, and at Venice he remained, in the service of the Comte de Montaigu, for about a year (1743–44). Long before the end of that time, however, his self-assertiveness and impudence, and possibly also his irresponsibility and licentiousness, had led to quarrels with his chief that culminated in his summary dismissal (autumn 1744). His sojourn in Venice had sufficed to give him a passionate devotion to Italian music, and to start him on that process of political speculation which terminated in the publication of his *Contrat social*.

He returned to Paris at the end of 1744, penniless and embittered. His furious attacks upon the Comte de Montaigu merely served to alienate his former acquaintances, and he found himself shunned by the great world. His enthusiastic advocacy of Italian music (soft and sensuous), and his vehement condemnation of French music (formal and mechanical), intensely irritated the Parisians, and caused dislike of him to approach the verge of physical violence. In vain he strove for some five years (1744–49) to rehabilitate himself in Society. He frequented such *salons* as continued to receive him; but he was socially impossible—shy, awkward, self-conscious, sensitive, quick to give and to take offence, wholly lacking in the grace of behaviour and the sparkle of conversation necessary for success in that world of etiquette and epigram. He wrote an opera, *Les Muses galantes*; but, though such talent as he possessed was undoubtedly musical, he had too little technical knowledge and too little capacity for systematic work to produce anything even tolerably good. Some of his compassionate acquaintances gave him secretarial occupation; but he found the regularity and the drudgery of the post irksome and threw it up. He sank into laziness and destitution.

Such happiness as he found in these distressful and unprofitable years he obtained when, quitting the *salons* of the great, where he was out of place and wretched, he frequented the taverns of the underworld and hobnobbed with the lost, with whom he had a natural affinity. In particular, about 1745, he struck up an acquaintance, which soon developed into cohabitation, with an illiterate and sensual barmaid, named Thérèse Levasseur, by whom he had five children—which children, since he could not afford to rear them, were at once sent anonymously to the asylum for foundlings, Rousseau himself never so much as setting eyes on any one of them.[1]

By the year 1749 it was abundantly clear that Rousseau was socially, economically, morally, and domestically a complete failure. If he had died then he would at once have passed into utter oblivion, like any other defunct pauper degenerate. Accident (the master determinant of his life), however, preserved him for a very different fate. Having vainly endeavoured to win the world by striving for it, he secured it by renunciation. When he ceased to run after Society, Society started to run after him.

4. *The Inspired Maniac* (1749–62). It happened by chance in October 1749 that he picked up a copy of the *Mercure de France* which contained an announcement that the Academy of Dijon offered a prize for an essay in answer to the question, "Has the progress of sciences and arts contributed to corrupt or purify morals?" The Academy probably expected that the successful essay would be a schoolboy dissertation on conventional lines glorifying the advance of civilisation.

---

[1] There is no reason to doubt the existence of these children, although the mystery surrounding their fate has given rise to many curious controversies and speculations.

But Rousseau perceived, as by a flash of inspiration, that a very much more original and effective treatise could be constructed by taking the opposite view; that an exceedingly strong case could be made out for the assertion that morals had deteriorated since the artless and unscientific state of nature had been abandoned; and that this was the case which it would best suit his temper to state and argue. For the presentation of this proposition to his mind revealed to him in a lucid instant how deep was his hatred and detestation of the polite Society which scorned and rejected him; which laughed at his gaucheries and caused him the most acute misery; which refused to redress his wrongs or recognise his pretensions. He was suffering from what in the psychological jargon of to-day is called an 'inferiority complex,' and he saw an opportunity for revenge upon his superiors—viz., the fine ladies of the *salons* and the proud scholars of the *Encyclopædia*. Ideas, inflamed by long-suppressed passion, crowded and jostled in his congested brain; the effort to catch them and clothe them in words raised his blood to fever heat. In a frenzy of inspired mania he poured forth from the depths of his infuriated heart a tremendous indictment of the society in which he lived. Man is by nature good, he said. In his primitive condition he was happy and innocent. The misery and corruption prevalent in the modern world are the consequences of so-called 'civilisation'—that is to say, of the increase of baneful knowledge and the excessive gratification of sense. To recover felicity man must return to the simple life.

Rousseau's first discourse not only won the proffered prize, it made a tremendous sensation in the artificial Society of the Age of Reason. It was the first rumble of the Revolution. Numerous replies, in which the obvious was emphasised, were penned—men so mighty (intellectually) as Lessing and (socially) as King Stanislaus of Poland, father-in-law of Louis XV of France, rushing into the fray in defence of a maligned civilisation. To these replies Rousseau wrote rejoinders, each more violent and extreme than its predecessor, and the net results of the wordy conflict were three: first, he vastly improved his literary style; secondly, he displayed himself as an exceedingly skilful, but entirely unscrupulous, controversialist, quick to discover the joints in his opponent's armour, and wholly merciless in driving his weapon home; and, thirdly, he was constrained not only to clarify his once muddy thought, and to commit himself to the defence of dogmas which at first he had not contemplated, but also to change his mode of life and to conduct himself in a manner consonant with his newly developed principles.

In 1750, in short, under the pressure of controversy and in the fervour of his novel faith, he passed through a process analogous to religious conversion, and emerged as a new anti-social creature. He severed his connexion with the great; he forsook the assemblies of the clever; he discarded the garments of polite Society and assumed the costume of the artisan; he sold his watch as an unnecessary product of craft; he declined gifts; he went to live with Thérèse in a slum, and earned a scanty living by copying music—mostly wrong.

In his new character as Man Friday in the Ile-de-France he excited far more interest and attention than he had done when he was striving to pose as a denizen of the great world. His boorish manners exactly accorded with the *rôle* of the simple savage in the state of nature which he was trying to play. Mme d'Epinay called him her "bear," and brought her friends to see him as though he had been an exhibit in a zoological garden. He got numerous orders for music-copying from persons of high degree who were not in the least concerned whether the copying was done accurately or otherwise.

For six years (1750–56) this state of things continued. Meantime, however, his mind was seething with new ideas, and not a few of them he put into writing. In 1754, in particular, he penned his second *Discours*, the subject being "The Origin of Inequality." This discourse, well says Professor C. E. Vaughan,

was and still remains the most complete expression of the revolt against human law and human convention—of the craving for a return to simple and freer conditions, for a renewal of man's communion with God and Nature—which was to breathe a new life into the thought, the imagination, the social ideals, of the civilised world.

The purport of the discourse was (i) that the origin of inequality was the institution of private property, and (ii) that for inequality there is in the nature of things no justification whatsoever. It is in this effusion that occurs that exaltation and glorification of the primitive state of nature that was to exert so powerful an influence upon the minds of the victims of an over-elaborated and decadent civilisation. Man in his original state of innocence, according to Rousseau, wandered naked in the woods, happy, healthy, carefree, solitary, peaceful, content. The fall came when he, tempted by the devil of cupidity, began to appropriate things (and in particular land) for himself; began to associate with his fellow-appropriators for the defence of his property; and began to organise states and governments for the more effective exploitation of his still innocent and impecunious neighbours. The whole thing was a wild fantasy of an undisciplined and exasperated imagination; but it made an immense appeal to a disillusioned and disgusted generation. It was, says M. Jules Lemaître, "the most extravagant, the most revolutionary, of all his works, the most pregnant, after the *Contrat social*, with future and fatal consequences."

This same seminal period saw also the publication of another work, strangely different from the second *Discours*, yet equally important as a manifestation of his thought. This was his (misnamed) article on political economy in the fifth volume of the great French *Encyclopædia* which Diderot and his friends—amid many perils from an obscurantist and persecuting Church—were then issuing. It appeared in November 1755. In this article—which anticipates in many respects its more famous successor, the *Contrat social*—Rousseau recognises and accepts the institution of private property, admits the naturalness of society and the necessity of government, formulates a theory of the State which is essentially organic, adumbrates his conception of the sovereignty of the people, and, above all, propounds (more clearly and effectively than in any other of his works) his great and most original idea, his doctrine of the general will. That the intense and anarchic individualism of the second *Discours* and the incipient collectivism of the *Encyclopædic* article could have flourished unharmonised, side by side, in the same mind at the same time, and could have received expression in two almost simultaneous coherent works is one of the many mysteries that surround Rousseau's curiously ambiguous personality at this date.

In 1756 the kindness of some of his friends enabled him to leave Paris (where he was increasingly unhappy) and take up his abode in the country (where for a time he went delirious with delight). For six years he dwelt in or near the forest of Montmorency, a dozen miles or so from Paris; first, at the Hermitage (1756–57), lent to him by Mme d'Epinay; secondly, at Mont Louis (1757–62), placed at his disposal by M. Mathas, Procurator-Fiscal; with intervals at the "Little Castle" of the Duke of Luxemburg.[1] These six years, in spite of the fact (or even because of the fact) that in his unhealthy solitude he fell a victim to erotomania, and was for a time in the possession of an unclean devil, were years of immense productivity. They were, indeed, the cardinal years of his literary activity. Seething simultaneously in his mind, and published almost at the same time, were his *Nouvelle Héloïse* (1761), his *Émile* (1762), and his *Contrat social* (1762)—his three greatest works; works that made an astounding sensation at the time of their publication, and works that have continued to be read in countless editions and innumerable translations down to the present day; works which, almost unsupported, sufficed to turn the Age of Reason to irrational sentiment, to charm *Encyclopædic* atheism into emotional deism, to convert passive obedience into a passionate enthusiasm for liberty, equality, and fraternity.

La Nouvelle Héloïse caused the fashionable world to weep

---

[1] During almost the whole of his life Rousseau lived in houses provided for him, rent-free, by other people.

to an extent which had no parallel until that notable day when the Walrus (in company with the Carpenter) beheld the quantities of sand that constitute the seashore. Weeping was a new sensation for the fashionable world, which was bored to death with gaiety, and it immensely enjoyed it. Rousseau touched the height of his popularity in 1761: he was visited in his forest seclusion by peers of the realm and princes of the blood, and still more frequently by their ladies. He was lionised and adored, his strange costumes, boorish manners, and unconventional utterances being regarded as manifestations of the unspoiled simplicity of his nature.

Very different, however, was the reception given to *Émile*, which dealt on highly original and novel lines with the problem of education. This book outraged the Church, first, by removing the training of the child out of the hands of the clergy; secondly, by prohibiting any teaching of religion until the period of adolescence; and, thirdly, by formulating a creed for use in pedagogy from which every distinctive article of Christian dogma was omitted—a sort of sentimental deism for sunny days dictated by the heart to the head. The Archbishop of Paris charged against the book and accused its author of heresy; the Sorbonne denounced it; the Parlement condemned it, and ordered the arrest of the writer; and—most devastating blow of all—the Government of Geneva consigned it to the flames. Rousseau's aristocratic patrons, alarmed at the ecclesiastical, academic, and legal hullabaloo, and fearing that if he were arrested they would be compromised, advised him to run away. He never needed to be told more than once to run away. He went; and, being denied an asylum at Geneva, at Berne, and at other Swiss cities, at last came to rest, under the protection of Frederick the Great of Prussia, at Môtiers, in Neuchâtel (summer of 1762).

5. *The Hunted Fugitive* (1762–78). Of the remaining sixteen years of his life—his second period of vagabondage—there is little need here to say much. It was a period of deepening gloom, failing health, broken spirit, haunting terrors, paralysing illusions, accumulating despair. His

sufferings and his suspicions unhinged his mind, and he had recurrent fits of sheer lunacy. It was during this period, and in the midst of one of his attacks of madness, that he visited England and had his famous quarrel with David Hume (1766–67). It was also during this period that he wrote those works of genius tinged with insanity, his *Confessions*, his *Dialogues*, and his *Reveries*. So, too, was it at this time, during more lucid intervals, that (having been consulted) he framed model constitutions for Corsica (just emancipated from Genoa) and for Poland (anxious by reform to avoid partition)—constitutions (never put into operation) remarkable for nothing so much as the total disregard displayed in them for all the abstract principles propounded in his theoretical works on politics.

Having lived in a dozen different places—but mainly in Paris—he moved finally, in May 1778, to Ermenonville, and there, in a cottage lent to him by the Marquis de Girardin, on July 2 he died.

III

The writings of Rousseau appear at first sight to consist of a mass of contradictions. In his *Discours*, in *Émile*, and in the opening chapters of the *Contrat social*, for instance, he displays himself as an extreme individualist, a passionate devotee of anarchic freedom, a mourner over lost liberty, an enemy of anything and everything that would restrain the solitary soul's uttermost eccentricity. On the other hand, in his *Political Economy* and in the later sections of the *Contrat social* he advocates a collectivism so complete as to establish the unqualified authority of the State over the citizen—an authority so comprehensive as to include the infliction of the death penalty for nonconformity to the civic religion.[1] Similarly, in some works he exalts and glorifies the pre-social state of nature, while in others he idealises the fully organised and highly developed state of political society. He denounces art and yet writes operas. He emphasises the fundamental importance of the family and the supreme need

---

[1] *Contrat social*, Book IV, Chapter 8.

to maintain the purity of all its institutions, and yet he lives with a woman to whom he is not married and he abandons all his children as soon as they are born. He advocates in *Émile* an education of an almost entirely negative kind, in which the prime function of the tutor is to prevent anything from interfering with the free operation of nature on the adolescent mind; whereas in the constitutions which he framed for the government of Corsica and of Poland he insists on the necessity of a State-controlled education intensely positive and directed deliberately to civic ends. He was a recluse, yet an ardent politician; a lover of humanity, yet a misanthrope; a man at once of ecstatic piety and of gross sensuality; a patriot and a cosmopolitan; an abstract logician replete with impracticable theories and a man of affairs with a shrewd eye to possibilities—and so on indefinitely. He was, in short, to all appearance, a mass of contradictions.

A study of the numerous commentaries that have been written upon the works of Rousseau during the past century and a half not only confirms the fact of his inconsistency, but also tends to engender the conviction that his contradictions are so serious and so bewildering as to baffle all attempts at harmonisation. It is, of course, impossible in our limited space to deal with them at length. Two examples must suffice. First, as to Rousseau's individualism. On the one side, M. Henri Sée (following M. Henri Michel) says:

C'est une conception individualiste, presque anarchiste, qui a inspiré le *Discours sur l'inégalité*. Mais, dans le *Contrat social*, Rousseau, en dépit des apparences, reste individualiste. Il se préoccupe aussi et surtout d'assurer à l'individu le plein développement de sa liberté, et ce sera l'organisation elle-même, ce sera le pacte social qui garantira aux citoyens le maximum de liberté. C'est en vertu de son individualisme que Rousseau a le premier nettement dégagé la doctrine démocratique de la souveraineté populaire.[1]

On the other side, Professor C. E. Vaughan (who has

[1] H. Sée, *L'Évolution de la pensée politique en France au XVIIIème siècle* (1925), p. 146.

rendered to all students of Rousseau an inestimable service by the publication of his magnificent edition of Rousseau's political writings) gives it as his mature opinion:

> Strike out the *Discours sur l'inégalité* with the first few pages of the *Contrat social*, and the individualism of Rousseau will be seen to be nothing better than a myth.[1]

So much for Rousseau's individualism and the irreconcilable divergence of opinion to which his statements respecting man and society have given rise.

A second example may be found in the antagonistic views of critics as to the position of the idea of a social contract in his political system. Professor Vaughan regards it as secondary and non-essential, and regrets that its irrelevant intrusion should have diverted the attention of students from the really fundamental matters of the sovereignty of the people and the supremacy of the general will.[2] Professeur René Hubert, on the contrary, in a brilliant monograph on the relation between Rousseau and the Encyclopædists, maintains that the social contract, which furnishes the title to Rousseau's most important book, is the very centre and keystone to the whole structure of his political fabric.[3]

The sum of the matter seems to be that Rousseau from time to time, and even at the same time,[4] uttered opinions diametrically opposite to one another concerning the individual and the State, concerning liberty and equality, concerning toleration and persecution, concerning primitive man and civilised society, and concerning countless other matters. He was an unsystematic thinker, untrained in formal logic. He was an omnivorous reader with undeveloped powers of assimilation. He was an emotional

---

[1] C. E. Vaughan, *Political Writings of Rousseau* (1915), i, 1. Similarly he contends in his introduction to the *Contrat social* (1918) that " Rousseau is the consistent enemy of individualism " (p. xiii), and that " those who have found in Rousseau the champion of political individualism are wholly mistaken " (p. xviii).

[2] *Cf.* C. E. Vaughan, *Political Writings*, i, 235, and *Contrat social*, p. lx.

[3] R. Hubert, *Rousseau et l'Encyclopédie* (1928), pp. 61, 87, 127–134.

[4] The second *Discours* and the article on *Political Economy* were composed simultaneously, as also were *Émile* and the *Contrat social*.

enthusiast who spoke without due reflection. He was an irresponsible writer with a fatal gift for epigram.[1]

His cosmos of ideas evolved itself extremely slowly out of a chaos of incongruous elements, and never did he succeed in giving a coherent exposition of the whole. The basal factor in all his thought was the Bible, which was, indeed, the foundation of all Genevan education; it will be recollected that one of the dreams of his youth was to become a Calvinistic preacher, and that one of the earliest of his attempts to find a career was his effort to qualify for the Catholic priesthood. Theology, as he learned it in his infancy, was, whether consciously or not, the master principle of all his speculation. To the scheme of salvation as propounded by the pastors of Geneva he gradually added the political philosophy of Locke, the theory of sovereignty of Hobbes, the *étatisme* of Plato, and the relativity of Montesquieu. The result was an appalling jumble; but ultimately it sorted itself out into a system with some approach to coherence. With the Bible as key let us seek to discern the main features of this system.

The Bible begins and the Bible ends with the picture of an ideal state, a Golden Age. On the one hand, the Old Testament seer gazing backward over the history of his race beholds through the mists of antiquity a garden planted eastward in Eden by the Lord, wherein the ancestors of humanity in primitive innocence live amid simple plenty a life of continual delight. On the other hand, the New Testament evangelist has an apocalyptic vision of a heavenly city, the New Jerusalem, into which are gathered the hosts of the redeemed, and wherein once again—the sinful earth having been consumed with fire—purity and happiness reign supreme. Paradise lost and Paradise regained—that is the summary of the history of mankind according to the Scriptures. The way in which Paradise was lost and the method by which it may be regained—that is the burden of Christian theology. Rousseau, brought up in a city dominated by

---

[1] The opening sentence of the *Contrat social*—" L'homme est né libre, et partout il est dans les fers "—has probably done more than any other misstatement to put readers off the track of the main argument of the book.

dogma, and always interested in religion, had a mind definitely cast in the theological mould. Even when he abandoned Christianity and became a deist he continued to think in terms of Paradise lost and Paradise regained. His political system, in short, is the rationalised plan of salvation; its essential factors are (i) the primitive state of innocence, (ii) the fall, (iii) the condition of sin and misery, (iv) the mode of redemption, (v) the new state of virtue and felicity. Let us briefly survey each of these factors in turn.

IV

1. *The State of Nature.* The second *Discours*, on the origin of inequality, is the Genesis of Rousseau's rationalised and secularised scripture. In it he depicts his intensely individualistic Garden of Eden, in which the noble savage, that ideal creature of eighteenth-century imagination, lives his simple, sinless, happy, and careless existence. He is an essentially solitary being, content to exist without any sort of society; he wears no clothes and feels no need of them; he has no property and does not want any; he finds his scanty necessities amply supplied by the lavish bounty of nature. He is devoid of knowledge of both good and evil; he is free from the diseases of civilisation, and he has no consciousness of the approach of death. There are no restrictions on his perfect liberty; his equality with his fellows is complete. Rousseau says:

> In this primitive state men had neither houses, nor huts, nor any kind of property whatever; every one lived where he could, seldom for more than a single night; the sexes united without design, as accident, opportunity, or inclination brought them together. . . . The produce of the earth furnished them with all they needed, and instinct told them how to use it.

2. *The Fall.* This is explained in the same seminal discourse. It was due to the growth of inequality; inequality was due to the abandonment of solitude for society; and the institution of society was due to the establishment of private property.

The first man who, having enclosed a piece of ground, bethought himself of saying "This is mine," and found people simple enough to believe him, was the real founder of civil society. From how many crimes, wars, and murders; from how many horrors and misfortunes might not anyone have saved mankind by pulling up the stakes or filling up the ditch, and crying to his fellows: "Beware of listening to this impostor; you are undone if you once forget that the fruits of the earth belong to us all, and the earth itself to no one."

Perhaps, we may suggest, the reason why this prophylactic speech was never uttered was the difficulty, in the absence of society, of summoning a public meeting; and the difficulty, before the evolution of language, in expressing such advanced ideas. In any case, however, private property, once having intruded itself, gave rise to inequality, generated jealousy and strife, led to the enactment of law, the organisation of police, and all the paraphernalia of government. Man's primitive freedom was wholly lost, and in its place was substituted a tyranny of the rich over the poor.

3. *The Condition of Sin and Misery.* Rousseau had no occasion to draw upon his imagination for a description of the condition of sin and misery into which (from whatever cause) mankind had fallen. He had but to look around him at the peasantry of France; he had but to recall his own experiences in his years of vagabondage. On all sides he saw wretchedness, violence, crime, disease. Why, he asks, when men saw the consequences of the Fall did they not return to the blissful state of nature once again? Why did they not do so, even in his own day? Ah, that was impossible! The gate of the Garden of Eden was closed, and an angel with a flaming sword prevented all approach. No longer were there forests wherein the noble savage could run wild; no longer was the population of the world so small that solitude for each and all was feasible; no longer could clothes be dispensed with without embarrassment and inconvenience; never again could the habits of civilisation be discarded, the knowledge of good and evil be forgotten, the fear of death eliminated. The Fall having taken place, and

its consequences being ineradicable, the New Jerusalem must be something wholly different from the Garden of Eden. It must recognise the existence of society; it must accommodate itself to science; it must admit of the continuance of private property; it must allow for advance of the arts and crafts of civilisation. How could this New Jerusalem be achieved?

4. *Redemption by Means of the Social Contract.* The problem to be faced was this: How could pristine liberty be recovered without the abolition of law; how could equality be restored without the surrender of property; how, in short, could individualism be harmonised with communalism; how could anarchic man and organised society be reconciled the one to the other? Rousseau found himself in the presence of the fundamental problem of political science—viz., the definition of the relation of personal freedom to collective authority. It is a problem analogous to that great culinary crux: How can omelettes be made without breaking eggs? He himself thus states the case:

> The problem is to find a form of association that will defend and protect with the whole common force the person and goods of each associate, and in which each, while uniting himself with all, may still obey himself alone, and remain as free as before.[1]

Rousseau's solution to this problem is the social contract. The social contract, then—as M. Hubert rightly perceived, but as Professor Vaughan failed to perceive—is central to Rousseau's scheme of social salvation, and is as indispensable to it as is the Cross to Christianity. The process by which the social contract is concluded is, indeed, closely modelled upon that by which conversion is accomplished and salvation attained in the Church. It involves a complete kenosis, or divestment of all individual rights, and regeneration as a member of a new communal personality. The old man with all his works is put off; the new man, the *moi commun*, is put on; a novel creation is effected; a political miracle is

---

[1] *Contrat social*, Book I, Chapter 6.

performed. Rousseau thus describes the process. The individuals who propose to transform themselves into a community meet together and simultaneously make the great surrender in the following terms: "Each of us puts his person and all his power in common under the supreme direction of the general will, and in our corporate capacity we receive each member as an indivisible part of the whole." This involves, Rousseau emphasises, "the total alienation of each associate together with all his rights to the whole community." It is an abnegation as complete as that which St Elizabeth, or any other sinner, ever made on admission to the community of the redeemed.

He adds:

> At once, in place of the individual personality of each contracting party, this act of association creates a moral and collective body, composed of as many members as the assembly contains votes, and receiving from this act its unity, its common identity, its life, and its will. This public person, so formed by the union of all other persons, formerly took the name of *Cité*, and now takes that of *Republic* or *Body Politic*. It is called by its members *State* when passive, *Sovereign* when active, and *Power* when compared with others like itself. Those who are associated in it take collectively the name of *People* and severally are called *Citizens* as sharing the sovereign power, and *Subjects* as being under the laws of the State.[1]

It will be at once recognised that this body politic of Rousseau is precisely the great Leviathan of Hobbes without its head. It is a body in which personality is completely transmuted into citizenship.

5. *The New Social State.* The main portion of the *Contrat social* is devoted to the task of unfolding the implications of the great transformation effected by the conclusion of the compact and by the consequent creation of the new communal organism. It might well be designated *The Gates Ajar*; it provides us with peeps into Rousseau's rationalised Paradise regained; it reveals to us the headless Leviathan and the city wherein he is supreme.

---

[1] *Contrat social*, loc. cit.

The first-fruit of the compact is, of course, the establishment of the sovereignty of the people; and to this conception of popular sovereignty Rousseau devotes a great many chapters of his book.[1] To us of the twentieth century the conception is—thanks largely to Rousseau himself—familiar enough; it is axiomatic to every form of democracy. But to men of the eighteenth century, particularly in France; to men brought up on Bossuet and his dogmatic statement of the divine right of kings; to men reared in a society in which ecclesiastical immunity and feudal privilege placed the first and second estates on platforms high above the third—a society in which a majority of the people were serfs without any political power whatsoever, and with few but the most elementary legal rights—to men of the eighteenth century, I say, Rousseau's great idea was revolutionary in the extreme. He boldly claims for the people, organised as a community and become a living whole, all those immense prerogatives and powers which Hobbes assigns to the despot, the great Leviathan, to whom in his visionary scheme the people, emerging from the state of nature, have surrendered themselves. He contends, as against Hobbes, that the people cannot, even if they wish, divest themselves of their sovereignty. "I hold," he says, "that sovereignty, being nothing less than the exercise of the general will, can never be alienated; and that the sovereign, who is no less than a collective being, cannot be represented except by himself."[2] And this inalienable and unrepresentable power is indivisible, illimitable, and in its proper sphere infallible. "The social compact gives the body politic absolute power over all its members."[3]

It would at first sight appear that this despotic monster, the many-headed multitude, is not less to be hated and dreaded by the liberty-loving individual than the unmitigated tyrant envisaged by Hobbes. But Rousseau sets to work to show that this is not the case. The State is an organism, he contends; it possesses a personality; it is characterised by a corporate mind, a communal conscience, and, above all, by

[1] *Contrat social*, Book I, Chapters 7–9; Book II, Chapters 1–12.
[2] *Ibid.*, Book II, Chapter 1.   [3] *Ibid.*, Book II, Chapter 4.

171

a general will. The essence of its sovereignty resides in this general will, and to the formation of this general will every individual contributes. Hence this general will of the community is the real will of every one of its constituent members. The general will is not the mere algebraical sum of the separate individual wills of the citizens; these wills in matters that concern the State have ceased to exist. It is the unitary will of the new body politic.

> There is often a great deal of difference between the will of all and the general will; the latter considers only the common interest, while the former takes private interests into account, and is no more than a sum of particular wills.[1]

This conception of the general will as the single and simple volition of the body politic regarded as a living entity is Rousseau's great contribution to political philosophy. It postulates an organic theory of the State, and it inevitably leads to a collectivist and even socialistic conclusion. It is, indeed, the source and origin both of the Hegelian system of politics, which culminated in the lectures of Treitschke, the ravings of Bernhardi, and the Great War; and also of the Marxian system of economics, which had issue in the dictatorship of the proletariat and Bolshevik communism. Rousseau gives a good deal of attention to it in the chapters relating to sovereignty in his *Contrat social*; but his fullest exposition of its characteristics and limitations is embodied in his *Encyclopædia* article on political economy. It is from this that we learn (i) that "the body politic taken as a whole may be regarded as an organised living body, resembling that of man"; (ii) that "the body politic is also a moral being possessed of a will," and that "this general will, which tends always to the preservation and welfare of the whole and of every part, is the source of the laws," and that it "constitutes for all the members of the State, in their relations to one another and to it, the rule of what is just or unjust"; (iii) that "the most general will is always the most just," and that "the voice of the people is, in fact, the voice of God"; (iv) that

---

[1] *Contrat social*, Book II, Chapter 3.

"the general will is always for the common good"; and (v) that "the general will is always on the side which is most favourable to the public interest," so that "it is needful only to act justly to be certain of following the general will."

Here, it is obvious, Rousseau is beginning to argue in a circle: the general will is the standard of justice; he who acts justly necessarily conforms to the general will! Is there, or is there not, a standard of justice, a moral law, extraneous to the general will? This ethical difficulty is not the only one in which Rousseau finds himself involved. How can the maintenance of individual freedom be reconciled to the assertion of the authority of the general will of the body politic? Rousseau replies: "In order that the social contract may not be an empty formula it tacitly includes the undertaking, which alone can give force to the rest, that whoever refuses to obey the general will shall be compelled to do so by the whole body," and he adds the amazing remark: "This means nothing less than that he will be forced to be free." Now to be thus forced to be free is in practice precisely the same thing as being forced to obey. In other words, in order to make the omelette of the State the egg of liberty has had to be broken. Rousseau has failed to solve the problem by which he, in common with all other political philosophers, was faced.

Nevertheless, he has made a permanently valuable contribution towards its solution, or, at any rate, to a working compromise between its opposite insolubilities; and there can be no question that just as he gathers into his system the ideas of most of his predecessors—e.g., Plato, Aristotle, Hobbes, Locke, Montesquieu—so he serves as the starting-point of much of the most fruitful political speculation of modern times—e.g., that of Kant, Fichte, Hegel, T. H. Green, Bradley, Bosanquet.

If we are asked what are the most enduringly important of his social and political ideas, we might reply, first, the idea that the people is the ultimate source of all legitimate terrestrial authority; secondly, that government is merely the agent and delegate of the sovereign people; thirdly, that the

common good is the criterion of sound legislation and satisfactory administration; fourthly, that the State is organic in
nature and not a mere mechanism; fifthly, that the true basis
of political obligation is consent, and hence, finally, that
there is in the last resort no antagonism between freedom
and authority, law and liberty, man and the State.

BOOK LIST

A. PRIMARY SOURCES

Collection complète des œuvres de Rousseau, edited by Du Peyrou. 17 vols.
  Geneva, 1782.
Œuvres de Rousseau, edited by Nargeoi, Fayolle, and Baucarel. 25 vols.
  Paris, 1801.
The Political Writings of Rousseau, edited by C. E. Vaughan. 2 vols.
  London, 1915.
Reveries of a Solitary, edited by J. G. Fletcher. London, 1927.
Lettres à Malesherbes, edited by G. Rudler. Paris, 1927.

B. SECONDARY SOURCES

BABBITT, I.: *Rousseau and Romanticism.* 1919.
BEAUDOUIN, H.: *La Vie et les œuvres de J.-J. Rousseau.* 2 vols. 1891.
BROCKENHOFF, F.: *J.-J. Rousseau, sein Leben und Werke.* 1863.
CHARPENTIER, J.: *Rousseau: the Child of Nature.* 1931.
CHUQUET, A.: *J.-J. Rousseau.* 1893.
COBBAN, A.: *Rousseau and the Modern State.* 1934.
DUCROS, L.: *J.-J. Rousseau.* 1908.
GEIGER, L.: *J.-J. Rousseau, sein Leben und seine Werke.* 1907.
GRAN, G.: *J.-J. Rousseau.* 1912.
HENDEL, C. W.: *J.-J. Rousseau: Moralist.* 2 vols. 1934.
HENSEL, P.: *J.-J. Rousseau.* 1907.
HÖFFDING, H.: *Rousseau og hans Filosofi.* 1898.
HUBERT, R.: *Rousseau et l'Encyclopédie.* 1928.
HUDSON, W. H.: *Rousseau and Naturalism.* 1903.
JOSEPHSON, M.: *J.-J. Rousseau.* 1932.
LEMAÎTRE, J.: *J.-J. Rousseau.* 1908.
MACDONALD, FREDERIKA: *Jean-Jacques Rousseau.* 2 vols. 1906.
MARITAIN, J.: *Trois Réformateurs.* 1928.
MORLEY, LORD: *Rousseau.* 2 vols. 1873.
NOURISSON, J. F.: *J.-J. Rousseau et le Rousseauisme.* 1902.
SÉE, H.: *L'Évolution de la pensée politique en France au XVIIIème siècle.* 1925.
SELLS, A. L.: *The Early Life and Adventures of J.-J. Rousseau.* 1929.
VULLIAMY, C. E.: *Rousseau.* 1931.
WRIGHT, E. H.: *The Meaning of Rousseau.* 1929.

VII

BURKE AND SUBLIMATED COMMON SENSE[1]

EDMUND BURKE has been described as "one of the greatest men, and—Bacon alone excepted—the greatest thinker who ever devoted himself to the practice of English politics." This high eulogy does not appear to be excessive, even if one, in repeating it, bears in mind that Burke has to stand comparison with men so eminent intellectually as Clarendon and Bolingbroke; Canning and Peel; Gladstone and Disraeli; Salisbury, Asquith, and Balfour. One cannot, indeed, rise from a perusal of Burke's voluminous writings without a profound conviction that their author was a man of pre-eminent character, lofty patriotism, superb intellect, fiery zeal, and that "infinite capacity for taking pains" which has been curiously termed genius.

The feature, however, that specially distinguishes Burke from the other writers dealt with in this series of studies is not his character, his ability, or his diligence; it is the fact that he was not only a thinker of the first rank, but also a practical politician who for the thirty most active years of his life played a prominent part on the stage of great affairs. Of other contemporary thinkers, Paine never reached in England a more exalted eminence than that of an excise officer; Godwin at the end of a long and unsuccessful career was nothing more lofty than a yeoman-usher of the

[1] From *The Social and Political Ideas of Some Representative Thinkers of the Revolutionary Era* (Harrap, 1931). The other studies in this volume are: "The Theorists of the American Revolution," by R. McElroy; "The Early English Radicals," by G. S. Veitch; "The Revolutionary Era in France," by J. Holland Rose; "Thomas Paine," by Norman Sykes; "William Godwin," by C. H. Driver; "Jeremy Bentham," by J. W. Allen; "The Socialist Tradition in the French Revolution," by Harold J. Laski; "The German Thinkers of the Revolutionary Era," by H. G. Atkins.

Exchequer, living in New Palace Yard, and drawing £200 a year as a sinecurist; Bentham, a man of independent means, lived to the age of eighty-four without holding any sort of public office—a semi-recluse, spending his days in a house appropriately called the Hermitage, occupied like a lonely spider in spinning utilitarian webs.

Some there were who regretted that Burke allowed himself to be lured from the calm heights of philosophical speculation down to the plains whereon party politicians contended noisily, "not without dust and heat." Goldsmith, for instance, in well-known lines lamented that he who was

> born for the universe, narrow'd his mind,
> And to party gave up what was meant for mankind.

In a similar strain, one of Burke's early biographers, Dr Robert Bisset, a deep-dyed Tory, confessed, not unnaturally, that he did not "rejoice at the commencement of his connexion with the Marquis of Rockingham" (1765), adding that "from that time he may be considered as a party man." "Burke," he continued, "ought not to have stooped to be the object of patronage. Like his friend Johnson, he should have depended entirely on his own extraordinary powers."[1] It is impossible not to sympathise with the spirit of these remarks. For on the one hand Burke had a philosophic mind of such strength and clarity that, if he had dedicated it to the unprejudiced pursuit of political principle, he could probably have produced works worthy to rank with the masterpieces of Plato and Aristotle, and far above the amateur lucubrations of Hobbes, Locke, and Rousseau. His essay on *The Origin of our Ideas of the Sublime and the Beautiful*, begun when he was an undergraduate in his teens and published when he was but twenty-seven, shows powers of independent thought of a high order. His ironical *Vindication of Natural Society*, issued anonymously in 1756, displays so complete and so contemptuous an acquaintance with both the reactionary principles of Bolingbroke and the revolutionary speculations of Rousseau as to indicate that

[1] R. Bisset, *Life of Edmund Burke* (1798), p. 69.

176

BURKE AND SUBLIMATED COMMON SENSE

even at that early date Burke stood fully equipped as a champion to defend civilised society against either those who would stop its steady advance or those who would stampede it into a reckless abandonment of its base. The story that at one time, the exact date of which is a matter of much controversy, he was a candidate for a philosophical chair at Glasgow University—whatever element of truth it may contain—suggests that in the fifties he was a figure of some prominence in the world of metaphysicians. On the other hand, there can, unfortunately, be no doubt that his immersion in party controversy, from 1765 to his death, thirty-two years later, adversely affected the quality of his work. He became an Old Whig apologist, and his zeal to maintain the Old Whig cause against all comers led him not infrequently to make assertions and develop arguments that in philosophical quietude he would emphatically have repudiated. From 1765 to 1783, perhaps, his official Whiggism put no strain upon his scientific conscience; the Whigs, as opposed to George III and the King's Friends, were the "men of light and leading." In 1783, under the reckless and unprincipled command of Charles James Fox, the Whigs made the fatal mistake of combining with the Tories of Lord North's reactionary rout for the purpose of driving Lord Shelburne from office and imposing their will upon the King. Burke, unhappily, although his alienation from Fox and the New Whigs had already begun, lent his support to the deadly Fox-North coalition, and for eight years his conduct in Parliament displayed a factiousness and unreason that no excuses can palliate. He attacked the younger Pitt with sustained and unpardonable animosity; he opposed his wisest measures—*e.g.*, the Eden treaty with France—and his various proposals for cautious Parliamentary reforms; he supported with sophistical arguments—*e.g.*, in the matter of the Regency Bill of 1788—principles plainly subversive of the Constitution; in general, he showed a passion and a prejudice that made even his friends ashamed of his aid. In 1790, however, the development of the French Revolution, by severing his uneasy and improper association with Fox and the New Whigs, restored him to sanity and sobriety and enabled him to do an imperishable service to humanity in exposing the true nature of the Jacobinism that was devastating the Continent.

If, then, Burke's political utterances—speeches, letters, dissertations, memorials—suffer from lack of detachment and philosophical impartiality, they gain from the fact that they are intimately associated with the actual course of current events. They are models of applied philosophy. They deal with the controversies of the passing moment *sub specie æternitatis*. They reveal the workings of a powerful mind that was never content until it had traced an argument back step by step to its ultimate source in "the eternal laws of truth and right."

This intimate association, however, in Burke's writings of the abstract and the concrete, the theoretical and the practical, the eternal and the temporal, has two consequences of an embarrassing nature. First, it compels every reader who wishes to understand Burke's works to make an exhaustive study of both his life and his times. Secondly, it imposes upon him the task of attempting to extract Burke's social and political ideas from masses of irrelevant and obstructive detail that have long since ceased to be either interesting or important. Thus Burke, in spite of his eloquence and lucidity, tends to be a weariness to the flesh. And the weariness is unnecessarily increased by the fact that there is no satisfactory life of Burke extant, and no properly edited collection of his works. In spite of the labours of Canon Murray, Dr Cobban, Mr Bertram Newman, Lord Morley, and Mr Thomas Macknight, the best biography still is that by Sir James Prior, first published in 1824. As to the various editions of the works of Burke, their name is legion and chaos. The first edition, sponsored by Lawrence and King (1792–1827), was never properly completed. Of the numerous later editions no two that I have examined are alike.[1] The four-volume edition of Burke's speeches, issued anony-

[1] My references in this essay are all made to Bohn's eight-volume edition of 1854–57.

mously in 1816, is beneath contempt. The four-volume edition of Burke's correspondence, laboriously collected by Earl Fitzwilliam and Sir Richard Bourke, and published in 1844, although incomparably better than the edition of the speeches, is painfully incomplete (especially for the period 1745–65) and lacking in adequate elucidation. Few greater services could be rendered by a scholar, or group of scholars, commanding leisure and money than that of preparing for the world a definitive edition of Burke's speeches and writings, accompanied by a critical survey of his life and times. For the rapid process of the world along the course which Burke with prophetical prescience foresaw, and the successive fulfilment of his predictions, makes it every day increasingly evident that he has still a message to deliver of primary significance to modern man.

II

The fact that Burke wrote no formal treatise expounding his political and social ideas, but left his principles to be discovered inductively from a study of his occasional words and his expedient deeds, renders it necessary for us—as in the case of Rousseau—to make a cursory survey of his career and of the circumstances in the midst of which it ran its course. For purposes of examination it may be divided into three periods, as follows : first, 1729–65, the period of preparation ; second, 1765–89, the period of advocacy of reform ; third, 1789–97, the period of opposition to revolution.

The date and place of Burke's birth have given rise to much controversy : seven places dispute the honour of having presented him to the world, while six different dates (ranging from January 1, 1728, to January 12, 1730) have been assigned for his nativity. It would be irrelevant to discuss the question here ; enough to say that the best opinion tends to support the claims of January 12, 1729, and of 33 Arran Quay, Dublin.[1] His father, Richard Burke, was a Protestant

[1] Those interested in this question will find the best treatment of it in A. P. I. Samuels' *Early Life of Edmund Burke* (1923), pp. 1–7.

attorney of good ability and high integrity, but of a passionate and overbearing disposition; he was a loyal member of the Episcopal Church of Ireland. His mother was, and remained, a devout Roman Catholic. Her maiden name was Mary Nagle; her parental home was Ballyduff, near Castletownroche, in County Cork. Her kindred had been among the most faithful and persistent supporters of James II in the conflicts of 1689–92, one member of her family, Sir Richard Nagle, having been James's Attorney-General. Of the fourteen or fifteen children of Richard and Mary Burke, only four—three sons and one daughter—survived infancy. The sons were brought up in their father's faith, the daughter in her mother's. But Edmund, the second of the three sons, although reared as a Protestant, spent (for reasons of health) five of his early years among his mother's relatives in Ballyduff, and he there learned that respect for Catholicism that made him so strenuous an advocate for the abolition of the penal laws in later life. His wide religious sympathy and his broad tolerance were further enlarged when he was sent, at the age of twelve, to an excellent school established some years before at Ballitore, in County Kildare, by a pious and scholarly Quaker, Abraham Shackleton by name.

In April 1744[1] Burke entered Trinity College, Dublin, and there he remained for some five years. During this period his genius unmistakably displayed itself. Not only did he win a scholarship (June 1746), carry off various college prizes, and secure a good degree; but outside the routine of the schools he read widely, wrote voluminously, and showed a keen interest in current affairs. In particular, he was one of four enthusiasts for controversy who, in April 1747, founded "The Club," the first students' debating society that history records, the minute-book of which (now treasured in Trinity College) is mainly in his writing. Occasionally he acted as president, and the minutes (not in his writing on this occasion) state that in that capacity he was "damned absolute." That he did not suffer fools, or

---

[1] Not 1743, as is sometimes stated. The T.C.D. year began on July 9.

even antagonists, gladly was admitted by himself in a naïve letter of this period to his friend Richard Shackleton, son of his old headmaster: "It is against my nature," he wrote, "to see people in an opinion I think wrong without endeavouring to undeceive 'em."[1]

Besides helping to found "The Club" (which still exists, under another name) he was prominent in the institution of a notable university magazine entitled *The Reformer*, of which thirteen numbers were issued between January and April 1748. The major part of the writing was from Burke's own pen. His contributions, the style of which was amazingly mature, show that at that time he was keenly interested in the morality of the theatre, the condition of the Irish peasantry, and the evidences of the Christian religion.[2]

In the last year of his college life (1748–49) he became involved in a furious controversy that convulsed not only the university, but the city of Dublin. It is known as the "Lucas Controversy." A certain Dr Charles Lucas made a fierce and sustained attack on the notorious corruption of the Dublin Corporation. The Corporation found a defender in the able but unscrupulous Sir Richard Cox, the honour of whose family was involved. Wigs were on the Green. Burke (aged nineteen) intervened "with holy glee" in the glorious hullabaloo, contributing four pamphlets on the side of Lucas the reformer which served very materially to pour oil upon the fire of Hibernian passion.[3] Like most of Burke's later political writings, they show how, in a curious way, Burke combined essential moderation of view with extreme violence of expression. That strange combination is, perhaps, characteristic of Irish sanity.

---

[1] Samuels' *Early Life of Edmund Burke*, p. 67.

[2] Samuels, *op cit.*, pp. 161–177, and Appendix II, where all the thirteen numbers are reprinted *in extenso*.

[3] The pamphlets are printed in full by Samuels, *op. cit.*, pp. 331–395. In both thought and expression they are of an incomparably higher order than any other of the utterances of the controversialists.

III

In 1750 Burke was sent by his father to London in order that, by way of the Middle Temple, he might enter upon the career of the law. For this career he had long been marked out. In 1745, during one of his vacations, as we learn from a letter of his, he had assisted his father at the Cork Assizes. In 1747 his name had been entered at the Temple. Mr Richard Burke, recognising his son's brilliant abilities, anticipated for him a lucrative practice, culminating in silk and the Bench. But Edmund disappointed his father's expectations. Although in London he acquired a knowledge of law that stood him in good stead all his life, he soon decided that the Bar was no place for him. Anticipating the young Disraeli—whose course in many respects was strikingly similar to Burke's—he gradually deserted law for literature, and literature for politics.[1] The elder Burke did not regard his son's abandonment of his profession with equanimity. He, like Edmund, was "damned absolute"; and the clash of two equal and opposite "damned absolutenesses," of the intense Irish variety, led to electrical discharges which in 1755 fused all connexions between them and left the young man penniless to his own resources.

For the next ten years (1755–65) Edmund Burke was adrift upon the surface of the world. It is not easy to follow his movements, or to discover how he managed to make a livelihood. He published anonymously his *Vindication of Natural Society* (1756); he refurbished and completed his essay on *The Origin of our Ideas of the Sublime and the Beautiful* (1757). Neither of these can have produced much cash.

[1] Not only did both Burke and Disraeli desert law for literature, and literature for politics; they both, before they entered Parliament, gained intimate acquaintance with its procedure by assiduous attendance in the Strangers' Gallery; both were outsiders who forced their way into the front rank of politics by sheer energy and ability; both were impecunious and harassed by debt all their days; both, in order to improve their status, bought landed estates that they could not pay for, and both in Buckinghamshire; both, when a peerage was offered to them, selected Beaconsfield as the seat of their dignity. So much for externals. In ideas and in political principles the parallel was still closer.

More lucrative was the *Annual Register*, a chronicle of the events of the preceding year, which he initiated in 1759 and continued to edit for nearly thirty years. Still more satisfactory, as a source of regular income, was a secretaryship which he secured that same year (1759). His employer was a member of Parliament, wealthy, and at the time well known, W. G. Hamilton by name. Secretary to Hamilton he remained for nearly six years, during three of which his duties took him back to Dublin, and renewed his acquaintance with the political and social problems of his native land.

Mr W. G. Hamilton, however, proved to be a hard master. He demanded the whole time and the undivided service of his servant. Hence Burke, who was seething with ideas—especially concerning Irish reform—and full of ambition, bade Hamilton a tempestuous farewell, early in 1765, and so once again, at the age of thirty-six, found himself at large.

IV

Burke had served a long and strenuous apprenticeship to politics. How different his fate from that of the favoured scions of the "governing class"! The younger Pitt, for instance, finished his apprenticeship in the nursery, entered Parliament while he was still legally an infant, and by the time he was thirty-six had already been Prime Minister for a dozen years. If, however, Burke's period of preparation was protracted, and his task of procuring an entry into the closed circle of official Whigdom one of prodigious difficulty, there can be no doubt that the experience in practical affairs which he gained under Hamilton, combined with the intimate acquaintance with current problems which his editorship of the *Annual Register* entailed, enabled him to embark on a public career in 1765 with an equipment of knowledge and wisdom such as none of his contemporaries possessed.

In the summer of 1765 George III, yielding to painful necessity, had called to office his enemies, the oligarchic Whigs, under the Marquis of Rockingham. Rockingham possessed rank, wealth, and character, without knowledge, intelligence, or experience. In a moment fortunate for both Burke was introduced to him as possessing precisely those endowments which he himself lacked. He made Burke his secretary, and before the close of the year helped to secure for him a seat in Parliament. Burke at once became, what he remained to the end of his days—the brain of the Old Whig party. Within a few days of his entry into the House of Commons he made a speech on American affairs that, said his friend, Dr Samuel Johnson, who surveyed him with benevolent eyes from the Strangers' Gallery, gained for him "more reputation than any man at his first appearance had ever gained before." He showed a mastery of detail combined with a grasp of underlying principle such as had rarely been seen up to that date. In force of oratory and command of language, as well as in some of his leading ideas, he recalled Bolingbroke. But he had a diligence, a sense of duty, a consciousness of responsibility, a freedom from the taint of self-seeking, that placed him in a class wholly above that of his great Conservative predecessor.

Burke had been in Parliament but little more than six months when (July 1766) George III found means to get rid of the uncongenial Rockingham Whigs. The tool of the King's malignant unfriendliness was the elder Pitt, who became at this date Earl of Chatham. Burke never forgave Chatham for his refusal to support Rockingham in 1765, and for his readiness to subvert him in 1766. On all essential points of policy Chatham and the Old Whigs were at this time in agreement. In union they might easily have averted the revolt of the American colonies. But an insane conceit, combined with a dislike of the party system of government, prevented Chatham from consenting to serve under the Whig leader. Numerous and immeasurably evil were the consequences of Chatham's intransigeance and intractability at this date.

Burke's first work in an opposition which endured for sixteen years was to write a brief but conclusive apologia for the Rockingham Government in his *Account of a Short Administration* (1766). More considerable was a detailed pamphlet, entitled *Observations on a Late Publication*, issued in 1769. The publication criticised was a dissertation by George Grenville, Rockingham's predecessor in office, on *The Present State of the Nation*, in which that disagreeable and disgruntled politician defended Lord Bute and himself, denounced both Rockingham and Chatham, proposed fresh schemes for taxing America (together with Ireland and the East India Company), and finally recommended various changes in the British Constitution. Burke fell upon Grenville's dissertation with devastating effect: exposed the errors and folly of Bute and his successor, defended the doings of the Rockingham Whigs, riddled with ridicule Grenville's financial proposals, and denounced his suggestions for laying impious hands upon the inviolable ark of the Constitution as set up by the Covenant of 1689. The *Observations* provide a magnificent example of Burke's encyclopædic knowledge, his complete comprehension of his theme, and his overwhelming mastery in argument. The crushed and abject Grenville could make no attempt at a rejoinder. The fact, however, that Burke in his *Observations* was compelled to follow the lead of the dissertation to which he was replying necessarily cramped his style and restricted his scope. In 1770, in a still finer utterance, unrestrained by any extraneous control, he let himself go. This new work was entitled *Thoughts on the Causes of the Present Discontents*. It began by describing the troubles that harassed the Government and the nation at that date—the dispute with America, the agitation that centred round Wilkes, the Radical programme propounded by the mysterious "Junius," and so on. It went on to examine and reject the explanations of these discontents advanced by the Ministry; the true cause, it contended, was the establishment of the "double-cabinet system" of the King—the system according to which the King and his friends exercised real control over affairs of State behind the backs of the nominal and responsible Parliamentary heads of the executive. It concluded by condemning as inadequate and undesirable such suggested remedies as a Triennial Bill or a Places Bill, and contended that the only effective corrective would be a frank and full return to the party system. No defence of the party system, or government by connexion, has ever been more convincing than that with which Burke concludes this masterly treatise.[1]

Of all the discontents of that distressful time the most menacing was that which was driving the thirteen American colonies to the verge of rebellion. It had been generated by the oppressive enforcement of the British Navigation Acts, by the restrictions placed on colonial industry and commerce in the interests of home manufacturers and merchants, and by the misgovernment of British officials; it had been raised to fever-heat by the attempt of the Mother Country to tax the dominions by means of the notorious Stamp Act (1765) and Imports Duties Act (1767); in 1774 it was rapidly passing beyond the sphere of argument into the sphere of war. The British Parliament, the American Congress, the Press and the Pulpit on both sides of the Atlantic—all were angrily debating the question of right: Had the Parliament the *right* to tax the colonies? Had the American settlers the *right* of resistance? and so on. In the midst of this juridical jangle Burke intervened with a superb speech which lifted the whole controversy on to a higher plane. Refusing so much as to consider the problem of abstract right, whether on the one side or on the other, he devoted himself to an unanswerable demonstration of the practical unwisdom of the policy which Lord North's Government was pursuing. Next year (March 22, 1775), in the same strain, in another inimitable oration, he urged a policy of conciliation. "The question will be," he remarked in ever-memorable words,

> not whether you have a right to render your people miserable, but whether it is not your interest to make them happy. It is not what a lawyer tells me I *may* do, but what humanity, reason, and justice tell me I *ought* to do.[2]

Burke's attempts at conciliation were, of course, unsuccessful. Passions on both sides of the ocean were roused to so intense a pitch of exasperation that nothing but blood-

[1] Burke's works, 1854-57, i, 372-381. [2] *Ibid.*, p. 475.

letting and separation could suffice to restore tranquillity. Nevertheless, even when the blood-letting had begun Burke still strove to avert separation. Very notable is the letter which he addressed in April 1777 to the Sheriffs of Bristol—the city for which at that date he had his seat in Parliament. This great letter is a passionate plea for pacification, a masterly argument for the reconciliation and harmonisation of *imperium* and *libertas*. In spite, however, of Burke's plea, and in spite of the labours of many other men of goodwill, the dreadful arbitrament of slaughter dragged on. In 1778 Britain's European enemies began to intervene, and by 1780 it was evident that the colonies were irrecoverably lost. Peace by surrender became the only possible issue of the conflict. But Lord North, the *bête noire* of the triumphant colonists, was not the man to negotiate peace on these terms. The Whigs, who under Burke's guidance had all along advocated moderation, were the only people who could do it. Hence in 1782 Lord North resigned, and the Marquis of Rockingham came back.

It is curious that when Lord Rockingham constructed his second Cabinet Burke had no place in it. After all the attempts of Lord Morley and others to explain the fact, it remains a mystery. But, though excluded from the responsible inner-circle of the Government, Burke received the lucrative appointment of paymaster-general of the forces—an office out of which some of Burke's predecessors had managed to extract more than £20,000 a year. One of Burke's most public-spirited and self-sacrificing acts was to reduce the emoluments of this office from fluctuating percentages, which could be made to yield almost anything that avidity could desire, to a fixed £4000 a year. This reduction he effected as part of a big scheme of economic reform which, outlined in a great speech on February 11, 1780, he was able partially to realise during Rockingham's brief tenure of power in 1782.

Brief tenure! Rockingham lived but three months after his recall to office in March 1782. His death bereft Burke of a faithful and lavishly generous friend. One of his last commands, as he lay dying at Wimbledon, was to order the cancellation of bonds for some £30,000 which represented Burke's indebtedness to him. After Rockingham's death Burke attached himself to Fox and Sheridan, rather than to Shelburne and the younger Pitt, who carried on the tradition of Chatham. Thus Burke became involved with Fox in the disastrous coalition that overthrew Shelburne in the spring of 1783, but was itself overthrown by George III and Pitt in the December of the same year.

The specific measure that enabled George III to evict the Fox-North coalition, just before Christmas 1783, was an India Bill, every item of which bears the impress of Burke's moulding hand. Burke was furious at the loss of this Bill, and still more furious at the enactment, in the face of his terrific tirades, of Pitt's very different measure for the reform of the East India Company's administration (1784). From that time onward, for the next five years and (though less exclusively) for a second five, Indian affairs occupied his attention. He was interested in India, first, as a shareholder in the East India Company, and one who had lost a good deal of money in the famous slump of 1769; secondly, as an enemy of Parliamentary corruption who resented and dreaded the hold over the constituencies which the Indian 'nabobs' (retired servants of the East India Company) were securing by means of their wealth;[1] thirdly, as a humanitarian who realised that the fortunes which the 'nabobs' were bringing back to England were not made by way of legitimate trade, but by cruel extortion and diabolical intrigue. With fiery zeal, unwearying diligence, and consummate skill he tracked these ill-gotten fortunes to their sources, and exposed them to the execration of mankind in a series of masterly speeches and writings. He came to the conclusion that the East India Company was rotten to the core and that it was totally unfit to exercise any sort of political authority.

[1] The most conspicuous of these 'nabobs,' Paul Benfield, who was said to have come back from India with wealth that yielded him £149,000 a year, purchased eight pocket-boroughs, the representation of which passed entirely under his control. See Burke's *Speech on the Nabob of Arcot's Debts* (works, 1854-57, iii, 174, 180-182, 185-189).

Further, he thought that he saw in the Governor-General, Warren Hastings, the *fons et origo* of all the tyranny and corruption that he discovered and denounced. Hence, when Warren Hastings returned from India in 1785 Burke and his friends at once proclaimed their intention to impeach him. The impeachment, as is well known, duly took place, dragging on its dreary length from 1788 to 1795. Although in the end Warren Hastings was acquitted—his doubtful deeds being excused by difficult circumstances and to some extent atoned for by conspicuous services—nevertheless the damning exposure of the nefarious practices of the East India Company's officials for ever prevented a repetition of their crimes.

V

The conduct of the later stages of the impeachment of Warren Hastings was greatly complicated by the fact that Burke and the other chief managers, Fox and Sheridan, had, while co-operating in the attack on Hastings, come into violent conflict respecting another matter of even greater magnitude and importance. This other matter was nothing less than the French Revolution and the attitude of the British Government towards it. Fox and Sheridan welcomed the Revolution with enthusiasm, rejoiced in the emancipation of the French people, excused their little exuberances, and wished Great Britain to proclaim itself whole-heartedly on their side in their struggle against a despotic king, an effete nobility, and an obscurantist Church. They saw in the French Revolution of 1789 an exact replica of the glorious English Revolution of a hundred years before.

Burke from the first took a wholly different view of the situation. He had visited Paris in 1773, had been introduced to some of the *salons*, and had come away from them profoundly perturbed by the anti-monarchic, equalitarian, and atheistic sentiments which he found dominant in their midst. He had predicted at the time that such sentiments, if persisted in, must subvert society. When, therefore, he saw them becoming operative in 1789 he realised that the movement just commencing was one wholly different from the cautious and conservative change of dynasty effected in England by the Whig magnates and the Anglican bishops in 1688–89. While still the movement was in its early and less violent stages he compared it with the Jacquerie in France, the Peasants' Revolt in England, and the Anabaptist eruption in Germany. Later, as it progressed in sanguinary terrorism, he realised that it was the manifestation of a more profound social upheaval than even these portentous events; that it was "a revolution of doctrine and theoretic dogma" comparable in its magnitude to nothing less epoch-making than the Reformation itself.

The sharp divergence of view respecting the French Revolution which separated Burke and Windham from Fox and Sheridan first openly displayed itself in a great speech which Burke delivered in the House of Commons in February 1790. But the final crash and definite breach did not come until May 6, 1791, when, as the sequel to a tremendous debate, Burke repudiated both his public association and his private friendship with Fox. He soon crossed the floor of the House, and took a seat near his old antagonist (henceforth his close ally), William Pitt. In 1794, under his inspiration, the leaders of the Old Whig group—Portland, Fitzwilliam, Windham—joined Pitt's Government, and thereby brought into existence the great Conservative Party. The foremost champion of party government wrecked the party to whose interests he had devoted the best energies of the major portion of his public career. In deliberately doing so, and in thus dooming himself to obloquy and impotence, he showed that to him, after all, party government was but a means to an end, and not an end in itself; that the supreme object of all government was the well-being of the nation as a whole; and that if party degenerated into faction and went astray it was necessary for the patriot to sever himself from it and by all means oppose it.

Whilst this gradual schism of the Whigs into 'Old,' or Conservative, and 'New,' or Radical, was taking place, Burke published the most famous of all his works—namely, to its chief; that he possessed a superb courage which enabled him without perturbation or flinching to face his angry constituents at Bristol, the raging rioters of Gordon's rout in London, the sullen hostility of the King's Friends, and the resentful fury of the Radicals and Revolutionaries; that in his speeches and writings he displayed an intellectual power of the highest order—a power of accumulating and digesting vast masses of material, a power of classifying and arranging it with masterly lucidity, a power of presenting it with overwhelming effect in the light of general principles; and that he combined with his splendid mental capacities a keenly sensitive, high-strung, emotional disposition. Such qualities, of course, had their defects. His nobility was such that he did not always detect the ignobility of some of his associates; his patriotism occasionally took the negative shape of mere hostility to foreigners; his loyalty to his party sometimes led him (especially during the lustrum 1784–89) into excesses of factiousness; his courage tended to degenerate into insensate obstinacy; his emotional sensitiveness led him (especially in his later years) into displays of unbridled passion that alienated the sympathy of even his most devoted friends. He had plenty of wit, but he lacked the saving grace of humour. He showed a marvellous command of all the resources of language, yet he failed in that supreme art of the orator which consists in the adaptation of the theme to the capacity of the audience. As his friend Goldsmith said in lines that have become hackneyed, he,

> too deep for his hearers, still went on refining,
> And thought of convincing, while they thought of dining.

He was a fine conversationist, not inferior to his friend and rival in the Literary Club, Dr Samuel Johnson. He was at his best in addressing his fellow-men, and it is noteworthy that all his greatest works are cast in the form of either speeches or letters. Even when he was writing he was never wholly at ease unless he had in his mind's eye a specific correspondent whom he was endeavouring to convince or to refute. Thus, as we have already remarked, he composed no

N   193

formal treatise on the science of politics or the theory of the State. He dealt with the current public affairs of the day. Most of his important utterances, whether of voice or of pen, grouped themselves round one or other of five great themes—namely, (1) Ireland, (2) the American colonies, (3) the British Constitution, (4) the East India Company, and (5) the French Revolution.

The most conspicuous general features of his political out-pourings are, first, his avoidance of abstract political specu-lation and his denunciation of the metaphysical treatment of practical affairs; secondly, his insistence on the empirical nature of the art of government; thirdly, his appeal to history and experience as the only satisfactory guides in administra-tive matters; fourthly, his emphasis on considerations of expediency, rather than on arguments based on rights, in all debatable problems of policy; and, finally, the essential moderation of all his opinions, even when he expressed these opinions with extreme immoderation of language.

When Burke began his public career he found himself in the midst of a furious battle of clashing ideologies. On the one side stood Rousseau and his followers vehemently pro-claiming the dogmas of the original liberty and the primitive equality of man; the natural rights of the individual; the sovereignty of the people; and the supremacy of a universal law, entirely different from the laws of civilised society, known only to the anarchic conscience of the illuminated. Over against this revolutionary rout stood the serried forces of the more or less "benevolent despots." These forces were entrenched for the defence of the dogma of the divine right of kings, with all its appendant doctrines of the duty of passive obedience and the invariable wrongfulness of resist-ance to the Lord's anointed. Burke felt himself to be entirely out of sympathy with both sets of combatants. He realised that the theories of each party—benevolent despots or male-volent democrats—if carried to their logical conclusions would lead to intolerable consequences. Was there no way of escape for suffering man from horrible alternatives of the Scylla of tyranny and the Charybdis of chaos?

He believed that there *was* a way of escape, and that it lay along the road of compromise and common sense. The end of government, he held, was not the realisation of idealistic theories, but the welfare of the nation. To this extent he was, like David Hume, a utilitarian before Bentham—but not before Bolingbroke. Intensely as he detested Bolingbroke's theology, in politics he was undoubtedly his disciple, and the developer of his ideas. Striking as are the superficial differences between the *Patriot King* and the *Thoughts on the Present Discontents*, there is in them a fundamental identity in motive and a broad agreement as to means. Bolingbroke had said in 1738, in words the novelty of which was more evident to his contemporaries than it is to us, "The ultimate end of all Governments is the good of the people, for whose sake they were made, and without whose consent they could not have been made."[1] No sentiment could possibly have been more consonant with Whiggism, and Burke constantly echoed and re-echoed it. In his American speeches, his Indian addresses, his Irish letters, his French reflections—everywhere it occurs and recurs. "All political power," he said in supporting Fox's India Bill in 1783, "which is set over men . . . ought to be some way or other exercised ultimately for their benefit." Again, in his *Reflections*: "Kings, in one sense, are undoubtedly the servants of the people, because their power has no other national end than that of the general advantage." So too in his letter to Sir Hercules Langrishe anent Ireland: "The good of the commonwealth is the rule which rides over the rest, and to this every other must completely submit." The application of this rule meant that measures were to be judged not by their accordance with systems antecedently constructed, but by their consequences as estimated by the standard of, not exactly felicity, and certainly not mere material comfort, but rather a real and comprehensive well-being that looked more to character and destiny than to circumstances and ephemeral pleasure. It was in this appreciation of spiritual values that Burke differed profoundly from the utilitarians of the schools of Hume,

[1] A. Hassall, *Bolingbroke on Patriotism*, p. 73.

Helvétius, Bentham, and—low be it whispered respecting the venerable archdeacon—Paley.

Bolingbroke, then, was Burke's great forerunner and teacher. But, although Bolingbroke in his later political writings had propounded principles of (considering the writer's antecedents) astonishing Whiggishness, it was scarcely possible for a prominent member of the Whig Party during the reign of the son of Bolingbroke's model "Patriot King" openly to avow himself a Bolingbrokian. "Who now reads Bolingbroke? Who ever read him through?" he asked in his *Reflections*; and a little later in the same work he remarked, "I do not often quote Bolingbroke, nor have his works in general left any permanent impression on my mind. He is a presumptuous and a superficial writer." These unkind observations recall the repudiations of Peter in the hall of the high-priest's house. For Burke, especially in his early and most impressionable years, was soaked in Bolingbroke; and his style never lost the form given to it by that Augustan master of resounding rhetoric.

Not Bolingbroke, however, but Locke was the oracle of the Whig Party. Locke was the philosopher of the "glorious revolution" of 1688, and upon the basis of that revolution, as interpreted and vindicated by Locke, the whole edifice of eighteenth-century Whiggism had been erected. Hence it followed that Burke, who in his fundamental political conceptions differed *toto cælo* from Locke, was compelled to render him lip-service; just as the modern Labour M.P., however sensible an individualist he may be, is bound to speak respectfully of Marx. One of the most interesting tasks that a student of political theory is called upon to perform in his perusal of the writings of Burke is to observe the way in which his author, when he comes face to face with a distinctive Lockian idea, bows down to it and worships, circumvents it, knocks it over from behind, and then goes on his way rejoicing. What are the principal Lockian ideas in the sphere of political theory? They are, of course, (1) the conception of the State and Government as artificial creations, based on contract, and built up by means of a series of legal enactments; (2) the inherence in the individual, anterior to the formation of the State, of a number of natural rights—especially the rights to life, liberty, and property— the protection of which is the prime function of the State; (3) the superiority of natural law to all laws of human origin; and (4) the complete separation of the functions of Church and State.

Perhaps the best example of Burke's attitude to Locke is to be found in his treatment of the contract theory. This theory is fundamental to Locke; for the whole Whig defence of the expulsion of James II in 1688 was based on the assertion that the Stuart monarch had "endeavoured to subvert the constitution of the kingdom by breaking the original contract between King and people."[1] The contract theory was the Whig riposte to the Tory dogma of the divine hereditary right of the ruler. Burke, therefore, as a member of the Whig party, as secretary to the Whig Prime Minister, and as the vindicator of Whig policy in Parliament and Press, could not be disrespectful to contract. But it was wholly alien from his system of thought. This is how, in a famous passage, he saluted and destroyed it:

Society is indeed a contract . . . but the State ought not to be considered as nothing better than a partnership agreement in a trade of pepper and coffee, calico or tobacco, or some other such low concern, to be taken up for a little temporary interest, and to be dissolved by the fancy of the parties. It is to be looked on with other reverence; because it is not a partnership in things subservient only to the gross animal existence of a temporary and perishable nature. It is a partnership in all science; a partnership in all art; a partnership in every virtue, and in all perfection. As the ends of such a partnership cannot be obtained in many generations, it becomes a partnership not only between those who are living, but between those who are dead and those who are to be born. Each contract of each particular State is but a clause in the great primeval contract of eternal society, linking the lower with the higher natures, connecting the visible and invisible world, according to a fixed

[1] Resolution of House of Commons, January 1689.

compact sanctioned by the inviolable oath which holds all physical and all moral natures each in their appointed place.[1]

If one asks what is the meaning of this sonorous passage, the answer is that as it stands it has none. It is resounding nonsense. In particular, the concluding sentence respecting "primeval contracts" and "inviolable oaths" is the emptiest verbiage. But its sheer vanity and vacuity has a profound significance; it sublimates Locke's contract theory into limbo. What could a sober lawyer make of an agreement between the dead and the unborn; from whom would he get his fee? What sort of an oath is that which holds the stars in their courses? Language has obviously lost its ordinary meaning. But, with the rest of the vocabulary, the term "contract" has virtually vanished away—that is to say, it has been so completely eviscerated and embalmed that it remains as a mere mummy of its Lockian self. With it has departed from the palace to the pyramid the whole attendant company of Locke's individualistic concepts. The way is made clear for the entry of the new (yet immemorially old) idea of society as an organism; of the State as arising from the will of God rather than from the wit of man; of the community as an entity claiming priority to each and all of its members. Burke, in short, was preparing the way for the transmutation of Old Whiggism into New Conservatism.

VII

Respecting the other Lockian fundamentals—that is, natural law, the inherent primeval rights of the individual, and the complete separation of the spheres of Church and State—it is not possible to quote quite so striking an example of formal acceptance combined with substantial repudiation as in the case of the contract theory. Nevertheless, they were all of them, in effect, eliminated from his system. The only laws that Burke in practice recognised were the laws of God and the laws of civilised society. The *lex naturæ* or *jus naturale*,

[1] *Reflections on the Revolution*, Burke's works, 1854-57, i, 368-369.

which had played so large a part in juridical speculation from the days of the Stoics and the early Christian Fathers down to the days of Aquinas, Suarez, Hooker, Grotius, and Locke, simply vanished ghostlike from the political stage. It was playing too prominent a part in Rousseau's travelling menagerie for Burke to have any place for it in his subsidised theatre.

The inherent primeval rights of the individual—the right to life, the right to liberty, the right to property—were in the same case. Burke did not—could not as a good Whig—definitely denounce them. Nay, he even appealed to them now and again, when it suited him to do so, as, for example, in his defence of the peoples of India against the tyranny of Warren Hastings. But as a rule he ignored them, and, in the case of the French Revolutionists, refused to allow them to be employed as weapons to rebut the claims of the French monarchy. The only rights that he commonly admitted as valid were rights based on the civil laws of the State, provided that civil laws accorded with the precepts of the eternal law of God.

But the law of God, the will of Heaven, the Divine Providence, he regarded as supreme over all. It was, indeed, in the eminent place that he assigned to religion that he differed most widely from the philosophical and semi-secular Locke. Locke's famous theory of toleration was based on the view that the State has nothing to do with religion. The State, he maintained, is wholly concerned with this world; religion with the next. The function of the State is to defend man's natural rights on earth; the function of the Church is to convey his soul to heaven. Hence, unless the Church trespasses upon the sphere of the State by promulgating immoral, anti-social, or anti-political doctrines, it should be left severely alone—neither fostered nor persecuted. This attitude of rather unfriendly aloofness was impossible for Burke. For he was profoundly religious, and he held that the very foundations of society were laid deep in the doctrines of God, free will, and immortality.

Thus, if we ask what was the system of thought that Burke

instituted in place of the individualistic, conventional, legalistic, contractual, and semi-secular system of Locke, the answer will, I think, be in substance as follows. First and foremost he emphasised the religious basis of society. Professor John MacCunn so clearly and tersely summarised his views that I cannot do better than quote his words. "Burke's political religion," he says,

> has its roots deep in three convictions. The first is that civil society rests on spiritual foundations, being indeed nothing less than a product of divine will; the second, that this is a fact of significance so profound that the recognition of it is of vital moment, both for the corporate life of the State and for the lives of each and all of its members; and the third, that, whilst all forms of religion within the nation may play their part in bearing witness to religion, this is peculiarly the function of an established Church in which the "consecration of the State" finds its appropriate symbol, expression, and support.[1]

It is in the *Reflections on the Revolution in France* that Burke most strongly expresses these views. He was horrified at the naked atheism that he saw rampant on the devastated fields of France. "We know," he cried, "and, what is better, we feel inwardly that religion is the basis of civil society, and the source of all good and of all comfort." Again: "We know, and it is our pride to know, that man is by his constitution a religious animal; that atheism is against not only our reason, but our instincts." The State, equally with society, is, he contends, of divine institution. God is its builder and maker. "He willed the State," he boldly asserts; "He willed its connection with the source and original archetype of all perfection." In another passage he adds: "All who administer in the government of men . . . stand in the person of God himself." Hence "the consecration of the State by a State religious establishment is necessary," and in England

> the majority of the people, far from thinking a religious national establishment unlawful, hardly think it lawful to be without one. . . . They do not consider their Church establishment as

[1] J. MacCunn, *Political Philosophy of Burke*, p. 122 (1913).

convenient, but as essential to their State. . . . They consider it as the foundation of their whole constitution, with which, and with every part of which, it holds an indissoluble union. Church and State are ideas inseparable in their minds, and scarcely is the one ever mentioned without mentioning the other.

An echo of the last sentiment occurs in the first letter to Langrishe:

> There is no man on earth, I believe, more willing than I am to lay it down as a fundamental of the constitution that the Church of England should be united and even identified with it.

A thinker so convinced as was Burke of the divine origin of society, state, and government could not take a merely mechanistic view of human institutions. Just as "poeta nascitur non fit," so, in his opinion, was community more akin to an organism than to an organisation. It was created rather than constructed; its development was a growth rather than an elaboration; it had the unity and continuity of life rather than the fortuitous complexity of an invention. In other words, Burke lifted political theory out of the category of law in which it had wallowed for a couple of centuries into the category of biology, wherein it was to run riot during the next hundred years. He constantly used such metaphors as "The physician of the State, who, not satisfied with the cure of distempers, undertakes to regenerate constitutions, ought to show uncommon powers." Metaphors like this imply that the body politic is an organism in the full and proper sense of the term; but metaphors often imply more than their employer intends. And Burke never in his discreet moments went farther than to say that the State was closely akin to an organism. He never so completely divested himself of his Old Whig individualism as completely to merge man in the State, or as utterly to reduce the citizen to the rank of a mere cell in a larger entity. Indeed, in his first letter on *Regicide Peace* he went so far as to argue against those who pressed the biological analogy to the point of contending that States had necessarily the same stages of childhood, manhood, and old age as had the individual man. "Parallels of this sort," he said,

> rather furnish similitudes to illustrate or to adorn than supply analogies from whence to reason. The objects which are attempted to be forced into an analogy are not found in the same classes of existence. Individuals are physical beings, subject to laws universal and invariable . . . but commonwealths are not physical but moral essences. They are artificial combinations and, in their proximate efficient cause, the arbitrary productions of the human mind. We are not yet acquainted with the laws which necessarily influence the stability of that kind of work made by that kind of agent.

In this passage Burke, in the heat of argument, approaches nearer to the Lockian position than in any other passage that I recollect. Commonly, however, all his metaphors and similes indicate that he conceived of the State as an entity possessed of some kind of life—a life transmitted from bygone generations, and a life to be passed on undiminished in abundance to succeeding ages. So essential, in fact, was the biological analogy to his system of political thought that it gives us the key to his attitude toward all the great practical questions that he was called upon to discuss. He was a reformer in respect of Ireland, India, America, and the England of 1770, because he realised that circumstances constantly change, and that as they change old institutions become obsolete and need to be modified or removed. In the later language of evolution, he perceived the continual need for an organism that wishes to survive to adapt itself to its environment. On the other hand, in respect of the France and the England of 1790–97, he was an anti-revolutionary, because he was acutely conscious of the fact that Jacobinism menaced the national existence itself. The body politic might be sick and need a physician; but Jacobinism was not a medicine, but a deadly poison. The body politic might be diseased and require an operation; Jacobinism, however, did not connote a remedial amputation, but a fatal decapitation. In other words, he realised the vital necessity of preserving the continuity of the national life; the peril of making too complete a breach with the past; the mortal error of sweeping away the whole heritage of the past and trying to create all things new.

Burke as a conservative reformer was equally opposed to Jacobitism and Jacobinism. In the interest of progress he advocated the cautious improvement in the working of old-established institutions. In the interest of order he resisted irreverent innovations that paid no regard to venerable tradition, but, in contempt of historic antecedents, proceeded

> to build Jerusalem
> In England's green and pleasant land.

In the sphere of practical politics Burke was entirely consistent throughout his career: he was always a reformer and never a revolutionary; always a Conservative and never a Tory. In the sphere of political theory it is not so easy to assert and prove his undeviating consistency. For he always had Locke, like the Old Man of the Sea, on his shoulders. Sometimes he says what the Old Man tells him, and at other times he says what he himself thinks. And, as we have seen, concerning such matters as contracts, rights, law, and religion the two voices did not naturally accord. But, considering the difference of spirit between the two, the divergence of language is not so great as might have been expected.

VIII

When Burke died Jacobinism seemed to be definitely in the ascendant in Europe. The "Regicide Directory" ruled in France; the Revolutionary armies, having broken up the great coalition formed against them, were sweeping victoriously over the Continent, and were menacing even England with invasion. In England itself sedition and treason, welcoming the expected Jacobin attack, threatened the total subversion of both throne and altar.

The very completeness, however, with which Burke's warnings had been justified, and his prophecies fulfilled, gave impressiveness to his reflections and appeals. His influence began to grow and to extend its range. Young statesmen, like George Canning, who for a moment had been carried away by the delusive hopes engendered by Jacobin enthusiasm, rallied to the defence of the old and tried constitution. Literary men, such as Wordsworth, Coleridge, and Southey, all of whom at one time or other had professed revolutionary principles, disillusioned by the excesses of the French, became avowed disciples of Burke, and in due course, as such, initiated the Romantic Reaction, which did something to repair the damage done by the wanton destroyers of antiquity. And from that time onward the power of Burke has continued to increase and to spread the scope of its operation, until to-day the great Whig thinker and statesman lives and moves in the minds of all men throughout the wide world who wish to combine devotion to liberty with respect for authority; hope for the future with reverence for the past; support of party with service of the nation; profound patriotism with sincere goodwill to all the "vicinage of mankind"; essential moderation with zealous enthusiasm; a sane conservatism with cautious reform.

BOOK LIST

A. PRIMARY SOURCES

BURKE, EDMUND:
1. Works. 8 vols. London, 1854–57.
2. *Speeches*. 4 vols. London, 1816.
3. *Correspondence*. 4 vols. London, 1844.

B. SECONDARY SOURCES

BAUMANN, A. A.: *Burke, the Founder of Conservatism.* 1929.

BISSET, R.: *Life of Edmund Burke.* 1798.

BURKE, PETER: *The Public and Domestic Life of Edmund Burke.* 1854.

COBBAN, A.: *Edmund Burke and the Revolt against the Eighteenth Century.* 1929.

CROLY, GEORGE: *A Memoir of the Political Life of Edmund Burke.* 1840.

HAZLITT, WILLIAM: *Political Essays.* 1819.

MacCUNN, JOHN: *Political Philosophy of Burke.* 1913.

MACKNIGHT, THOMAS: *History of the Life and Times of Edmund Burke.* 3 vols. 1858–60.

MORLEY, JOHN: *Burke, a Historical Study.* 1867.
—— *Burke, a Biography.* 1879.
MURRAY, R. H.: *Edmund Burke: a Biography.* 1931.
NAPIER, SIR JOSEPH: *Lecture on the Life of Burke.* 1862.
NEWMAN, BERTRAM: *Edmund Burke.* 1927.
PAYNE, E. J.: *Burke's Select Works.* 3 vols. 1874.
PRIOR, JAMES: *Life of Edmund Burke.* 1824.
ROSEBERY, EARL OF: *Appreciations and Addresses.* 1899.
SAMUELS, A. P. I.: *Early Life of Edmund Burke.* 1923.

VIII

AUSTIN AND STATE SOVEREIGNTY[1]

THE fifty years of punctuated peace that followed the Napoleonic wars—the period that has been named "the era of reaction and reconstruction"—was divided into two unequal portions by the *annus mirabilis*, 1830. Up to that date reaction was dominant throughout Europe: after that date reform, revolution, and reconstruction became ascendant. The outstanding events that marked the turn of the tide were, first, the final expulsion from Paris of the Bourbon dynasty, which failed and fell because of the proved incapacity of its members either to learn anything or to forget anything; secondly, the successful revolt of the Belgians against the Dutch ruler of the United Netherlands—a revolt that initiated the disintegration of the treaty system elaborately constructed at Vienna in 1815; thirdly, the death of the obstructive George IV, and the accession of his more mobile brother, William; and, finally, the resignation of the Wellington Ministry in November, followed by the return of the Whigs, under Grey and Russell, to office and to power, after a long and weary period of exclusion.

In respect of England the period of reaction may be said to have begun as far back in history as the accession of George III in 1760. For not only did George III himself —trained as he was by Bute in the principles of Boling-

[1] From *The Social and Political Ideas of Some Representative Thinkers of the Age of Reaction and Reconstruction*, 1815–65 (Harrap, 1932). The other studies in this volume are: "The Age of Reaction and Reconstruction, 1815–65," by Norman Sykes; "Chateaubriand and the French Romantics," by Constantia Maxwell; "Hegel the German Idealist," by A. D. Lindsay; "Coleridge and the English Conservatives," by Keith Feiling; "Robert Owen and the Early Socialists," by Frances M. Page; "John Stuart Mill and the Philosophical Radicals," by Robert S. Dower; "Auguste Comte and the Positive Philosophers," by Theodora Bosanquet; "Thomas Hodgskin and the Individualists," by C. H. Driver.

broke—make it his prime endeavour to drive out the Whigs, and to emancipate himself from the control of their Cabinet; but Whigs and Tories alike were taught by such high authorities as the French Montesquieu, the Swiss de Lolme, and their own countryman, Blackstone, that the English constitution was—by reason of the division and balance of its powers—perfection, and that the cry for reform was but the voice of ignorance or perversity. On the Continent, however, where despotism—occasionally benevolent, but more often the reverse—prevailed till 1789, reaction did not set in until, near the end of the century, the failure of the Revolution to fulfil its promises drove the disillusioned majority to turn its eyes and fix its hopes once more on the overturned thrones, the desecrated altars, the despoiled nobilities, and the disendowed priesthoods of the *Ancien Régime*.

No three writers better represent the composite spirit of the reaction than the French Chateaubriand, the German Hegel, and the English Coleridge. The first sought to stem the rising tide of secularism by re-erecting the demolished dam of mediæval faith; the second endeavoured to counter the encroaching anarchy by exalting the authority of the State; the third strove to provide an antidote to revolutionary novelty by reviving and re-interpreting all "the old perfections of the earth." In a striking manner, indeed, Coleridge resembled the Neo-Platonic philosophers of the days of dying Rome, the men who endeavoured to put the new wine of rationality into the old bottles of pagan superstition.

Similarly, no three writers more adequately typify the varied aspects of the genius of reconstruction than do Owen, Mill, and Comte. The enthusiastic but unbalanced manufacturer of New Lanark, who dreamed of building a new society on the four pillars of communism, co-operation, culture, and currency reform, stood for all that was most representative of the wild utopianism of the age. The Utilitarian servant of the East India Company, who employed his ample leisure in demonstrating how a new world could be peacefully evolved out of the old by means of education, freedom, and democratic government, stood for all that was most representative of the mild meliorism of the age. The religious and philosophical Frenchman, who denounced and repudiated both theology and metaphysics, and yet founded a school and initiated a cult, stood for all that was most representative of the agnostic materialism and positive science of the age.

For the age—roughly 1830–65—was one in which profound and numerous changes were rapidly taking place. The Industrial Revolution was transforming the arts and crafts not only of England, but of all Continental countries, and of America; the vast economic upheaval that ensued was transmuting the face of society, giving rise to a new middle class, converting also, as by the spell of an evil magician, the peasantry into a proletariat, and herding it into pestilential urban slums. On the other hand, the spread of education and the consequent "march of mind" were generating a new speculation into the meaning of life. Biblical criticism was shaking men's faith in orthodox religion. The revelations of natural science—in particular geology and biology—were opening up new vistas of probability to the imagination of thinkers. The dreams of political reformers and social revolutionaries were stimulating in the minds of the unhappy and oppressed proletariat visions of a radically regenerated earth. On the Continent men undisciplined in intellect and inexperienced in the conduct of affairs were carried away by the wild fantasies of Saint-Simon, Fourier, Proudhon, Cabet, Lassalle, and Marx. In England, on the other hand, although the writings of men like Charles Hall, William Thompson, and Thomas Hodgskin show that fantastic speculation was not unknown, the dominant progressive influence was that of Jeremy Bentham and his school of Philosophical Radicals.

Jeremy Bentham was not a great original thinker. His Utilitarian ethics, which taught that the ultimate test of conduct is its consequences, he learned from Hume, and from Hume's great predecessor, Hobbes. His Utilitarian politics—between which and the ethics a deep logical gulf yawned—he picked up from Beccaria, Helvétius, Priestley, Paley, and other contemporaries: it was in the air. It taught that the aim of government *ought to be* "the greatest happiness of the greatest number"; but, since the idea of obligation is absent from Utilitarian ethics, why the Government should have this aim, or, indeed, how its individual members could conceivably have so altruistic an aim, is not evident. Man, however, or at any rate the Englishman, is not a severely logical animal, and the "greatest happiness" formula, with its implication of human equality, exactly suited the requirements of the time. It provided the magic phrase—the "Open Sesame"—before which the barriers of privilege and prerogative, of monopoly and nepotism, of iniquity and inequity, went down, leaving the way free for the unimpeded advance of individual energy and initiative.

Bentham had disciples in many walks of life, and of many shades of politics. His most wholehearted admirers and enthusiastic followers were, of course, the so-called Philosophical Radicals, headed by James Mill and his eldest son, John Stuart Mill: they shared both his zeal for drastic political reform and his rejection of intuitional religion. The Manchester School of economists, also, were Benthamites in their denunciation of Government interference and their advocacy of *laissez-faire*. Sir Robert Peel and his favourite pupil, the young Gladstone, were profoundly influenced by Benthamite humanitarianism. Nearly all moderate English opinion in the early Victorian age was, indeed, Benthamite. Only the more extreme opinion remanied alien—on the one side the Conservatism of Lord Eldon, and on the other side the Communism of Karl Marx. Numerous, however, as were the groups of Benthamites, solitary and unique among them stood the figure of John Austin.

II

Of John Austin's career it is not necessary to say much. Unlike Rousseau, Austin was not a man whose opinions reflected mirror-like the changes and chances of an ever-shifting environment. Unlike Burke, he did not play a great part in practical affairs, or express his ideas in forms determined by the exigencies of the political problems of the moment. He lived, indeed, a life singularly remote from the common ways of men; his habitual abode was the spaceless and untimely realm of thought. He himself once remarked, "I was born out of time and place; I ought to have been a schoolman of the twelfth century or a German professor." It is doubtful, however, whether he would have felt at home even in a mediæval Benedictine monastery or in a modern German university; for his intense individualism would have rebelled against the rigid curriculum of the cloistered school, while his ingrained lethargy and untidiness would have sought and found escape from the systematised labour expected of a Teutonic professor. He was, in fact, according to any terrestrial standard, a failure. He had, in the judgment of all who knew him, great, though slow-moving, powers of mind; but they were rendered inoperative by defects of character—by laziness, by unpunctuality, by lack of a sense of proportion, and by a curious incapacity to bring to a conclusion any work that he attempted. His only chance of success would have been to be compelled to earn his own living; but from this saving chance he was excluded by the too kind Providence that gave him a wealthy father, a prosperous brother, and a capable wife. "It is doubtful," says his biographer, "whether he even made in the last forty-two years of his life, by his profession, by his pen, or as a lecturer, a hundred pounds."[1]

Born in 1790, the eldest son of a Suffolk miller who became rich by means of war-contracts, he entered the Army with a purchased commission in 1807, and served for five years in Malta and in Sicily under Lord William Bentinck. These years—the period of the great Napoleonic struggle that began at Tilsit and ended at Moscow—were a lustrum of intense agitation; but almost all we know of the young Lieutenant Austin's share in the hurly-burly is that during his term of service in the Mediterranean he managed to get and to read

[1] Sir John Macdonell in the *Dictionary of National Biography*, ii, 268.

Dugald Stewart's *Philosophical Essays*, Drummond's *Academical Questions*, Enfield's *History of Philosophy*, and Mitford's *Greece*. Having learned so much, we are not surprised that the next information we receive is to the effect that in 1812 he himself and the military authorities concurred in thinking that he had completed such contribution as he was qualified to make towards the resettlement of Europe, and that he might therefore with advantage be released for civilian pursuits. Consequently, at the age of twenty-two, he sold his commission and began to read for the Bar. That is one reason why he could not claim to share with Bill Adams the glory of winning the battle of Waterloo! Soon his military experiences faded into the dim, indefinite background of his life; but they probably impressed upon his mind a permanent tendency to over-emphasise the element of command in law, and to stress unduly the indivisible and illimitable character of supreme authority. His jurisprudence always smacked of the drill-sergeant.

In 1818 he was called to the Bar by the Inner Temple, and for seven years he strove to secure a practice, partly on the Norfolk Circuit, and partly in chambers at Lincoln's Inn. But practice eluded him. He was too slow, too heavy, too meticulous, too conscientious, too much behind time, too unpractical. In 1825 he gave it up for ever. At that date his younger brother, Charles, then twenty-six years of age, was just at the beginning of his brilliant and unprecedentedly successful forensic career. It would be difficult to conceive two brothers more strikingly different: John, ponderous, laborious, hesitant in judgment, ineffective; Charles, light, facile, even more cocksure than his friend Macaulay, over-whelmingly decisive in argument or debate.[1]

Charles Austin, called to the Bar in 1827, took silk in 1841, made over £100,000 in the one year of the railway crisis (1847), retired with a fortune at the age of forty-nine, and lived for another quarter of a century in cultured comfort. Concerning his brother, nine years his senior, Charles

[1] See the sketches of Charles Austin given in Mill's *Autobiography* and Trevelyan's *Macaulay*.

remarked, "John is much cleverer than I, but he is always knocking his head against principles." Every one seems to have been impressed by John's cleverness. "He was a man of great intellectual powers," said the younger Mill, who had him as a tutor, and attended his lectures. "If John Austin had had health," said Lord Brougham, "neither Lyndhurst nor I would have been Chancellor." But no two critics could agree as to precisely why so much talent should have resulted in such complete futility. His brother attributed his failure to conscience; his wife to shyness and reserve; Mill to melancholia; and Brougham to indigestion. Whichever of the four was correct, the fact remains that (if the logical process of rule of three be sound) it would have taken him, at his rate of earning, 42,000 years to make the sum of money that Charles made in 1847.

The success of a thinker, however, is not measurable in terms of cash. Charles is now forgotten, save as a name associated with the more enduring names of Mill and Macaulay. John lives, by his own merit, as a legal philosopher who, as the result of much-protracted, often-intermitted, intolerably prolix, and never-completed labours, did a permanently valuable piece of work in determining the province of jurisprudence, defining its vocabulary, and clearing away the fogs of many bewildering misconceptions that clung around it. His main tasks as a jurist were accomplished during the eight years 1826–34. In the first of these years he was appointed, through the influence of Jeremy Bentham and James Mill, to the chair of jurisprudence in the newly constituted University of London (University College). Since the college was not to be opened until the autumn of 1828, Austin had two years in which to think of what to say. He occupied the time in going to Germany and—particularly at the Universities of Heidelberg and Bonn—in sitting at the feet of the great modern civilians who there taught the revived and rejuvenated Roman law. His wife accompanied him, and helped him with the language.

John Austin's wife, Sarah, has already been mentioned twice, and it is necessary here to pause a moment in order to

note a few things about her. She was a remarkable woman
—beautiful, talented, brilliant, fascinating, high-souled.
That she was attracted by the judicially minded John is the
best evidence we have that he was possessed of a charm
which he conspicuously failed to impart to his writings. She
herself secured, and continues to hold, an independent place
in English literature. As translator of Ranke's *History of the
Popes* and of Guizot's *English Revolution*, as author of a work
on *Germany from 1760 to 1814*, and as editor of her husband's
unliterary remains, she displayed abilities of a high order.
John and Sarah (three years his junior) were married in 1820.
They settled in Queen Square Place (now Queen Anne's
Gate), Westminster, close to Bentham and the Mills, and
there in 1821 was born their only child, Lucie, who became
Lady Duff Gordon.[1]

From Queen Square Place in 1826 John and Sarah set out
for Germany, and in Germany they remained for nearly two
years—that is, until it was time for John to begin his course
of lectures. The lectures, on the province of jurisprudence—
toilsome, slow-moving, over-elaborated, arid, burdened with
irrelevancies, and incalculably remote from the practice of
the law—in spite of their novelty, originality, and high logical
power, failed to attract students. And since the professors at
University College were at that time dependent for their
salaries on the fees paid by their pupils, after four years, when
the class had dwindled to five, Austin had to resign. His
pupils, however, although few, had included a striking proportion of young men destined to eminence in the worlds of
law and politics—*e.g.*, J. S. Mill, G. Cornewall Lewis, Lord
Belper, Lord Romilly, Charles Villiers, Charles Buller, and
Sir W. Erle. They all spoke with profound respect of their
teacher, and all confessed that they owed him an incalculable
debt for the clarification of their legal ideas.

Nevertheless he had, for the third time, failed. Sarah

[1] It is a curious coincidence that precisely at the time when Sarah Austin in
Queen Square Place was encouraging and befriending the young John Stuart
Mill in Guilford Street, not very far away, Sara Austen, wife of a prosperous
solicitor, was assisting the youthful Benjamin Disraeli, of Bloomsbury Square,
to get his first novel, *Vivian Grey*, into shape for publication.

Austin, in the memoir which she prefixed to her husband's posthumous works, says:

> Such was the end of his exertions in a cause to which he had devoted himself with an ardour and singleness of purpose of which few men are capable. This was the real and irremediable calamity of his life—the blow from which he never recovered.

The remaining failures of his career can soon be chronicled. In 1833 he was made a member of a commission to inquire into the criminal law: The report, issued in June 1834, showed that he had failed to convince the Commissioners that a code and not a mere digest was requisite. In 1837 he was appointed to lecture in the Inner Temple on "the general principles of jurisprudence and international law," but he failed to keep an audience, and the course was suspended within a few weeks. In 1836 he went to Malta, the scene of his early military inactivities, together with his old pupil G. Cornewall Lewis, in order to inquire, on behalf of the Government, into the condition of the laws and into the grievances of the natives. In his search for the ideal constitution he failed to keep in contact with the realities of the situation, and his report (1837), though juridically interesting, was practically useless. Then his health failed, and for ten years he was taken about by his devoted wife from one resort to another—Carlsbad, Dresden, Berlin, and Paris. Finally, the 1848 upheaval in Paris drove him back to England. He settled at Weybridge, and, failing to find anything to do, he spent the concluding eleven years of his life in placid, and not unhappy, idleness. In December 1859 he failed to remain alive.

III

Seeing that John Austin lived to the mature age of sixty-nine, and considering that during two-thirds of his existence he was supposed to be studying law, we must admit that his output was surprisingly small. In 1832 he published the substance of his University College lectures under the title of *The Province of Jurisprudence Determined*. The book, described by Lord Melbourne as the dullest he had ever read, fell flat; few lawyers took any notice of it; no second edition was called for during its author's lifetime; even to-day it is scarcely known outside the English-speaking world. Nay, in England itself its solid worth has been recognised only since, in the sixties, it began to be vehemently attacked. No other book than this ever came from his pen. He wrote, however, occasionally for the reviews. Mill tells us in his *Autobiography* that Austin contributed one article to the *Westminster* criticising McCulloch's defence of primogeniture. He published at least two in the *Edinburgh*; one (1842) adversely reviewing List's *National System of Political Economy*, and the other (1847) advocating a strong central Government, supplemented and moderated by an extensive system of local devolution. Towards the close of his life (1859) he was invited by the editor of the *Quarterly* to furnish an article opposing Russell's projected scheme of Parliamentary reform. He produced the article; but he prefaced it with so voluminous a survey of the whole English constitution that the editor had to decline to publish it. Austin therefore issued it as a separate pamphlet (Murray, 1859). It is extremely interesting as showing how a good Benthamite Utilitarian could be a sound and thoroughgoing Tory. In the pamphlet Austin, after completing his survey of the constitution, expatiated on the inexpediency of any change, enlarged on the evils which any extension of the franchise would entail, dwelt (with obvious recollection of Paris in 1848) on the horrors of mob-rule, and concluded by showing the beneficent consequences of even the anomalies of the existing system of representation. After his death his devoted wife, with infinite toil, collected and arranged his chaotic manuscripts, supplemented them from the old notebooks of quondam pupils (especially those of Mill), and produced the two-volumed *Jurisprudence* (Murray, 1863) which remains the chief monument to his fame.[1]

Austin's *Jurisprudence* is a curious work, unique of its kind.

[1] *Cf.* John Stuart Mill's "Austin on Jurisprudence," originally published in the *Edinburgh Review*, October 1863; reprinted in *Dissertations and Discussions*, vol. iii (1867).

It consists of four completed sections, and a collection of *disjecta membra*. Of the completed sections the first, and incomparably the most important, is the old (1832) *Province of Jurisprudence Determined*. The other three sections deal respectively with (1) pervading notions—that is, the connotation of legal terms such as right and duty, person and thing, will and intention, negligence and inadvertence; (2) law considered in relation to its sources; and (3) law considered in respect of its purposes and subjects. The defects of the book, apart from its intolerable style, are numerous and glaring. Its arrangement is imperfect; its basis of classification indefensible; its omissions numerous; its repetitions tedious beyond measure; its over-elaboration ridiculous; its irrelevancies many and protracted; its disfigurement by italics excessive; its occasional truculence of language disturbing, if now and again diverting. But over against these defects it had merits which those who first read it in the sixties were more ready to recognise than some of the pundits of this later age. It clarified once for all some of the fundamental notions of law; it swept away finally many pernicious confusions, the practical consequences of which had been serious; it dammed certain current metaphors whence for generations had flowed streams of nonsense whereby, as he expressively remarks, "the field of jurisprudence and morals had been deluged with muddy speculation."

Mill had no doubt as to the value of Austin's work. He considered that it "placed him in the estimation of all competent judges in the very highest rank of thinkers." He regarded it as an incomparable discipline in "the difficult and precise art of thought," adding that, "though the merit and worth of his writings as a contribution to the philosophy of jurisprudence are conspicuous, their educational value as a training-school for the highest class of intellects will be found to be still greater." His reasoned conclusion was that "no one thoroughly versed in these volumes need ever again miss his way amidst the obscurity and confusion of legal language." [1] Sir Henry Maine, twelve years later, although

[1] J. S. Mill, *Dissertations and Discussions*, iii, 206–274.

he dissented emphatically from some of Austin's views, agreed with Mill as to the sterling value of Austin's analysis. "There is not," he said,

> the smallest necessity for accepting all the conclusions of these great writers [*i.e.*, Bentham and Austin] with implicit deference; but there is the strongest necessity for knowing what these conclusions are. They are indispensable, if for no other object, for the purpose of clearing the head.[1]

Sir Thomas Erskine Holland, no more a disciple of Austin than was Maine, concurs in Maine's eulogy. The *Jurisprudence*, he asserts, is

> a book which no one can read without improvement. It presents the spectacle of a powerful and conscientious mind struggling with an intractable and rarely handled material, while those distinctions upon which Austin after his somewhat superfluously careful manner bestows most labour are put in so clear a light that they can hardly again be lost sight of.[2]

Austin, in short, had a mole-like mind. Its operations were subterranean, tedious, and obscure. It rarely ascended to the surface, and it never rose into the air. Hence it remained oblivious to scenery, and failed to see things in their entirety. But it did invaluable work in grubbing about among the roots of thought, and in tracing ideas to their sources. Nevertheless a mole-like mind is a muddled mind; and Austin, if with wearisome burrowing he succeeded in unravelling some of the radical tangles that he found in the legal underworld, undoubtedly himself created others. To be specific: if he elucidated the meaning of 'law' he still further confounded for us the connotation of 'sovereignty.' But of that more anon. Suffice it here to say that his influence as an analyser of fundamental legal ideas was far-reaching and beneficent. His book opened a new era in the science of jurisprudence—that is to say, in the study of the abstract or formal philosophy of positive law. It served, moreover, as a model to all workers in the realm of the moral and social

---

[1] Maine, *Early History of Institutions*, p. 343 (1875).
[2] Holland, *Jurisprudence*, preface to first edition (1880).

sciences, impressing them with the supreme importance of the exact use of words and of the employment of rigid logical processes. In the world of legal practice it powerfully assisted the causes of simplification, codification, and reform. Above all, it stimulated further research into the meaning of the three great terms, Law, Sovereignty, and State. And, if it be argued that research into the connotation of abstract nouns is an insignificant occupation for all persons except infants at school, the reply is that there have been few graver causes of civil conflagrations and international conflicts than precisely these terms which are so hard to define. One could draw many parallels from the realm of theology; for all theological controversies are logomachies. For example, as is well known the difference of meaning between *homo-ousios* and *homoi-ousios* caused the streets of Constantinople, in the fourth, fifth, and sixth centuries of the Christian era, to flow with blood. It is, however, sufficient for our purpose to note, by way of illustration, that the Hundred Years War between England and France was fought to decide the question whether the Salic Law was a law or not a law; that the Civil War between Charles I and his Parliament was fought to decide the question whether the English sovereign was a sovereign or not a sovereign; and that the great nineteenth-century struggle between the North and the South in America was fought to decide the question whether an American state was a state or not a state. In other words, the conceptions represented by the terms Law, Sovereignty, and State lie at the very foundation of political principle and governmental institution. Just as Tennyson truly says, respecting the "flower in the crannied wall" which he has plucked and examined (reversing the process followed in respect of students at universities):

> Little flower—but *if* I could understand
> What you are, root and all, and all in all,
> I should know what God and man is,

so if political idealists could but say precisely what are the nature, the source, and the sphere of supreme authority they would have solved the problem of the governance of men.

IV

THE THEORY OF LAW[1]

The term 'law' has from the first been an ambiguous one:
it has connoted two ideas, closely connected, yet distinct—
namely, (1) a causal authority and (2) a consequent uniformity of behaviour. In other words, it has stood for both
force and order; for both will and regularity; for both
general command in the imperative mood and general statement in the indicative. Not until the dawn of the modern
scientific age did this ambiguity cause much inconvenience.
For, on the one hand, among men general commands
resulted in general conformities of conduct; and, on the
other hand, in the realm of nature the undeviating regulari-
ties of the behaviour of such bodies as the sun and the moon
were regarded as consequent upon the direct fiat of some
supernatural will. The development of physical science,
however, from the time of the Renaissance, necessitated the
bifurcation of the term. (*a*) '*Law*,' *in the scientific sense of the
word*, became simply and solely a general statement, entirely
devoid of any implication of command. A good example is
the so-called law of motion which runs: "Action and reaction
are equal and opposite"; or the law of gravitation, first
formulated by Newton and now modified by Einstein, to the
effect that "Every particle of matter in the universe attracts
every other particle with a force whose direction is that of the
straight line joining the two, and whose magnitude is pro-
portional directly as the product of their masses, and in-
versely as the square of their mutual distance." General
statements such as these may be true or may be false; but
either to obey them or to disobey them is impossible. They
lie wholly outside the sphere of the will. They are nothing
more than provisional hypotheses, based on observation and
experiment, which men of science accept as true pending
further investigation. (*b*) '*Law*,' *in the juridical sense of the word*
on the other hand, gathered to itself exclusively the idea of
command, authority, and force. It came to connote a

[1] *Cf.* also above, pp. 98–104.

general injunction addressed to the will, without any implication whatsoever as to any consequent uniformity of behaviour.
Austin well defines it as "A rule laid down for the guidance
of an intelligent being by an intelligent being having power
over him."

It is decidedly unfortunate that, since 'law' in the scientific
sense and 'law' in the juridical sense have come to mean
things so wholly different and distinct, a new term has not
been adopted in place of one or other of them. For confusion
between the two connotations has persisted in spite of all the
efforts of grammarians and logicians to keep them apart. Even
in the eighteenth century eminent thinkers like Montesquieu
in France and Blackstone in England gave general definitions
of 'law' in which the two uses of the words were hopelessly
confounded. It was, indeed, directly due to their copious
effusions of muddled nonsense respecting 'law' that Austin
was compelled to remark, as before noted, that "the field of
jurisprudence and morals had been deluged with muddy speculation." Austin did much to clarify the flood and to separate
its elements. Yet even to the present day it is possible to hear
occasionally, mainly from the pulpit, such expressions as "a
violation of the law of gravitation"—expressions as devoid
of rational meaning as any in *Alice in Wonderland*, and un-
redeemed by Alice's charming irresponsibility and humour.

The jurist, then, regards laws scientific as laws in a merely
metaphorical sense, and he dismisses them from his purview.
But, even so, within the proper limits of his subject there are
so many laws claiming to be imperative as to give him plenty
to do when he attempts to define and to classify. There are
laws divine and laws human; laws revealed and laws unrevealed; laws customary and laws statutory; laws moral and
laws social; laws municipal and laws international; laws civil
and laws criminal; laws natural and laws conventional; laws
of honour; laws of fashion; and countless other varieties.
How can he reduce these numerous categories to system and
simplicity? How can he grade them in order of authority?

The task of the modern jurist has been immensely facilitated by the labours of a long line of eminent predecessors.

For us it is unnecessary to go back beyond the great Roman Imperial lawyers who flourished in the early centuries of the Christian era; although it is true that they themselves owed much to the ancient Greeks, as the Greeks owed much to still more venerable Oriental *prudentes*. The Roman lawyers distinguished three kinds of authoritative commands—namely, (1) *jus civile*, (2) *jus gentium*, and (3) *jus naturæ*. The *jus civile* was the law peculiar to Roman citizens, and inapplicable to any other persons. The *jus gentium* may roughly be described as the highest common factor of the laws that prevailed among the *peregrini*, or strangers, who frequented the great city: it was a system of rules marked by simplicity, equity, intelligibility, and freedom from technicalities and traps. The *jus naturæ* was essentially the dictates of conscience and common sense sublimated by the Stoic philosophy into an authoritative system of precepts regarded as emanating from the primal and universal reason. It tended to be identified with the *jus gentium*, and probably would have become merged and lost in it, but for the fact that the *jus gentium* recognised the ubiquitous institution of slavery, while the Stoic conscience repudiated and denounced it as incompatible with the natural liberty and equality of men.

Mediæval Christendom—in law, as in so much else, the heir of Imperial Rome—accepted the classification of the great Latin jurists, but supplemented it and redefined its terms. First and foremost, it added the category of *jus divinum*, the supernaturally revealed law of God. Secondly, it explained the *jus naturæ* as the unrevealed law of God—the law made known to all men in all lands and in all ages by means of the inner monitor of conscience.[1] Thirdly, it regarded the *jus gentium* as the nearest actual approach among sinful men to the ideal standard of the *jus divinum atque naturale*. Finally, it relegated the *jura civilia*, the numerous and varied legal systems of the many peculiar peoples within the pale of Christendom, to the lowest grade of commands, treating them with contempt, and denying to them all validity when they conflicted with the precepts

[1] *Cf.* Romans ii, 14–15.

of the higher laws. The best epitome of the mediæval conception of law is that given by St Thomas Aquinas in the second part of his great *Summa Theologiæ*.

The early modern jurists, such as the Spaniard Suarez and the English Hooker, were ecclesiastics brought up in the school of St Thomas. Hence they accepted in the main the mediæval legal categories. That is to say, they regarded the *jus divinum* as the most authoritative, and the *jus civile* as the least authoritative, of the commands that regulated human conduct. The first important thinker radically to dissent from this view was Jean Bodin, the author of that remarkable work, *De Republica Libri Sex*.[1] The cause of his dissent was that since 1562 he had seen his country, France, torn by ferocious civil wars and disgraced by such appalling atrocities as the Bartholomew massacre, simply because Catholics and Calvinists could not agree in their interpretation of the *jus divinum*. When he had come to the conclusion that no concord was possible he wrote his book to show that the only way of peace and national salvation was the recognition of the sovereignty of the State and the primary obligation of its *jus civile*. Nevertheless, even though he exalted the *jus civile* to the highest place, he was so much still a denizen of the Middle Ages as to admit (with bewildering inconsistency) that the validity of the *jus civile* depended on its harmonisation with the *jus divinum*, the *jus naturale*, the *jus gentium*, and even with a novel class of peculiarly French *leges imperii*, by which he seems to have meant such constitutional fundamentals as the so-called Salic Law. Bodin prepared the way for Hobbes, Bentham, and Austin; but he did not himself advance far along the path of clarity.

Before, however, Hobbes brought his Leviathan on to the path to trample down with ruthless weight the lingering entanglements of mediæval ideology, the great Dutch jurist Grotius had boldly appropriated two of the four mediæval categories of commands, and had combined them to constitute a code of universally obligatory international law.[2]

[1] Issued first in French in 1576, and secondly in a revised and improved Latin version in 1586. [2] See above, pp. 98–104.

222

He had taken the *jus gentium* and had converted it from a system of private law common to the peoples of all nations into a system of public law binding upon states *inter se*. He had also taken the *jus naturale* and, dropping its peculiarly Christian definition as the unrevealed law of the God of the Bible, had secularised and universalised it by describing it as "the dictate of right reason" (*dictatum rectæ rationis*), and as such imperative for Jew, Turk, infidel, and pagan, equally with Christians of all the warring sects.

Hobbes, however, was, as we have noted, the person who broke most completely with the mediæval and Roman tradition respecting law. He nominally accepted the fourfold classification of the schoolmen—just as he nominally accepted the Huguenot idea of the social contract as the basis of society and the State—but he turned it inside out and entirely emptied it of its former content. The *jus divinum*, he said (professing profound veneration), applied solely to the other world beyond the grave; the *jus gentium*, in Grotius's sense of the term, was non-existent, since nations in respect of one another were in a state of nature—that is, of chronic war; the *jus naturæ* consisted merely of the dictates of common sense tending towards self-preservation, and as such was devoid of all ethical or juridical character; only the *jus civile* remained in any way imperative. The will of Leviathan is the only source of valid law on earth, and "no law can be unjust"!

It is not surprising that Hobbes's drastic treatment of the ancient and sacrosanct categories of law met among his mediævally minded contemporaries with general reprobation and repudiation. John Locke, in particular, who strove in his *Two Treatises on Government* (published in 1690) to steer a middle course between the divine right of Filmer's *Patriarcha* and the profane wrong of Hobbes's *Leviathan*, reasserted the reality and supreme authority of natural law, and contended that the very end and object of civil government was the formulation and protection of the natural rights of the individual to life, to liberty, and to property. In the eighteenth century, indeed, largely under the influence of Locke, the cult of nature and natural law had an immense vogue. It captured romancers like Defoe; it took possession of sentimentalists like Rousseau; it inspired a whole school of philosophers and theologians, among whom Bolingbroke and Voltaire stood eminent; it served, in the hands of Pufendorf and his compeers, as the main source of international law. Nay, more, it even reinvaded the province of jurisprudence. Blackstone, in particular, freely readmitted it. The law of nature, he said, "is binding over all the globe, in all countries, and at all times. No human laws are of any validity if contrary to this."[1] This was serious: in an English law-court could a person accused of violating one of the laws of England plead successfully that the law was invalid because contrary to the law of nature? What, again, of the divine law? Sir Thomas More, in the sixteenth century, when convicted of high treason had pleaded that the statute under which he had been condemned was "directly repugnant to the laws of God and His Holy Church." His plea had been disallowed. Ought it to have been so? In Blackstone's opinion, apparently not. For he said, "Human laws are of no validity if contrary to divine laws—all valid laws derive their force from that divine original."[2]

Here undoubtedly was a problem that needed clearing up. What laws could claim validity in the English courts? Could Acts of Parliament or cases adjudged be set aside by the plea that the law which they laid down was contrary to the divine law, or natural law, or customary law, or constitutional law, or international law, or moral law, or any other code of human conduct? Austin, who, like Bentham, was filled with intense disgust at the sloppiness and incoherence of Blackstone's thought, set himself to clarify the mess. And most effectively did he succeed in doing so. First he delineated the three features that, in his opinion, characterise all laws properly so called. They are as follows: (1) Every law properly so called must emanate from a determinate source; (2) it must be the expression of a command; (3) it must be

---

[1] W. Blackstone, *Commentaries on the Laws of England*, i, 41 (1765).
[2] Blackstone, quoted by J. Austin, *Jurisprudence*, i, 214.

enforced by a sanction—that is, by a penalty in case of dis-obedience. Applying this triune test he discovered three great classes of laws proper—namely, (*a*) laws of God, whether revealed or unrevealed; (*b*) positive laws—*i.e.*, laws of the State, whether enacted directly or enacted indirectly; (*c*) other commands—*e.g.*, the rules of clubs and similar voluntary associations. Outside the range of laws proper he placed such rules of human conduct as lacked either deter-minate source or one or more of the other marks of true law —*e.g.*, customary law, laws of honour, laws of fashion, and (shades of Grotius!) international law. Beyond these again, wholly beyond the pale of jurisprudence, he relegated to the limbo of mere metaphor the laws of science, political economy, etc.[1]

Of Austin's "laws proper" some are enforced by one kind of sanction, others by other kinds. Thus, the revealed law of God is enforced by religious sanctions; the unrevealed law of God, known to men partly by means of the moral sense and partly by means of the test of utility, is enforced by ethical sanctions; the rules of voluntary associations are enforced by social sanctions. But the only kind of law sanctioned by the State and enforced in its courts is positive law. And positive law is within the law-courts final and supreme even though it conflicts with all and every other code of law whatsoever. "To say," says Austin, rebuking Blackstone, "that human laws which conflict with the divine law are not binding—that is to say, are not laws—is to talk

---

[1] The following table summarises the Austinian scheme of law. Its relation to the mediæval scheme is indicated by means of the names printed in parentheses.

    I. LAWS PROPER
        1. Laws of God: (*a*) revealed (=*jus divinum*).
                    (*b*) unrevealed (=*jus naturale*).
        2. Positive laws (=*jus civile*).
        3. Other commands.

    II. LAWS IMPROPER—*e.g.*:
        1. Laws of honour or fashion or custom.
        2. International law (=*jus gentium*).

    III. LAWS METAPHORICAL—*e.g.*:
        1. Laws of science.
        2. Laws of political economy.

stark nonsense."[1] Austin, of course, is absolutely right. The courts of the land must enforce the law of the land, or legal chaos would supervene. If in the opinion of any subject the law of the land conflicts with the divine law, or with the moral law, or with any code of law regarded as having superior authority, three courses lie open to him: (1) he may use his political power and his social influence to get the law changed; (2) he may refuse to obey and pay the penalty; (3) he may, if he regards the situation as serious enough, organise a rebellion and endeavour to destroy the State, in the hope of setting up a new one more in accordance with his conscience. But meantime the courts of the State must enforce positive law—the law, the whole law, and nothing but the law.

Austin rendered an inestimable service to the cause of clear legal thinking by sweeping away from the field of jurisprudence all the antiquated lumber of natural law and natural rights by which it had long been littered and encumbered. There are some who hold that, in his definition of law, he over-stressed the idea of force and under-stressed the elements of order and justice. There are others who resent his exclusion of international law from the category of laws proper. Others, again, maintain that, especially in respect of primitive societies, he under-estimated the importance and authority of custom. But none of these criticisms carries much weight. All of them are of historical and philosophical, rather than legal, significance. They do not affect the main point—namely, that positive law is the only kind of law that can possibly be recognised as valid in the law-courts of the State. Let us note, then, Austin's definition of positive law. It is, he says, "law set by a sovereign person or body of persons to a member or members of the independent political society [*i.e.*, State] wherein that person or body is sovereign or supreme."[2] This brings us to Austin's second great conception—namely, that of State sovereignty. To that we will now turn.

---

[1] Austin, *Jurisprudence*, i, 215.   [2] *Ibid.*, i, 177.

V

The Theory of Sovereignty

It cannot be said that Austin was so successful in elucidating the theory of sovereignty as he was in elucidating
the theory of law or in defining the province of jurisprudence. He was successful in his delimitations of law and
jurisprudence because he was able to distinguish more clearly
than any of his predecessors the sphere of legality from the
sphere of morality. He was less successful in his attempts
to define sovereignty because he was not able to distinguish
with sufficient clarity between three separate and distinct
forms of sovereignty—namely, the legal, the political, and
the ethical. The only question which he, as a jurist, was
called upon to answer was the legal question: What is the
ultimate or supreme authority recognised by the law-courts
as the source of positive law? But he confused this simple,
straightforward, and easily answered question with the more
complicated and difficult political question: What, as a
matter of fact, is the ultimate or supreme power which
actually controls or governs the State? Nor did he wholly
keep these legal and political questions from confusion
with the still more disputable ethical question: Where
ought the ultimate and supreme sovereignty to reside? In
respect of Great Britain, for example, he said that the
sovereign—legal, political, and ethical—was the composite
body consisting of King, Lords, and *electors*—a body which
no law-court could recognise; a body which demon-
strably has never exercised actual governmental control; a
body whose ethical claim to supremacy no one has ever
maintained.[1]

That Austin confused the legal sovereign with the political
sovereign and with the ethical sovereign is no doubt due to

[1] It is worth noting that this amazing muddle perpetrated by Austin in 1832
was repeated by him in the pamphlet which he published in the last year of his
life (1859). In his *Plea for the Constitution*, p. 9, he says that " the sovereignty
resides in the King, the House of Lords, and the electoral body of the Commons.". The more one reads of Austin the more one is impressed by the difficulty
and slowness with which he escaped from his mental confusions.

the fact that his predecessors had done the same. Bodin, the first thinker to deal systematically with the subject, had accurately (if not adequately) defined sovereignty, as a legal conception, in the statement: *Majestas est summa in cives ac subditos legibusque soluta potestas.*[1] But his further discussion of *majestas* showed that his prime concern was the political problem—where in France actual sovereignty resided—and the ethical problem—as to whom the ultimate loyalty of Frenchmen was properly due. Similarly Hobbes, the second great theorist to treat of sovereignty, had dealt with the matter almost wholly from the political point of view. He was concerned not so much to clarify the procedure of the law-courts as to save the Commonwealth from a devastating civil war due to the contentions (1) of Parliamentarians, that sovereignty could be divided: (2) of philosophers, that natural law took precedence of civil law; (3) of jurists, that the common law was unchangeable even by statute; (4) of democrats, that the limits of obedience were determined by an original contract between sovereign and subjects; and (5) of ecclesiastics, both Catholic and Calvinistic, that the State was subordinate to the Church. He vehemently maintained on prudential grounds the political supremacy of the State, and on utilitarian grounds its ethical claims to ascendancy. Finally, Jeremy Bentham, Austin's immediate predecessor and master, had been primarily a law-reformer, and not a legal theorist. His *Fragment on Government* (1776), which is mainly an essay on sovereignty, had been devoted to a destructive attack upon the introductory sections of Blackstone's *Commentaries*, wherein Blackstone had eulogised the English constitution as almost flawless; had exalted English law as ideal; had deprecated change; and had attributed the virtues of the English system of government precisely to that division and separation of the sovereign powers of legislation, administration, and adjudication whose division and separation Hobbes had declared to be impossible. Bentham had demolished Blackstone and reaffirmed with striking emphasis the necessary indivisibility of sovereignty. But it

---

[1] J. Bodin, *De Republica, Lib. I, cap. 8.*

had been political, not legal, sovereignty of which he had treated.

Since all Austin's great predecessors had treated sovereignty from the political or ethical point of view, rather than from the legal point of view, it is not astonishing that Austin did the same. Nevertheless it is a misfortune that he was not able to emancipate himself from the influence of his masters, because, since he had determined the province of jurisprudence, it was essential for the completion of his system of thought—his philosophy of positive law, as he called it—that he should consider and define sovereignty purely as a legal conception, without any reference to either politics or ethics. His problem was simply, as we have already remarked: What is the ultimate or supreme authority recognised by the law-courts—the authority from which there is no legal appeal?

Now this is a problem which, as a rule, when once its limitations are recognised, is fairly easily solved. Rarely, indeed, is its solution more difficult than that of an ordinary crossword puzzle. In Great Britain, for example, the legal sovereign is obviously the King in Parliament—that is to say, the composite body consisting of King, Lords, and Commons. A statute of this body passed in due form cannot be questioned in any British court; and if stress is laid upon the words "in due form" as limiting the legal omnipotence of the King in Parliament, the answer is that this sovereign body can determine its own form and procedure. In the case of such a federal body as the United States of America, which necessarily has a rigid constitution, the solution to the puzzle is not quite so simple. It is not, however, very difficult; and if a great deal of misapplied ingenuity has been expended over it, this has been mainly owing to the fact that the would-be solvers have tried to discover a legal sovereign which is at the same time the political sovereign. Those who can dismiss the irrelevant problem of political sovereignty from their minds will soon come to the perception that the legal sovereign in America is the composite body (part central, part provincial) which has power to amend or

229

definite formulation of the legal theory of Parliamentary sovereignty. The second is that of Jean de Lolme in his *Constitution d'Angleterre* (1771) to the effect that "it is a fundamental principle with English lawyers that Parliament can do everything except make a woman a man, and a man a woman." This may be funny; but it is sheer nonsense. Parliament can do nothing except make laws; and it can as easily make a law to the effect that every man must become a woman and every woman a man as it can make any other law. If it does make such a law the law-courts can do nothing but regard it as valid. They cannot, of course, compel either men or women to do the impossible—although the spectacle of long-haired men and short-haired women at the present day raises doubts as to whether or not this particular feat *is* impossible. But, assuming it to be impossible for an interchange of sex to take place, the law-courts can still impose the legal penalties enacted against those who do not do the impossible. And to impose penalties is all they can do in the case of the infringment of any law whatsoever. For the law is equally satisfied by the rendering of obedience or by the payment of the penalty of disobedience: it shows no preference whatsoever for the one as against the other. This brings us to the seventh and last mark of legal sovereignty: it is unaffected by any question of obedience or disobedience on the part of its subjects. A law duly enacted is a law even if no one obeys it at all; it is and remains a law, indeed, even if no one can possibly obey it.

With these marks of legal sovereignty in our minds let us examine Austin's definition of sovereignty. It is couched in singularly circumlocutory terms. "If," it runs,

> a determinate human superior, not in the habit of obedience to a like superior, receive habitual obedience from the bulk of a given society, that determinate superior is sovereign in that society, and the society (including the superior) is a society political and independent.[1]

Here, it is obvious, is a hopeless confusion between the legal and the political sovereign—a confusion due, appar-

[1] Austin, *Jurisprudence*, i, 221.

ently, to the baseless assumption that the two are identical. The *legal* sovereign must be "a determinate human superior": the law-courts must know precisely from whom emanate the commands which they are precluded from treating as invalid. The *political* sovereign, however—that is, the power which actually exercises supreme control in a State—need not be determinate, and, in fact, very rarely is so. As the American jurist J. C. Gray well says, "The real rulers of a political society are undiscoverable. They are the persons who dominate over the wills of their fellows."[1] They may be a single crowd-compeller, such as Lenin or Mussolini; they may be a group of demagogues, such as the French Committee of Public Safety; they may be a gang of conspirators, or the leaders of an army, or the organisers of a general strike; they may be a band of newspaper proprietors; they may be the electors; or they may be a host of men, unknown even to one another, who by speech and writing mould that vague but potent thing called public opinion. Austin, then, starts his definition with his eye correctly fixed on the determinate legal sovereign, and not on the indeterminate political sovereign. But he immediately shifts it. For the requirements of habitual obedience within the State, and habitual freedom from obedience to extraneous authority, although vital to the existence of political sovereignty, are totally irrelevant to legal sovereignty.

If we ask what are the distinguishing marks of the *political* sovereign—that is, of the actual controlling power in the State, as distinct from the legal sovereign—the answer is that the *political* sovereign, as distinct from the legal sovereign, (*a*) is generally indeterminate; (*b*) is generally incapable of precise location; (*c*) cannot be in abeyance, any more than a mass can be devoid of a centre of gravity; (*d*) is incapable of division, just as the centre of gravity of a mass cannot be divided; but (*e*) is subject to all kinds of effective limitations and restrictions.

The last is, perhaps, the only point that calls for explication. Is not a limited or restricted sovereignty a contradiction

[1] J. C. Gray, *The Nature and Sources of the Law*, p. 79 (1921).

233

in terms? No; in the sphere of politics it is not. For political sovereignty—the actual control of a State—is a shifting, unstable, impermanent thing. A stroke may incapacitate Lenin, a shot may remove Mussolini, a mistake in tactics may overthrow a trade union or newspaper oligarchy, a parrot-cry or a panic may revolutionise public opinion. Hence there are certain things which no political sovereign-of-the-moment dare do, if he wishes to remain sovereign. Political sovereignty is always precarious. Not even Lenin dared to take the land from the Russian peasants. Not even Mussolini dared to break with the Papacy and occupy the Vatican. No political sovereign, in short, however highly exalted above all subjects he may be, can hope to retain supreme authority unless he recognises that there are certain things he cannot do, certain spheres into which he must not enter. The penalty for the ignoring of these restrictions and limitations is that he ceases to be sovereign. That is to say he ceases to receive that "habitual obedience from the bulk of a given society" which Austin might have correctly noted as a mark of the *political* sovereign, even though it had no relevance to the *legal* sovereign to whom he seemed to apply it.

This sharp and all-important distinction between legal and political sovereignty, which Austin so fatally ignored, gives rise to three questions. First, if the doctrine of legal sovereignty has no significance outside the law-courts is it worth while to pay so much attention to it? Secondly, what, if any, is the relation of the legal to the political sovereign in a State? Thirdly, what is to be said concerning the ethical question, Where *ought* supreme power to reside? The answers to these questions must be brief and summary.

I. The problem of the nature and location of the legal sovereign is important simply because the law and the law-courts play so prominent a part in our communal life. Law lies at the very base of our civilisation; all our social and economic institutions are founded upon it; upon its exist-ence and stability the continuance of all our liberties and felicities depend. Almost every act of our lives is conditioned by law; in the atmosphere of law we for ever move and have our being. Hence the law-courts and the rules they administer and enforce determine the ways of life of the whole community, even though but a small fraction of the community actually passes through their formidable portals. The main subject of Parliamentary debates and divisions, and the main object of general elections, is to decide the nature of the laws which the country shall impose. Thus the problem of legal sovereignty is not an abstract question, of interest only to philosophical jurists: it is a practical question of the closest personal concern to every subject.

II. Since the question of the nature and location of legal sovereignty is a matter of such urgent moment to every citizen, it is clear that the political sovereign—*i.e.*, the person or body of persons that actually exercises dominant control in the State—will not tolerate the continued existence of a legal sovereign (*e.g.*, in Great Britain a Parliament) that does not conform to its wish. If no constitutional means exist for keeping the legal sovereign in harmony with and—outside the law-courts, wherein alone it is supreme—in subjection to the political sovereign, a revolution is likely to ensue. In Great Britain the electors are assumed to be the political sovereign, and periodical general elections are the device adopted for the maintenance of harmony between them as a body and the legally sovereign Parliament. But the precise seat of political sovereignty, as we have already observed, is extremely difficult to locate, and the assumption that it resides in the electors as a body is by no means unchallenged. In 1926, for instance, it was challenged by the trade unions, or, rather, by a certain company of trade-union officials, syndicalists, and communists, who acted in the name of the unions. If their general strike had been successful and they had destroyed Parliamentary government in this country they would have been compelled to institute a new legal sovereign, a new system of law-courts, and a new body of law. By some means or other, in short, the conventional sovereign within the law-courts must be kept in harmony with, and in subordination to, the political sovereign who actually exercises dominant authority in the world outside the law-courts.

235

III. What, finally, is to be said concerning the ethical question, Where *ought* supreme power to reside in a community? We have already remarked that the political sovereign, however great his power, is practically restricted by numerous limitations of a prudential kind. In other words, there are certain things which no despot, however autocratic, could possibly do with any hope of being allowed to retain his place and power. As David Hume well observed, "It is on opinion only that Government is founded; and this maxim extends to the most despotic and most military Governments, as well as to the most free and most popular."[1] Political sovereigns who abuse their power are faced by rebellion, which, if it is sufficiently widespread, deprives them of their sovereignty and sets up another sovereign in their stead. And just as there are certain things that they cannot or dare not do, so there are other things which (on moral or religious grounds) they *ought* not to do. These things, no doubt, vary from age to age as ethical standards change. At the present time it would perhaps be generally agreed that the political sovereign *ought* not to persecute its subjects in the matter of religious belief, and, on the other hand, that it *ought* to seek so far as its power extends to secure "the greatest happiness of the greatest number" of those within the scope of its authority.

But, since political sovereignty cannot be divided, the problem remains, when all has been said concerning moral and other limitations of sovereignty, where in the last resort *ought* this supreme authority to reside? This is the problem that Austin discusses in his *Plea for the Constitution* (1859). He solves it in a conservative sense; but he is as emphatic as the most convinced democrat that the ultimate sovereignty must reside, and ought to reside, in the State. For the State represents the community as a whole, and, as the world is at present constituted, it is the only institution that does so. Hence, however large an autonomy the State may leave to Churches, to trade unions, to universities, and to other voluntary associations of a sectional kind, in the last resort its authority must, in the interest of the community as a whole, override

---

[1] D. Hume, *Essay on the First Principles of Government* (1741).

them all. So long as the primary division of mankind is the present division into nations, so long must each nation, organised as a State and acting through its Government, be supreme within the territorial limits of its jurisdiction in all causes and over all persons. Political sovereignty cannot be partitioned. There cannot within one and the same territorial area be more than one authority employing the sanction of physical force. The conduct of international diplomacy and the power of waging war and making peace also demand a central and final authority. The right of levying taxes by compulsion cannot reside in multiple hands.

In short, in so far as the community of the nation is valuable as a maintainer of justice, a keeper of peace, an organiser of the conditions of the good life, it demands for its executive Government the obedience of all good men. But it must never be forgotten that the benefits of community are not the supreme values. The supreme values of truth and righteousness concern the individual conscience alone. As it has often happened in the past, so it may happen again in the future that the lonely soul will have to decide whether or not the ineluctable claims of truth and righteousness demand that the authority of the community be defied and the higher authority of the individual conscience be obeyed. No well-balanced mind will lightly challenge an authority upon which so much that is essential to human felicity depends as the State. No sane man will wantonly precipitate the anarchy that any formidable defiance of the will of the Government necessarily entails. Nevertheless, in the last resort the individual conscience is supreme.

> Whoso has felt the Spirit of the Highest
> Cannot confound nor doubt Him nor deny:
> Yea, with one voice, O World, tho' thou deniest,
> Stand thou on that side, for on this am I.

POSTSCRIPT

Other questions concerning the sovereignty of the State have risen since Austin's day, questions which it would be irrelevant for us to discuss here. Such questions are, for example, the problem of the relation of the British Parliament to the Parliaments and other legislative assemblies of the Empire; and, still more vital, the place of the sovereign national State in general in a League of Nations or a Federated World. These are large and complex problems of prodigious practical importance. All we can or need say about them here and now is that their solution will be immensely facilitated if those who have to deal with them come to their treatment with an adequate acquaintance with their Austin, and with clear ideas as to the true nature of Law, of Sovereignty, and of the State.

BOOK LIST

A. PRIMARY SOURCES

AUSTIN, JOHN:
    1. *The Province of Jurisprudence Determined.* 1832.
    2. *A Plea for the Constitution.* 1859.
    3. *Lectures on Jurisprudence.* 2 vols. 1863. 5th edition, edited by Robert Campbell, 1885.

B. SECONDARY SOURCES

ANSON, W.: *Law and Custom of the Constitution.* 1886.
BROWN, W. J.: *The Austinian Theory of Law.* 1906.
BRYCE, JAMES (LORD): *Studies in History and Jurisprudence.* 1901.
CLARK, E. C.: *Practical Jurisprudence.* 1883.
DICEY, A. V.: *Law of the Constitution.* 1885.
GRAY, J. C.: *The Nature and Sources of the Law.* 1921.
HARRISON, F.: *Jurisprudence and the Conflict of Laws.* 1919.
HOLLAND, T. E.: *The Elements of Jurisprudence.* 1880.
LEWIS, G. C.: *Use and Abuse of Political Terms.* 1832.
MAINE, H. S.: *Early History of Institutions.* 1875.
MARKBY, W.: *Elements of Law.* 1871.
MILL, J. S.: *Dissertations and Discussions.* 1867.
—— *Autobiography.* 1873.
POLLOCK, F.: *A First Book of Jurisprudence.* 1896.
RITCHIE, D. G.: *Principles of State Interference.* 1902.
SALMOND, J. W.: *Jurisprudence, or the Theory of Law.* 1902.
SIDGWICK, H.: *Elements of Politics.* 1919.

IX

SPENCER AND ADMINISTRATIVE NIHILISM[1]

AMONG the eminent political thinkers of the nineteenth century few have differed more markedly than Thomas Carlyle and Herbert Spencer. They were extremely antipathetic each to the other. Carlyle was a notable historian and a firm believer in the historic method; Spencer's method was the reverse of historic, and Spencer himself despised history as a subject fit only for the attention of "immature minds." To Carlyle the most fruitful of all human studies was biography; to Spencer biographies were but empty verbiage, and the only human study of value was "descriptive sociology." Carlyle's philosophy of society centred round the 'hero' or great man; Spencer, curiously for so strong an individualist, poured contempt upon the 'hero' and repudiated the great man theory as "ridiculous." Above all, Carlyle exalted the State and its autocratic rulers, while to Spencer the State was anathema—man's worst enemy and the irreconcilable foe of personal freedom. Finally, Spencer spoke of Carlyle as "arrogant" and "despotic," while Carlyle retaliated by describing Spencer succinctly as "an immeasurable ass."[2]

In truth neither of these two notable and typical Victorians was teachable or tractable. Both were prophets commissioned, the one by the Immensities and Infinities, the other

[1] From *The Social and Political Ideas of Some Representative Thinkers of the Victorian Era* (Harrap, 1933). The other studies in this volume are: "Introductory: The Victorian Age, 1837-1901," by G. P. Gooch; "Thomas Carlyle," by Robert S. Dower; "Sir Henry Maine and the Historical Jurists," by J. E. G. de Montmorency; "Alexis de Tocqueville and Democracy," by Harold J. Laski; "Karl Marx and Social Philosophy," by J. L. Gray; "T. H. Green and the Idealists," by A. D. Lindsay; "Matthew Arnold and the Educationists," by J. Dover Wilson; "Walter Bagehot and the Social Psychologists," by C. H. Driver; "Taine and the Nationalists," by R. A. Jones.

[2] D. Duncan, *The Life and Letters of Herbert Spencer*, p. 378.

239

by the Unknowable and Absolute, to instruct rather than to learn. They were better equipped to strike at each other's heads than to sit at each other's feet. Each had his vogue in Victorian days; each attained wide popularity and considerable influence. But both alike suffered swift and extensive eclipse as the twentieth century dawned. Carlyle's inequalitarianism offended the democratic sentiments of the Edwardian age, while Spencer's hard individualism outraged its soft collectivism. Carlyle was fortunate in dying before the decline of his cult set in; Spencer, unhappily, lived to see and feel his isolation in a new world of hateful institutions and alien ideas.

Until about 1860 Spencer was ahead of his generation: a pre-Darwinian evolutionist; a republican Radical with leanings towards Chartism, feminism, and Godwinian anarchism; a formidable, sceptical, unconventional, revolutionary reformer. After 1860, for some quarter of a century, while he was working out the great scheme of his synthetic philosophy, he was—as the arch-agnostic, and as the supreme interpreter of the universe (within the limits of time and space) in terms of evolutionary science—one of the prime representatives of his contemporaries. He marched with his generation, holding aloft their banner of scientific affirmation and religious negation. From 1885, however, when he sank into chronic invalidism, he fell out of the ranks of the progressives. Even as an exponent of evolution he, with his continued insistence on the inheritance of acquired characteristics, fell behind Darwin and Weismann. Still more did his pacificism, secularism, little-Englandism, and administrative nihilism alienate him from a new generation dominated by militarism, irrationalism, imperialism, socialism, and sentimentalism. Abandoning his juvenile adhesion to the causes of Chartism, feminism, and land-nationalisation, he became the exponent of a reactionary conservatism, the guide, philosopher, and friend of the leaders of the Liberty and Property Defence League.

He himself, it is true, changed singularly little. In his last book, *Facts and Comments* (1902), he repeated with senile emphasis many of the things that he had uttered with juvenile enthusiasm sixty years before in his first book, on *The Proper Sphere of Government*. He did not, indeed, change enough. He did not read enough. He did not sufficiently keep abreast of the swift movement of current thought. His ideas became fixed in middle life, and he lost the capacity to modify them. Nevertheless he was a great man and a notable thinker. Many of the principles to which he gave expression were principles of permanent validity and importance. Some, too, of the late Victorian and early Edwardian novelties to which he closed his mind were probably pernicious errors and dangerous aberrations. Certainly not a few of his painful prophecies have been fulfilled, and not a few of his solemn warnings justified by the course of events. There are many welcome signs that thoughtful men are beginning to open his books again in the search for social and political guidance in these difficult and anxious days. Just as the doings of modern democracy have vindicated many of the most mournful forebodings of Carlyle, so has the swift descent of recent socialism towards the abyss given a new relevance to the danger-signals hoisted by Spencer in the long series of his individualistic manifestos.

II

The life of Spencer need not detain us long, for it was singularly uneventful and unattractive. Spencer, indeed, was not so much a man as an intellectual organism, and his passage through this world was rather an existence than a life. It would be almost enough to summarise it under the five captions (1) Integration, April 27, 1820; (2) Evolution, 1820–60; (3) Equilibration, 1860–85; (4) Dissolution, 1885–1903; (5) Disintegration, December 8, 1903.

Spencer, said one of his early acquaintances, was "all head and no heart." He was never in love; he was never even married. Not till he was thirty-six years old, as he himself tells us, did he ever "give vent to an oath."[1] Now this was abnormal and unnatural. By the time a man is thirty-six he ought to be finishing, not beginning, his career as a venter of

[1] *Autobiography*, i, 486.

oaths. For the only excuse for the practice of swearing is the coexistence of violent emotion with a defective vocabulary. By the time a man has fulfilled three dozen years he should, on the one hand, have got his emotions under control, and he should, on the other hand, have acquired a vocabulary adequate to his needs. Hence, if for a person not to have emitted an oath when young argues emotional poverty, for him to continue to do so, or to begin to do so, when no longer young suggests mental deficiency. This belated lapse into profanity, however, on Spencer's part indicates that in 1856 he had not become wholly desiccated and dehumanised. Fish, at any rate—for it was in pursuit of them that he vented his oath—if not men and women, were able to generate a passing flash of emotion. After 1860 he seemed entirely to dry up, and to become a mere organic machine for the production, in somewhat incongruous alternations, of synthetic philosophy and individualist propaganda.

But, although Spencer's life was flat, solitary, and uninteresting, it cannot be wholly passed over by any student who wishes to comprehend his social and political ideas. For if anyone ever inherited ancestral traits it was he; and if anyone ever retained throughout the whole of his career the impress of his early environment again Spencer was the man. He was a descendant on both his father's and his mother's side of a long line of Nonconformists and rebels—Hussite, Huguenot, Quaker, Methodist. His father, George Spencer, a Quaker schoolmaster of Derby, and his father's four brothers—and particularly one Thomas Spencer, a radical and individualistic clergyman of the Church of England—were all men of striking personality, pronounced independence of judgment, and extreme contentiousness. Their frequent and frank discussion of all political and religious problems of their day was undoubtedly the best education that Herbert Spencer received. For Herbert's father, although a schoolmaster, seems to have exercised no sort of discipline or restraint over his son—who was the only one of his nine children to survive infancy. He let him run wild; he left him to the guidance of Nature; he allowed him to evolve on much the same lines as

Rousseau marked out for the ineffable Émile. This anarchic liberty in which George Spencer permitted the adolescent Herbert to grow up presents the sharpest possible contrast to that sleepless despotism which James Mill had, a few years earlier, exercised over the servile mind of the young John Stuart. All originality had been crushed out of John Stuart Mill by the ponderous loads of erudition with which his infant intellect had been burdened: he had read Greek at three; he had taught the classics to his brothers and sisters at eight; before he came of age he had mastered more subjects than most men are able to comprehend in a lifetime. Spencer, on the other hand, could not so much as read his own language when he was seven; at thirteen he remained almost completely ignorant; all his life he continued to be handicapped by a lack of knowledge of the merest rudiments of culture. There was never sufficient grist in his mill. For not all the lumber which his faithful collaborators collected and presented to him in sacks labelled "Descriptive Sociology" could take the place of the fine grain of thought stored in the garners of such master-minds as Plato and Aristotle, Augustine and Aquinas, Locke and Berkeley, Kant and Hegel. Nevertheless, in Spencer's case deficiency in ordinary education, aggravated in later life by an incurable indisposition to systematic reading, had its advantages. It was not wholly to the bad that a mind which proved itself to be one of the most powerful and original that the world has ever known should spend its energies in going over ground that—unknown to it—had been traversed and worked by a long line of the ablest predecessors. Of course, much waste of time and power was involved, and of course many long-buried errors were turned up again and displayed as epoch-making novelties. But, by way of compensation, many old truths were presented in new lights, and not a little new truth was discovered in regions regarded as exhausted. In short, on the whole it suited Spencer's strong and original genius to be allowed to roam at large in a world unclassified. As was said of a great contemporary of his (Benjamin Disraeli), whose education had also been unsystematic, "he escaped the permanent infantile paralysis which is often the consequence of a public school curriculum; he evaded the premature senile decay that is sometimes the painful sequel to a university career."

At the age of thirteen Herbert Spencer was not only almost completely ignorant, he was also disobedient, bad-tempered, and unsociable. Even his easygoing father felt that something ought to be done. So he sent him (1833) to the parsonage of his uncle, Thomas Spencer, at Hinton Charterhouse, near Bath, in order that the rudiments of discipline, decent behaviour, and learning might, if possible, be instilled into him. He at once ran away, and traversed the whole 115 miles from Hinton to Derby on foot in three days. But on being sent back he settled down, and for three years submitted to a process of semi-civilisation at his uncle's hands. He showed himself completely impervious to Latin and Greek; but he took to mathematics and physics as a fish takes to water, and he displayed a passionate interest in nature. His radicalism and individualism were nourished by his uncle's conversation and example; in particular he came to share his uncle's enthusiasm for the New Poor Law of 1834.

On returning home in 1836 he was faced by the problem of finding a career. Twelve years were occupied in unsuccessful experiments. He was a teacher 1836–37; an engineer 1837–41; a journalist and other things 1841–44; and again an engineer 1844–48. He made some money during the railway boom in the early forties; but he lost a good deal of it in the promotion of inventions which the public refused to patronise. His originality was at its height, and it manifested itself in the production of all sorts of ingenious novelties— a velocimeter, a dynamometer, a cyclograph, type-founding machines, sewing-machines, electromagnetic machines, pumping machines, planing machines, devices for binding music, devices for hurling mail-bags from moving trains—all sorts of contrivances for all sorts of purposes. But, if his pioneering genius was displayed by his inventions, not less clearly was his aloofness from his fellows revealed by the fact that not a single one of his inventions was a permanent success. Some subtle defect of inutility or over-elaboration or excessive expense made them all abortive. Hence in 1848 and at the age of twenty-eight he was still unsettled, impoverished, and at large.

Then in 1848 he took the step which put him into his right place and determined the remainder of his career. He secured, and for five years held, the appointment of sub-editor to *The Economist*, a magazine whose contributors included some of the most eminent men of the day. In the office of *The Economist* (340 Strand) and in the neighbouring parlour of Mr Chapman, the publisher, he met such men as Huxley, Tyndall, Froude, Francis Newman, G. H. Lewes, and Horace Greeley, together with such women as Anna Swanwick, Bessie Parkes (mother of Hilaire Belloc), Mrs Lynn Linton, Madame Bodichon, and George Eliot. The conversation of these advanced thinkers did much to stimulate his inquiring mind: it also supplied him with material on which his mind could work. Spencer's originality as a thinker consisted largely in his ingenious development of novel ideas which he derived from the intellectual atmosphere wherein he moved during this seminal lustrum. And among all the sources of his inspiration none was more important than the ideas of one of his colleagues on the staff of *The Economist*—namely, Thomas Hodgskin, the amiable anarchist, disciple of William Godwin. He it was who suggested to Spencer the title of his first notable work, *Social Statics* (1851), and probably no small part of its contents owed their form to Hodgskin's anti-political bias.[1]

In 1853 Spencer felt his position in the literary and scientific world to be sufficiently strong to warrant his resigning his sub-editorship and embarking in his own canoe on the ocean of authorship. As events turned out, he found to his cost that he had cut himself adrift prematurely. For fifteen years he had a dire and doubtful struggle with adversity. His early works yielded him little or nothing in the form of

[1] See C. H. Driver's article on Hodgskin in *The Social and Political Ideas of Some Representative Thinkers of the Age of Reaction and Reconstruction* (Harrap, 1932).

money, and but for the fact that three lucky legacies
descended upon him to refresh him he would almost certainly have been compelled to land and take to some
terrestrial sort of work. Even as it was, he contemplated
emigration to New Zealand. Nay, he was reduced so low
as—after publishing *Social Statics!*—to consider the possibility of seeking employment in a Government office! Had
not William Godwin eaten his principles, together with the
necessaries of life, during the closing years of his existence, as
yeoman-usher of the Exchequer? To make matters worse for
Spencer, his health broke down in 1885. The number of his
daily hours of work had continually to be reduced. Those
who tend to criticise severely his *Synthetic Philosophy* should
not forget that it was the product of insomnia, dyspepsia,
and neurasthenia. He obviously did not manage his body
well. If he had married, if he had read more and thought
less, if he had taken more exercise, and, above all, if he had
had his teeth attended to, he would probably have been a
healthier, a happier, and a more permanently influential
man.

In 1868, however, the tide of financial adversity turned.
His books began to sell and to command good prices both in
England and in America. He came into vogue as a con-
tributor to the more weighty magazines. In 1868, too, he
was elected to the Athenæum Club, and so was able to sleep
in peace during the afternoons as well as to divert himself with
billiards before going to bed. Finally he became rich enough
to afford to live in lodgings in Brighton. Thither he moved
in 1898, and there he died, in his eighty-fourth year, on
December 8, 1903.

Of his character little need be said. It was estimable,
honourable, but unattractive. There can be no doubt that
Spencer's outstanding features were his high intellectual
power, his originality, his unconventionality, his independence of judgment, his disinclination to bow to any sort of
authority. This intense individuality was accompanied by a
courage, a sincerity, a hatred of shams, and a contentiousness
that made him ready for any and every fray, rendering him,

moreover, a formidable and persistent opponent. His famous controversies with Harrison, with Huxley, and with Weismann were particularly prolonged and acrimonious affairs. He was vain, egoistical, and sensitive. True, he had good grounds for vanity. For alone, and without any aid from education or patronage, he fought his way into the front rank of the intellects of his age. He possessed in a remarkable degree three powers not commonly found in combination— namely, the power of accumulating facts, the power of generalising from them, and the power of expounding his conclusions. He was dominated by two leading ideas which he expressed, iterated, and reiterated with almost fanatical zeal during sixty years of authorship. These two ideas were, first, in the sphere of politics, Liberty; secondly, in the sphere of science, Evolution. Such inconsistencies as marked his thought were due to the clashings of the corollaries of these two disparate principles. Of the two, his first love was Liberty; with this love he was born, and his early environ- ment tended to foster it. His intellectual passion for Evolu- tion was a later and an acquired characteristic. He saw in Evolution the veritable tree of knowledge; but to him Liberty was the incomparably superior tree of life.

III

Si monumentum requiris, circumspice. So Spencer might have said (if his uncle had been able to teach him Latin) when, at the close of his career, he surveyed the twenty substantial volumes that were the product of his pen. They represented the result of sixty years of arduous mental toil, or, as he would have preferred to call it, cerebration. In them he had worked out the implications of his two dominant ideas. They can be classified into two groups—namely, (*A*) the creative works written before 1860, (*B*) the explicative works written after 1860. To these must be added his posthumous *Autobiography*, written between 1875 and 1895, but not published until 1904. The following is a brief *catalogue raisonné* of his principal writings:

247

A. THE CREATIVE PERIOD, 1842–60

1. *The Proper Sphere of Government* (1842). This juvenile work consisted of twelve letters written for *The Nonconformist*, a periodical inaugurated the year before, and edited, by Edward Miall, in order to advocate the cause of disestablishment. Spencer's unmitigated epistles maintained not only that the State had no business to meddle with religion, but also that it lay outside its proper function to regulate industry and commerce, to relieve the poor, to control education, to encourage colonisation, to enforce sanitation, and even (*mirabile dictu*) to wage war. Its sole concern, it would appear, was to administer justice and enforce contracts. This uncompromising utterance struck the keynote of all Spencer's political effusions. He himself has told us, in one of the most interesting passages of his *Autobiography*, how the apparent chance that led him to write these letters determined the whole course of his subsequent literary activity; for the letters gave rise to *Social Statics*, from that flowed *The Principles of Psychology*, and that in its turn generated the whole *System of Synthetic Philosophy*.[1]

2. *Social Statics* (1851), which has rightly been described as "one of the most original books since Plato and Aristotle," traversed the same ground as the twelve letters, but it surveyed it more carefully, and it descended below the surface in its search for fundamental principles. The argument is as follows: Man is by nature—like Spencer himself—a solitary animal. Circumstances, and especially the growth of population, compel him to live in society. Hence his relations to his fellows need defining. As an aid to this necessary definition he is provided with a "moral sense." This moral sense enunciates four general principles of conduct—namely, the principles of (*a*) justice, (*b*) negative beneficence, (*c*) positive beneficence, and (*d*) self-realisation. Of these four principles the first is incomparably the most important. "What, then, is justice?" asks Spencer, apparently unaware that Plato has asked and answered the question in the greatest of his dia-

---

[1] *Autobiography*, i, 212.

logues. To Spencer justice is that principle which ensures to each man in society, as though he were still living in solitude, the natural rewards of his energy and efficiency, and the natural penalties of his slackness and inefficiency. In order that this law of conduct and consequence may operate it is necessary that each individual should have the largest possible measure of freedom. The only legitimate limit, indeed, to the liberty of the individual is the equal claim to liberty of every other individual. Hence the primary and cardinal "law of equal liberty," which Spencer formulates in the words: "Every man has freedom to do all that he wills, provided he infringes not the equal freedom of any other man."[1] From this primary law of equal freedom (the first and foremost of the natural rights of the individual) are derived many secondary or particular natural rights, which Spencer then proceeds to specify—e.g., the right to the use of the earth, the right to property, the right to freedom of trade, the right to free speech, and so on. The enumeration of the natural rights of the individual leads logically to a consideration of the proper limits of State action in a perfectly balanced society. Spencer no longer excludes war from the appropriate activities of government. On the contrary, he deliberately adds defence of the community against external foes to administration of justice and enforcement of contracts within the community, to the proper duties of the political organ. But he repeats with emphasis his warning to the State to keep its freedom-destroying hands off commerce, religion, poor relief, education, colonisation, sanitation, and even off currency, banking, and the Post Office. The assumption throughout—not unlike that made by Mill in his *Liberty*—is that the individual and the State are necessary enemies, the one to the other; that any extension of State activity involves an inevitable restriction of personal freedom; and that the ideal condition of mankind is one of

---

[1] *Social Statics*, chapter vi. Criticisms of this 'law,' as thus inadequately formulated, leap to the mind. For instance, has every man freedom to brawl in church, to keep pigs in his garden, to walk naked through the streets, etc., etc., provided he infringes not the equal freedom of others to do the same? Obviously more definition is necessary.

amiable anarchism. How different an assumption from that underlying the *Republic* of Plato, the *Politics* of Aristotle, and the works of the writers of the modern schools that look to Hegel as their lord!

3. *The Principles of Psychology*, regarded by Mr W. H. Hudson as Spencer's "greatest achievement," followed in 1855. Of its filiation to *Social Statics* we are informed by Spencer himself. "Had there been no *Social Statics*," he says, "those lines of inquiry which led to *The Principles of Psychology* would have remained unexplored."[1]

Although the connexion may not at first appear obvious, it is nevertheless real. Spencer's social and political system, like that of Hobbes,[2] is based on psychology. Spencer, like Hobbes, starts from the individual man, his desires and apprehensions, his search for pleasure and his flight from pain. Hobbes, whose dominant emotion was fear, constructed his monstrous Leviathan as a safeguard against besetting perils: he did not object to regulation and regimentation, provided only he were protected from danger. Spencer lived in less alarming days. Amid the *Pax Victoriana* he felt secure and comfortable. He needed no Leviathan to defend him: a policeman, and he a long way off, and mainly active at night, was enough. Hence Spencer's dominant emotion was resentment at restraint. The passion for liberty possessed him, and his chief desire was to find a bit to place in Leviathan's jaw. And out of the same materials as Hobbes had employed in the construction of his Leviathan—namely, hedonism and contract—Spencer fabricated the chain of natural rights that should be capable of curbing the overgrown monster. Spencer's psychology—like that of Hobbes as set forth in his *Humane Nature* and in the first part of his *Leviathan*—was highly original. It was, indeed, mainly evolved out of his inner consciousness; for he had singularly little knowledge of what Hobbes or anyone else had written on the subject. It was based on a study of the nervous system and of the principles of phrenology. It included the study of the minds

[1] *Autobiography*, loc. cit.
[2] And, one might add, those of Spinoza, Locke, and Rousseau.

of children and even of animals. The whole conception of the work was evolutionary, although the evolution, unfortunately, was of the pre-Darwinian type, the inheritance of acquired characteristics and not natural selection being taken as the key to the evolutionary process.

But the most remarkable feature in this astonishing effort of genius was the way in which it suggested a mode of reconciliation between the sensationist and the intuitionist schools of mental philosophy. Sensationists, such as Locke, had maintained that the mind is originally a *tabula rasa*, and that all knowledge is derived from experience. On the other hand, intuitionists, like Descartes, had asserted the existence of innate ideas; or, like Kant, had contended that at least the forms of thought are innate. Spencer's reconciliation of their apparent incompatibles was effected by the brilliant and penetrating suggestion that ideas that transcend the experience of the individual are yet derived from the experience of the race and are transmitted by inheritance. The importance of Spencer's suggestion is well explained by Mr Hector Macpherson,[1] and also by Mr Hugh Elliot.[2] The latter ends an able summary with an eloquent paragraph that contains the words:

> Spencer's *Psychology* is of the first importance in the history of the subject; even now it is far better worth reading than the great majority of text-books that have been produced since his time. For the general point of view and the general method are quite beyond criticism: it is only minor points that have been affected by the progress of knowledge.

4. *Essays:* First Series (1858), Second Series (1863), Third Series (1874). Much of Spencer's time and energy during these seminal years was spent in the production of a remarkable series of essays, which securely established his fame as a thinker. Twenty-four were written during the eight years 1852–60, and about one-half of these were published in a volume that was dated 1858. Their themes

[1] H. Macpherson, *Herbert Spencer, the Man and his Work*, chapter vii, "The Evolution of Mind."
[2] H. Elliot, *Herbert Spencer*, chapter xi, " Psychology."

were very various, but all showed the workings of a mind of exceptional power and independence. Two principles dominated them: in the sphere of politics individualism; in the sphere of science evolution. Under the first heading may be mentioned *Over-legislation* (*Westminster Review*, 1853), *Representative Government* (*Westminster Review*, 1857), and *State-tampering with Money and Banks* (*Westminster Review*, 1858) —an essay full of warning, strikingly relevant to present-day politics. Under the second heading come *The Development Hypothesis* (*Leader*, 1852-54), *Progress: its Law and Cause* (*Westminster Review*, 1857), *The Nebula Hypothesis* (*Westminster Review*, 1858), and *The Social Organism* (*Westminster Review*, 1860)—an essay indicating that Spencer's politics and his science were getting painfully mixed up.

5. *Scheme of the Synthetic Philosophy* (1860). The same year as saw the publication of the notable essay on *The Social Organism*—the cardinal year of Spencer's existence—saw also the issue of the prospectus of his great projected *Synthetic Philosophy*, the elaboration of which occupied the major portion of his remaining forty-three years of successive equilibration, dissolution, and disintegration. The important point for us to note is that the whole colossal scheme was designed to elucidate and confirm precisely those principles of ethics and politics which Spencer had first enunciated in his letters of 1842, and his treatise of 1851. He himself tells us in his *Autobiography* (vol. ii, p. 314) that "the whole system was at the outset, and has ever continued to be, a basis for a right rule of life, individual and social." And he repeats this statement with emphasis in his preface to *The Data of Ethics* (1879). The scheme—which on the whole was closely followed during the succeeding thirty-six years—envisaged a series of volumes treating respectively of (*a*) first principles, (*b*) biology, (*c*) psychology, (*d*) sociology, including politics, and (*e*) ethics. The whole was inspired and unified by the idea of evolution.

6. *Education* (1861) really belongs to this same creative period, for this volume, although issued in book form at the beginning of the next period, consists of four essays originally

published in various magazines during the years 1854–58. The first essay is the ablest and most important of the four; when first published it struck a resounding blow at the classical curriculum of the day, and powerfully furthered the cause of scientific education. "What knowledge is most worth?" it asked. In reply it classified the aims of education as preparation successively for life, health, livelihood, parentage, citizenship, and the right use of leisure. It showed the uselessness of the ordinary grammar-school, gerund-grinding for the realisation of any one of these aims, and advocated a new curriculum dominantly scientific.

IV

B. THE EXPLICATIVE PERIOD, 1860–1903.

7. *The Synthetic Philosophy* (1862–96). Spencer himself in his *Autobiography* has told us in minute detail the marvellous story of his achievement, in substantial completeness, of the gigantic task which he set himself in 1860. Hampered by chronic ill-health, harassed for many years by grave financial anxieties, depressed by the indifference of the reading public, irritated by the unfriendliness of the learned, distressed by the animosity of the pious—steadily he pursued his plotted path until he attained his projected goal. It was a pity that he called his system a "philosophy," for it was really only a synthesis of the sciences. It dealt wholly with the phenomenal, and not at all with the noumenal; it was concerned with processes, not with essences; its scope was less wide than even epistemology, from ontology it deliberately held aloof. It was a still greater pity that Spencer inaugurated his great series with a long dissertation on the Unknowable. The dissertation was irrelevant to his main concern, which was to interpret the known universe in general, and the moral and political phenomena of human society in particular, in terms of evolution. It needlessly offended theologians, who professed to have information respecting the Unknowable; it wantonly alienated metaphysicians, who considered that the Unknowable should also be the Unmentionable. In any

case, it said too much: it asserted, respecting the Unknowable, (*a*) that it exists; (*b*) that it is infinite; (*c*) that it is absolute; (*d*) that it is impersonal; (*e*) that it is inscrutable; (*f*) that it is unconditioned; (*g*) that it is indestructible. By the time the end of the dissertation is reached the reader feels that the Unknowable is an old familiar acquaintance. *First Principles* (1862) is unquestionably the weakest portion of the System of Synthetic Philosophy. *The Principles of Biology* (1864–67) also is not wholly satisfactory. For Spencer's knowledge of his subject was amateurish and second-hand, and he did no experimental work. He felt that he had to treat biology as a basis for psychology, but he had little interest in it for its own sake. Huxley, however, kept him from gross errors. Spencer's strength first fully displayed itself in *The Principles of Psychology*, which incorporated the work of 1855 and greatly extended it (1872). The crown of the system, however, consists of the series of five volumes comprising the *Principles of Sociology and Ethics* (1876–96). To the science of society and to the science of human conduct Spencer made contributions of real and permanent importance. Precisely what these contributions were we shall have to note in a later section.

8. *The Study of Sociology* (1873). While Spencer was at work on *The Principles of Sociology* he received a request from Professor E. L. Youmans, an American friend who had been of great service to him, asking him to contribute a volume on *The Study of Sociology* to the "International Scientific Series" which he was then inaugurating. After some hesitation Spencer decided to suspend for a short time his work on the *Principles*, and to comply with his friend's desire. He thought that it might be well, on the one hand, to unify his ideas by making a preliminary survey of the whole sphere of sociology, and, on the other hand, to prepare the public for his more detailed investigation of a subject that was then new to the orbit of science. Hence in 1873 he produced his highly original and intensely interesting monograph, *The Study of Sociology*. It treated, first, of the need for a science of society; secondly, of the possibility of such a science; thirdly, of its

nature; fourthly, of the peculiar difficulties—objective and subjective—that it had to face; and, finally, of the bases of sociology in biology and psychology. Spencer did not seem to realise that, in demonstrating the possibility of a social science, in stressing the constant factors in human nature and its terrestrial environment, in depreciating the influence of great men, and, above all, in treating society as akin to an organism, he was laying the axe to the roots of his individualism. Yet so he was. Nevertheless, in his next publication —apart, of course, from the successive sociological and ethical volumes of the *Synthetic Philosophy*—his individualism was once more set forth in its most naked and aggressive form. This publication was the four essays, originally contributed to the *Contemporary Review*, collected and issued under the title

9. *The Man versus the State* (1884). In the first essay, "The New Toryism," he laments the drift of the Liberal Party from individualism and defence of freedom towards collectivism and coercion; in the second, "The Coming Slavery," he demonstrates convincingly the trend of the times towards regimentation, bureaucracy, excessive taxation, and socialism; in the third, "The Sins of Legislators," he collects—with a bias amazing in an exponent of the science of society—examples of the disasters that have flowed from the meddling and muddling of politicians; finally, in "The Great Political Superstition," he attacks the theory of Parliamentary sovereignty, refurbishing, as a bit for the jaws of Leviathan, the antiquated illusion of "natural rights." The book is a powerful although partial one. It is replete with facts and arguments serviceable to those engaged in the tasks of maintaining the liberty of the individual and resisting the encroachments of socialism.

10. *The Nature and Reality of Religion* (1885) deals with matters outside our scope. It contains a record of a public controversy concerning agnosticism and positivism into which Spencer entered with Mr Frederic Harrison. It might have been entitled "The Unknowable *versus* Humanity." Mr Harrison objected to the publication of his letters without his knowledge or consent, and the volume was withdrawn from circulation.

11. *Various Fragments* (1897) and *Facts and Comments* (1902) consist of miscellaneous odds and ends. They are interesting mainly as showing that Spencer had learned nothing and forgotten nothing since 1860. His remarks on State education, patriotism, party government, imperialism, rebarbarisation, regeneration, and sanitation bear the same marks of individualistic radicalism as had his utterances of 1842. But, by a strange process of social evolution, what was called individualistic radicalism in 1842 had come to be regarded as anti-socialistic conservatism in 1902!

12. *An Autobiography*, begun in 1875 and continued at intervals until 1893, should also be mentioned. It was undertaken as a relief from the more serious work of the *Synthetic Philosophy*. Although prolix and inorganic, devoid of literary charm and emotionally cold, it is well worth reading as a record of Spencer's intellectual development, and as an unconscious revelation of his harmless egoism and childlike vanity. He defined it as "a natural history" of himself. It should, indeed, be classed, not with biographies, but with works of descriptive sociology.[1]

As one surveys the writings of Spencer in the mass one cannot but concur in the justice of the judgment eloquently expressed by Mr Hugh Elliot in the concluding paragraph of his excellent volume on Spencer in the "Makers of the Nineteenth Century" series. He says:

> If we wish to estimate his real greatness, apart from the adventitious fluctuations of his environment, we shall enquire, not what was thought of him at different times, but what he did. We shall find that, without money, without special education, without health, he produced eighteen large volumes of philosophy and science of many diverse kinds; that he invented an entirely new system of philosophy which for half a

[1] Closely associated with Spencer's *Synthetic Philosophy* were the successive volumes of *Descriptive Sociology*, prepared under his direction by Dr David Duncan and other coadjutors. These ponderous volumes provided data respecting the customs and institutions of mankind drawn from world-wide sources. Eight volumes were published during Spencer's life (1873–81), at a loss of some £4000. The series was resumed in 1910, and it is still in process. The total number of volumes at the moment is fourteen (1937).

century filled the attention of all thinking people; that he led the chief controversies on evolution and biology without ever having received any tuition in those subjects; that he wrote perhaps the most important text-book of psychology of his century, without any acquaintance with the works of his predecessors, and scarcely any with those of his contemporaries; that he established the science of sociology in England; that in all branches of so-called moral science he was recognised as a leader; that he became the philosophic exponent of nineteenth-century Liberalism; that he published a variety of mechanical inventions; and that on endless other subjects, great and small, he set forth a profusion of new and original ideas. A stable judgment will recognise in these achievements a true greatness that may withstand all passing gusts of popular opinion.

V

Spencer's general philosophic position does not call for our examination, except in so far as knowledge of it is needful for a comprehension of his social and political ideas. It may suffice to say that its outstanding features can be summarily indicated by the six words agnosticism, naturalism, dualism, intuitionism, evolutionism, and individualism.

First, Spencer was an agnostic who repudiated the investigations of metaphysics as useless and the revelations of theology as illusory. Into the ultimate realities that lay behind the phenomena of time and space he held that it was for ever futile for man to inquire. The finite human mind, necessarily restricted in its scope to the data provided by experience, was, he contended, devoid of capacity to comprehend anything beyond the reach of the senses. Hence, as we have already remarked, his "philosophy" was improperly so named. It was merely generalised science. It dealt wholly with relations; it knew nothing, and maintained that it was impossible to know anything, about the absolute.

Secondly, Spencer was a naturalist, in the sense that he held that observation and reflection constitute the only sources of human knowledge.

Thirdly, he was a dualist who accepted the equal reality

of, and the fundamental difference between, the self and the not-self. As Mr Hector Macpherson well expresses it:

> What Spencer did was to start with two universal intuitions, which cannot be proved, and which must be accepted as necessities of thought—belief in personal identity, and belief in the permanence of the constitution of things which we call Nature. By starting with the intuitive beliefs—subjective existence and objective existence—Spencer escaped the sceptical conclusions of Hume and Mill.[1]

Spencer's attitude was happily epitomised by the epigrammatist who exclaimed, "What is mind? No matter. What is matter? Never mind."

Fourthly, as Mr Macpherson indicates in the passage just quoted, Spencer was an intuitionist. He revolted against both the psychological sensationalism of Locke and the ethical utilitarianism of Bentham and the Mills. He revived the cult of innate ideas; he reasserted the authority of a moral sense; he reintroduced into the sphere of jurisprudence and politics the long-banished conception of natural rights. Not only, moreover, did he resuscitate these antiquated notions, he gave them—perhaps without knowing much about their antecedents—a new meaning, a new vitality, a new rationality. For he interpreted and explained them all in the light of his master-doctrine of evolution.

Fifthly, then, he was an evolutionist, although an evolutionist of a pre-Darwinian type. The doctrine of evolution, of course, was in the air during all the early part of the nineteenth century. Lamarck had introduced it into the study of biology; Hegel had made the gradual realisation of the idea of freedom the keynote of his philosophy of history; Newman had, in his masterly dissertation on *The Development of Christian Doctrine* (1845), offered an evolutionary defence of Catholic theology; and in many other spheres the conception of an unfolding by slow degrees had taken the place of the older idea of sudden creation or catastrophic change. To Spencer the evolutionary principle presented itself as the key to the whole cosmic process. As early as 1842 his *Letters on*

[1] Quoted by D. Duncan, in *The Life and Letters of Herbert Spencer*, p. 517.

the Proper Sphere of Government show that he conceived of society as a growth rather than a construction; that he attributed social changes to natural causation; and that he saw among the phenomena of ethics and politics the operations of uniform law. Still more clearly does *Social Statics* (1851) display the influence of the ideas of adjustment, adaptation, inheritance, survival, and so on in the interpretation of the doings of man in community. The famous essay on *Progress: its Law and Cause* (1857) is a sustained proclamation of the doctrine of evolution, and of its universal applicability. "From the earliest traceable cosmical changes down to the latest results of civilisation," it asserts, "we shall find that the transformation of the homogeneous into the heterogeneous is that in which progress essentially consists." And it proceeds to illustrate this general assertion by reference to the latest scientific views respecting the origin and development of the stars, the earth, plants, animals, man, the social organism, and human civilisation in all its branches. Finally he devoted the thirty-six years of his mature manhood and old age to the explication of the evolutionary idea, in the successive volumes of his *Synthetic Philosophy*. He aimed at showing that all the transmutations in both nature and society could be explained as changes "from an indefinite incoherent homogeneity to a definite coherent heterogeneity, through continuous differentiations and integrations." Yet in spite of this evolutionism, which compelled him to regard society as an organism, he remained,

Sixthly, an individualist. In the sphere of practical affairs he continued to the end, as he had begun, a passionate devotee to the cause of personal freedom. He resented restraint; he repudiated authority; he denied that he was his brother's keeper; and he declined his brother's offer to keep (and control) himself. He looked forward to a day when State interference should be as obsolete as religious persecution; a day when every man would be wise enough and good enough to be allowed to do what he liked, and when amicable anarchism would prevail universally throughout the human race.

R 2   259

VI

It will already be evident that Spencer was the exponent of two different and incompatible systems of politics. On the one hand, he was an evolutionary sociologist, to whom the community appeared as an organism or quasi-organism, and to whom, therefore, the course of social development naturally tended to display itself as a gradual movement away from primitive, anarchic individualism towards the unity of a complete communism—a unity in which the legislature (the organ of social cerebration) would be omnipotent and omnicompetent. On the other hand, he was an anarchic individualist, or "administrative nihilist," continually on the alert to discover and denounce the "sins of legislators," regarding every act on the part of the State as an "interference" with the freedom of the subject, and constantly asserting the "natural rights" of the individual to be exempt from the molestation of the organised, but inorganic, masses of his fellows.

Now it is almost incredible that two systems so distinct and so conflicting as these could coexist for a lifetime in a mind so strong, so clear, so courageous, and so unconventional as Spencer's. Yet so they did. It is necessary, therefore, for anyone who would give a full account of Spencer's social and political ideas to expound the two systems separately. When this separate exposition is undertaken it will soon be found that the one system—namely, the individualistic system—is complete, coherent, fully realised, and set forth with passionate conviction by its author over a period of sixty years. It will be found, on the other hand, that the second system—namely, the sociological system—is incomplete, incoherent, imperfectly realised, and set forth with hesitations and confusions that are eloquent of intellectual uncertainty. In particular, when Spencer is asked (through his works) to say what sort of organism society is, or resembles, his various answers in their inconsistency and absurdities verge upon the comic. But of that more anon. We must first examine Spencer the individualist.

A. Spencer's Individualistic System

As we have already observed, Spencer's individualism was both innate in his blood and derived from his environment. He was, as his ancestors for many generations had been, by nature a religious dissenter and a political rebel. And his natural bent towards nonconformity and radicalism was increased by his early association with his disputatious and sceptical relatives, as well as by his later friendship with that notable Godwinian anarchist, Thomas Hodgskin. Hence,

1. *Man the individual* was the basis of this primary system of his. Like Hobbes, he regarded man as solitary, rather than social, by nature. Like Hobbes, too, and like Hobbes's disciples, the Utilitarians, he considered that happiness was the end or purpose of man's being. But he differed from both Hobbes and the Utilitarians in conceiving the prime source of happiness to be, not the reception of agreeable sensations from without, but rather the development and exercise of faculties from within. The evolution of capacity, the employment of growing powers, the realisation of latent potentialities, the fulfilment of the purpose of creation—such he considered to be the deep fount of felicity. And for this process of self-realisation the one thing needful is freedom. Hence freedom is a natural right of the individual—indeed, the one supreme natural right, from which all other natural rights flow, and to which all merely civil rights are inferior.

2. *Natural rights*, then, returned to the fields of ethics and jurisprudence, whence they had been banished as "anarchic fallacies" by Bentham and his followers. They had, indeed, for many generations before Bentham's day played a prominent part in these and kindred fields, even if their tendency was, as Austin severely remarked, to "deluge them with muddy speculation." Originating, perhaps, in Greek sophistry and cynicism, the theory of natural rights had maintained itself in Stoic philosophy, Roman jurisprudence, and mediæval Christian theology. Natural rights had been

recognised by modern thinkers such as Hooker and Locke;
even Hobbes and Spinoza had rendered them formal obei-
sance; they had formed the very foundation of Rousseau's
system; they had been exalted and affirmed in the eighteenth
century by both American rebels and French revolutionaries.
But when the nineteenth century dawned the excesses of their
devotees had discredited them, the squabbles of their
defenders had cast doubt upon them, and the Utilitarians had
utterly repudiated and rejected them. Spencer brought them
back, knowing, it would appear, but little respecting their
historical antecedents. Certainly his attempt to demonstrate
their existence and to maintain their authority is perfunctory
and unsatisfactory in the extreme. The German jurists, it
appears, admit them—or, at any rate, admit "the idea of
Naturrecht," which, we may remark, is by no means the same
thing. Moreover, the customs of savage peoples—the
Bechuanas, the Korana Hottentots, the Araucanians, the
Kirghizes, the Dyaks, the Chippewayans, the Ahts, the Com-
anches, the Eskimos, the Brazilian Indians, the peaceful
Arafuras, the peoples of Java, Sumatra, Madagascar, and
Ashanti—illustrate them (or, to be more exact, something
entirely different).[1] Spencer does not seem to realise that, if
natural rights are to be reinstated in serious political speculation, arguments much more relevant and conclusive than
these are necessary. He appears to take the natural right to
freedom as granted, and from this postulate he deduces all
the detailed secondary rights of which he treats at length in
Social Statics, in the *Principles of Ethics*, and elsewhere. Such
secondary rights are the right to physical integrity, to free
motion and locomotion, to the use of natural media, to
property, to reputation, to gift and bequest, to free exchange
and free contract, to freedom of industry, freedom of belief
and worship, freedom of speech and publication.[2] All these
"natural rights" the natural man, isolated in an anarchic

[1] See the article on "The Great Political Superstition" in *The Man versus
the State*.
[2] Cf. *Social Statics*, chapters vii–xvii, and *Principles of Ethics*, Part IV, "Justice,"
pp. 64–147.

world, is supposed to possess independently of any organised society or any promulgated law. Society does not, according to Spencer, create these rights; it merely—when organised as a State, and when acting by means of a Government—defines and defends them. What, then, of society?

3. *Society* in this individualistic system is not an organism, or even a quasi-organism, but merely an organisation; not a growth, but a construction; not natural, but artificial. "The nation," says Mr A. W. Tillett, paraphrasing Spencer's argument, "is but an aggregate of individuals whose individual welfare is the only end to be subserved."[1] Society—this late and lamentable curtailer of personal freedom—came into existence by mere force of circumstances, and particularly owing to the growth of population. Since it is no longer feasible for people to keep out of one another's way, unrestricted liberty is no longer possible. Hence the problem arises: how to reconcile personal freedom with social harmony; how to adjust the relations between the individual and the community in which he inevitably finds himself.

4. *The Harmonisation of Man and Society*. The doctrine of natural rights inhering in the individual almost necessarily involves the doctrine of some sort of social contract as the basis of society. If the contract is not a formal and precise one, as envisaged by Rousseau, it is a tacit and implied one, as in the systems of Hobbes, Spinoza, and Locke. In Spencer's individualistic system, too, the contract is tacit and implied. It is founded on the universal recognition and acceptance of two primary principles or "laws"—namely, first, the "law of conduct and consequence," and, secondly, "the law of equal freedom." The "law of conduct and consequence" is thus formulated by Spencer:

> Each individual ought to receive the benefits and the evils of his own nature and consequent conduct, neither being prevented from having whatever good his actions normally bring to him, nor allowed to shoulder off on to other persons whatever ill is brought to him by his actions.[2]

[1] A. W. Tillett, *Introduction to Spencer's Synthetic Philosophy*, p. 54.
[2] *Principles of Ethics*, Part IV, "Justice," p. 17.

The second law—namely, "the law of equal freedom"—
to which Spencer constantly recurs, is briefly stated as follows
at the beginning of Chapter VI of *Social Statics*—a chapter
devoted to its exposition:

> Every man has freedom to do all that he wills, provided he
> infringes not the equal freedom of any other man.[1]

The extreme rigour of these two fundamental social laws is
modified by two supplementary principles which Spencer
terms respectively the "law of negative beneficence" and the
"law of positive beneficence."[2] According to the first of these
laws, each person in seeking his own self-realisation should
refrain, so far as possible, from causing injury or unhappiness
to his fellows. According to the second, he should actively
aid and comfort his fellows, at any rate in so far as he can do
so without inconveniencing himself. By observance of these
ethical and prudential maxims, thinks Spencer, the nearest
practicable approach to harmony between man and society
will be attained, and the individual will reduce to a minimum
the inconveniences that must necessarily ensue from the compulsion, placed upon him by circumstances, to mingle with
his kind.

5. *The State*, according to this view, is an evil, even if, for
the time being, a necessary evil. It originated in war, and its
essence is force—that is to say, the very negation of individual
freedom. Hence in the ideal industrial and pacific society of
the future it will vanish away. It is a temporary and transitional institution, needful only during the period in which
man is passing from solitude to sociability, from savagery to
civilisation, from the egoism of barbarity to the altruism of
community. The first great step towards the abolition of the
State will be its reduction to the rank of a voluntary society,
corresponding to the modern Church. The Church was once
a compulsory institution, which enforced obedience, promulgated positive laws, and levied taxes, punishing heresy and

---

[1] Some embarrassing applications of this law, as thus stated, can, as we have
already remarked, easily be imagined. See above, p. 249.
[2] Cf. *Social Statics*, chapter iii.

schism with excommunication and death. It no longer remains such: its imperative commands have given place to negligible exhortations; its devastating exactions have been mitigated to pathetic appeals; its ferocious penalties have been reduced to mild expressions of disapproval. The individual now can (and generally does) ignore the Church. In the idyllic future he will, says Spencer, be equally able to ignore the State.[1]

Viewed from this standpoint, the Aristotelian classification of States into monarchies, aristocracies, and democracies is almost meaningless. It relates to mere external forms, not to inward essences. The vital question to ask concerning any State is: Does it interfere much or little with individual freedom? According to this basis of classification there are two, and only two, distinctive kinds of State, namely, the militant type on the one hand and the industrial or pacific type on the other.

The militant type, the product of war, and the embodiment of all the most barbaric and primitive of men's passions, is necessarily despotic and authoritarian. It is organised for combat, and consequently it is characterised by rigid discipline, by regimentation, by universal regulation. It necessarily subordinates the individual to the community, the citizen to the soldier. It is stiff with status; and the features that mark its subjects are obedience, dependence, loyalty, patriotism, conservatism. On the other hand, the industrial type, towards which (in Spencer's earlier and more optimistic opinion) mankind is tending, is characterised by features diametrically opposite. It is marked by a minimum of governmental control. It is organised for peace and for voluntary co-operation. It is free from unnecessary rules and regulations, contract and not status determining the conditions of its members. Flexibility, not rigidity, characterises its institutions. The individual takes precedence of both soldier and citizen, and the outstanding features of the industrial individual are the meek and gentle virtues of the cosmopolitan, the pacificist, the philanthropist, the humanitarian,

[1] See *Social Statics*, chapter xix, on " The Right to ignore the State."

the free-trader, the free-thinker, the free-liver, the amiable anarchist of the type of Tolstoi.[1]

The industrial State, as described by Spencer, is obviously an extremely unstable and transitory institution. It is merely a momentary halt between militarism and anarchism. Its functions are reduced almost to vanishing-point: it must not interfere with commerce, religion, poor relief, education, colonisation, currency, banking, post office.[2] Indeed, its only proper duties are two—namely, first, to defend the community against external foes, and, secondly, to administer justice within the community. Hence when, on the one side, wars —those irrational relics of barbarism—cease, and when, on the other side, men obey the natural law of equal freedom, the State will have nothing to do, and so, by mere atrophy, will disappear. For

6. *Government*—the instrument of the State—*i.e.*, of society politically organised—is, in Spencer's individualistic view, an evil; a necessary evil due to the persistence in man's present communal condition of existence of those egoistic and purely selfish qualities proper to his condition of solitary savagery, the qualities of the cave-man. "Thus, as civilisation advances," he says,

> does government decay. To the bad it is essential: to the good, not. It is the check which national wickedness makes to itself, and exists only to the same degree. Its continuance is proof of still-existing barbarism. What a cage is to the wild beast, law is to the selfish man. Restraint is for the savage, the rapacious, the violent; not for the just, the gentle, the benevolent. . . . Magisterial force is the sequence of social vice; and the policeman is but the complement of the criminal. Therefore it is that we call Government a necessary evil.[3]

Such, in outline, is Spencer's individualistic system, the system that dominated all his political thinking from the day

---

[1] For Spencer's detailed study of these two types of State see his *Principles of Sociology*, Part V, " Political Institutions," chapters xvii–xviii. It may be noted that he speaks of the munder the heading of " Societies " rather than " States "; but as he is treating of political institutions States is the proper term to employ.

[2] See *Social Statics*, chapters xxii–xxix.

[3] *Ibid.*, Introduction, p. 25.

of his earliest publication (1842) to the day of his latest utterance (1902). It is obvious that it is based on a narrow and one-sided view of man; for man is not by nature a solitary animal. He is at least semi-social. If he sometimes wants to be alone, and can for a period remain self-sufficient, it is equally true that on other occasions he pines for fellowship, that he goes mad in isolation, and that he needs the presence and the co-operation of his kind. It is obvious, further, that this individualistic system of Spencer involves equally narrow and inadequate conceptions of Society, State, and Government. Society is not a mere congeries of human atoms; it is at least quasi-organic. The State is not mere coercion; it is also co-operation. Its action is not always "interference"; it is more commonly beneficent assistance. Government is not necessarily an evil or the product of evil; it is capable of becoming a good, and even the supreme instrument of good. Even if it vanishes as a means of coercion it will certainly remain and increase as a means of co-ordination: the policeman, even if no longer needed to arrest criminals, will continue to be needed to regulate traffic, to collect lost children, and to comfort cooks.

Spencer, himself, indeed, amid all the narrowness, rigidities, and aridities of his individualistic system, had curious and incongruous visions of a larger and more living world—a world in which the antithesis of Man *versus* State did not exist; a world in which organism took the place of organisation; and a world wherein the unity of communal life superseded the harmony of mere compromise between the individual and his fellow-individuals. To his second or sociological system we must now turn.

VII

B. SPENCER'S SOCIOLOGICAL SYSTEM

The intrusive idea that disturbed the tranquillity, broke the unity, and destroyed the finality of Spencer's individualistic system was the idea of evolution. In the doctrine of evolution, as we have already remarked, Spencer thought

267

that he had found the key to all the processes of both physical and human nature. By means of it he attempted to explain the present constitution and condition not only of the starry universe, the planetary system, the face and figure of the earth, the flora and fauna of the world, together with the bodies of men, but also of the minds of men, the morals of men, the customs and institutions of men, and the forms of human society. Indeed, the primary aim of the *Synthetic Philosophy* was precisely the solution on naturalistic and evolutionary lines of the problems of ethics and politics. Hence the vitally important sections of *The Principles of Sociology* are those that treat of domestic institutions, ceremonial institutions, ecclesiastical institutions, and political institutions. Now if society is to be explained on evolutionary lines it must possess some sort of unity and some sort of continuity. It cannot be a mere fortuitous concourse of atoms devoid of all coherence or interrelation, without past and without future. And, since the phenomena of society are the phenomena of will, intellect, and emotion, it is clear that the unity of society must be either organic or quasi-organic—that is to say, if not organic in the strict sense of the term, it must be at least more akin to the organic than to the mechanical. Spencer, in his acquired and unnatural zeal to apply his evolutionary key to the phenomena of community, and to develop a science of sociology, did not hesitate to 'go the whole hog' and formally to proclaim society to be an organism. The idea of the "social organism" first appeared, most incongruously, in the midst of the extreme individualistic atomism of *Social Statics* (1851), which marked the dawning of the light of evolution in Spencer's mind.[1] The idea was fully and most elaborately explicated in the famous essay entitled *The Social Organism* (1860).[2] When Professor Huxley in *The Fortnightly Review* pointed out the disharmony between the "administrative nihilism" of Spencer's individualistic system and the collectivist implications of his doctrine of the

[1] *Social Statics*, chapter xxx, pp. 5 and 6.
[2] Spencer's *Essays*, Second Series, No. 5 (1863). *Cf.* also Spencer's *Autobiography*, ii, 48.

social organism, Spencer tried, quite ineffectively, to reply in a supplementary essay, entitled *Specialised Administration*.[1] He recurred to the theme in *The Study of Sociology* (1873) and in *The Principles of Sociology*, Part II (1876). Finally, he reverted to it in his last work, *Facts and Comments* (1902). Thus we see that for over half a century this evolutionary conception of a social organism existed in Spencer's mind side by side with, and in unresolved antinomy to, the individualistic atomism of his primary political system.

If we ask Spencer to what sort of an organism society is to be likened he is in a difficulty. As an individualist who anticipates the ultimate disappearance of government he tends to compare society to an "indifferentiated jelly," in which individuals, like protozoa, float about. As an evolutionist who sees society in transformation from the incoherent, indefinite, and homogeneous to the coherent, definite, and heterogeneous, he is bound to compare it to one of the higher vertebrates, even if he refuses to go higher than the ass.

And if we ask him what is likely to be the future course of social evolution he is in a still greater difficulty. For as a politician he has definitely prophesied the disappearance of the militant type of State, with its high centralisation and unified control, and has predicted that the industrial type will universally prevail—the type which is marked by anarchic individualism. But as an evolutionist he is bound by all the analogies of nature to see the line of progress leading to increased unification, growing differentiation of function, closer interdependence of parts, and the final complete ascendancy of that "cerebral mass" the legislature.

The truth is that the conception of society as an organism cannot be made to accord with the radical *laissez-faire* individualism of Spencer. It is more in harmony with the conservatism of Burke, who, in spite of his lip-service to the contractual doctrine of Locke, viewed the nation as a living entity with the memory of a glorious ancestry and the hope of a splendid posterity. It is still more in harmony with the

[1] *The Fortnightly Review*, December 1871. Republished in Spencer's *Essays*, Third Series, No. 5 (1874).

collectivism of Sidney Webb, the socialism of William Morris, and the communism of Karl Marx. For in all these systems the individual withers and the body politic or economic is dominant. It is for Webb, Morris, and Marx, rather than for Spencer, the individualist, to develop the view that society is an entity; that it undergoes growth and decay; that it displays differentiation of structure and of function; that its parts are and remain mutually dependent; that it adapts its constitution to its environment; and that, generally, it follows the normal process of evolution and dissolution. Similarly, it is rather for Comte than for Spencer, the dissenter and rebel, to talk of a science of sociology, to dismiss the doctrine of free will as an illusion, and to treat the phenomena of man in community as coming within that sphere of positive and unvarying law wherein no volitions, human or superhuman, interfere. Again, it is for Buckle rather than Spencer—Spencer, the asserter of personality and the maintainer of the doctrine of the individual's natural right of self-realisation—to repudiate the "great man" theory, to denounce hero-worship, and to contend that the men who apparently make history are themselves but the products of their environment.

In short, in accepting and developing the dogma of the organic nature of society, Spencer, while he put the crown upon his system of synthetic philosophy, cut the ground from under the feet of his political individualism. And—if we may pursue the metaphor further—the sociological crown which he placed on the head of his philosophy was speedily appropriated by his chief enemies, the Socialists, and was by them melted up into weapons by means of which they were able to harass and destroy the individualistic disciples of Spencer.

Nevertheless, in spite of inconsistencies and confusions, Spencer was a great man and a notable thinker. His contributions both to the science and to the philosophy of the nineteenth century were of the highest importance. In the sphere of ethics and psychology he will be principally remembered as the man who found in evolution the key to the reconciliation of the inductive and deductive schools of thought. In the sphere of social and political ideas he will rank high, not as the founder of a science of a visionary 'sociology,' but as the dauntless champion in a collectivist and servile age of the claims of the individual and the cause of personal freedom.

BOOK LIST

A. PRIMARY SOURCES

SPENCER, HERBERT:

The Proper Sphere of Government. 1842.

Social Statics. 1851.

The Principles of Psychology. 1855.

Essays, First Series. 1858.

Education. 1861.

The Synthetic Philosophy. 1862–96.

Essays, Second Series. 1863.

The Study of Sociology. 1873.

Essays, Third Series. 1874.

The Man versus the State. 1884.

Facts and Comments. 1902.

An Autobiography. 2 vols. Published posthumously. 1904.

B. SECONDARY SOURCES

BARKER, E.: *Political Thought in England from Herbert Spencer to the Present Day.* 1915.

BEARE, J. J.: *Organic Morality, or the Ethics of Mr Herbert Spencer.* 1889.

COLLINS, F. H.: *An Epitome of the Synthetic Philosophy.* 1889.

DUNCAN, D.: *The Life and Letters of Herbert Spencer.* 1908.

DUNNING, W. A.: *A History of Political Theories from Rousseau to Spencer.* 1920.

ELLIOT, H.: *Herbert Spencer.* 1917.

HUDSON, W. H.: *An Introduction to the Philosophy of Herbert Spencer.* 1894.

LICHTENBERGER, J. P.: *Development of Social Theory.* 1924.

MACPHERSON, H.: *Herbert Spencer, the Man and his Work.* 1900.

MARTINEAU, J.: *Types of Ethical Theory.* 1885.

MORGAN, C. L.: *Spencer's Philosophy of Science.* 1913.

RITCHIE, D. G.: *Principles of State Interference.* 1891.

SIDGWICK, H.: *Lectures on Ethics.* 1902.

TILLETT, A. W.: *Introduction to Spencer's Synthetic Philosophy.* 1914.

WERNER, E. T. C.: *Herbert Spencer.* Shanghai, 1913.

INDEX

273